Howling Wilderness:

The Indian Captivity of Ollie Spencer

Janet E. Nelson Rupert

Howling Wilderness Press

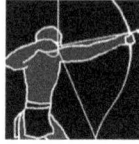

Howling Wilderness Press
Suite 140
118 Graceland Blvd.
Columbus, Ohio 43214

Howling Wilderness Press is a registered trade name

Designed by Janet E. Rupert

Manufactured in the United States of America
by Lightning Source Inc. (US)
1246 Heil Quaker Blvd.
La Vergne, TN USA 37086

Cataloging Data
Howling Wilderness: The Indian Captivity of Ollie Spencer/Janet
E. Nelson Rupert
Includes bibliographical references and index.
1. Indian Captivities.   2. Shawnee Indians.
3. Iroquois Indians. 4. Indians of North America--Wars--Ohio.
5. Ohio--History.

ISBN 978-0-9891034-0-4

Illustration sources on page 307.

FOREWORD

Oliver (O.M.) Spencer was born in New Jersey in 1781. Known as Ollie as a youth, he was the son of Colonel Oliver Spencer, a wealthy tanner and noted Revolutionary War officer, and Anne Spencer, the daughter of Robert Ogden, who headed the New Jersey Assembly before the war. Due to post-war poverty, when Ollie was nine years of age, his family went west to the new villages of Columbia and Cincinnati to make a living from farming. This was a dangerous enterprise, as the local natives were still numerous and in possession of the land.

Ollie was one of many thousands of settlers who Native Americans kidnapped. Doing so enabled them to replenish their numbers, depleted by war deaths and illnesses, while they battled for their land. The natives were particularly fond of taking children and bringing them up as their own.

The original text of Oliver Spencer's story, The Indian Captivity of O.M. Spencer, while lyrical, is difficult for all but the most dedicated readers to follow. I have rewritten it in more modern English and added extensive supplemental text.

I have written the quoted material with the original spelling, grammar, and syntax, without noting errors present when compared to modern writing. I have noted factual discrepancies with the word "*sic.*"

In memory of my father

CONTENTS

vii

MAPS, ILLUSTRATIONS, AND SIDEBARS

Then to have sat down upon the bench at the evening sun, and told one's children how we raised this flourishing settlement from the howling wilderness.

—Francis Bailey, 1797

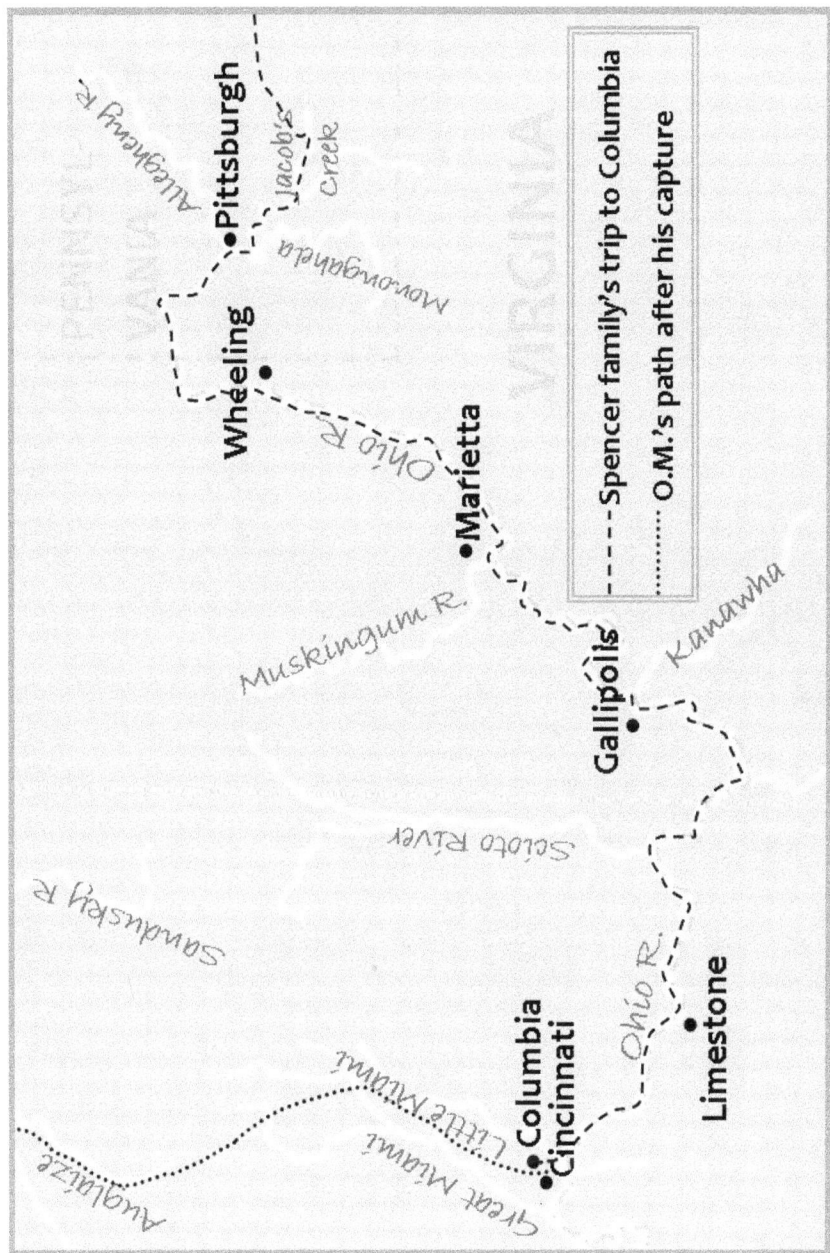

PENNSYLVANIA

Allegheny R.

•Pittsburgh

Jacob's Creek

Monongahela

VIRGINIA

- - - - Spencer family's trip to Columbia

.... O.M.'s path after his capture

•Wheeling

Ohio R.

•Marietta

Muskingum R.

Gallipolis

Kanawha

Scioto River

Sandusky R.

Columbia
Cincinnati

Little Miami

Great Miami

Ohio R.

Limestone

Auglaize

CHAPTER ONE

COLONEL SPENCER'S JOURNEY WEST

ON A PLEASANT DAY in October of the year 1790, when Oliver Marlborough Spencer, then called Ollie, was only nine years of age, he mounted the leading horse attached to the foremost of two wagons in which his mother and sisters sat. Their destination was the "far West." In the wagons, they had stowed articles of household furniture indispensable to the comfort of a family and not then easily procured west of the Allegheny Mountains.

Pleased with the novelty of traveling, from which he anticipated a great deal of pleasure, the few tears that he shed on leaving forever the home of his childhood soon dried up. Possessing spirits naturally buoyant, he wondered not a little at the sober sadness of his father, the deep sighs of his mother, and the frequent sobs of his sisters, whose feelings and expectations he supposed would naturally correspond with his.

His father, Colonel Oliver Lecar Spencer, had made an exploratory trip to the West in May of 1789. Colonel Spencer traveled on horseback to a wild lush land between the Great and Little Miami Rivers just north of the Ohio River, barely explored by white settlers. Little did he know as he traveled through Maryland and Virginia that his actions would lead to Ollie's capture by Indians.

Colonel Spencer, then fifty-three years old, did not blithely contemplate uprooting his wife and family for a life on the frontier. "Near poverty" drove him in his search for a better life. He was once a wealthy man whose money had come through affiliation with his wife's family, and he had lost it, in a sense, paying and clothing the men of his command, a regiment in the Continental Army in the American Revolution. After the war, he trusted in the honor and justice of the government to pay his equitable claims against it; but in this hope and confidence, he was deeply disappointed. The United States repaid his patriotism with $10,000 in continental currency, made worthless by inflation.

Following the war, he had done adequately for a while with his own small shipping business and the family tannery, once the largest such establishment in New England, but Loyalists had stripped it of all its content and hardware during the revolution, making it difficult to operate. In the running of it, apprentices placed as many as fifteen hundred hides a day in vats filled with water and tree bark, used for its tannic acid and ground at the site in a mill with two large iron-teethed wheels powered by two horses. One journeyman and five apprentices emptied the vats by using wooden buckets on long poles, a method so labor intensive that one of the apprentices, a teen-aged nephew, became malnourished and exhausted from overwork and short rations, forcing him to quit and go home to Connecticut. Money was so scarce that Colonel Spencer could not properly run his business.

He managed better with the shipping business, and he and his son Robert had two ships, the *Dove* and the *Spencer*, operating out of the port of Burlington on the Delaware River, which in the early days of shipping matched New York and Boston as a port of entry.

Unfortunately, Robert had set sail for the West Indies in 1787 and never returned. News of a hurricane that struck his destination filled the local paper. A "most violent hurricane" had blown into the Bay of Honduras from the north northwest on a Sunday in the late summer of 1787. "Out of fifteen square rigged vessels, sloops and schooners, including a number of craft . . . which were riding at anchor in Belize road, at the commencement of the gale, not a single one was to be seen; the whole having either sunk or been [driven] on shore, and many of their hands perished."

Even with this dismal news, the Spencer family knew nothing for certain of Robert's fate, but two years had passed since he set sail without word of him. Colonel Spencer said of Robert, "[He] sailed from hence to the West Indies better than a year ago, without any certain, or authentic accounts of him tho' some report gives us some encouragement of his still being among the living, but we are much afraid they are lost."

With the loss of a ship and the loss of a son, Spencer had to find a new means of subsistence, and perhaps a change of scene would help assuage the grief he never spoke of, but surely felt. With aching war wounds and hope in his heart, he headed for a territory still claimed by wild Indians. He was not afraid; this wasn't the first time that his family had encountered them.

Colonel Spencer was the fifth generation of Spencers in America. Their ancestor Gerard was the youngest of five Spencer siblings who had arrived with the Winthrop fleet in 1630 in Massachusetts. This Puritan family had "left England on account of the persecutions for religious opinions, in the reign of the second Charles, to seek in the unbroken wilds of New England an asylum from oppression, and to rear a temple to the God of their fathers, in which they might worship him 'according to the dictates of their own consciences'."

They arrived to a wilderness where a few traders and fishermen had come before, their governor writing of the task before them, "If there be any endued with grace and furnished with means to feed themselves and theirs for eighteen months, and to build and plant, let them come over into our Macedonia and help us." From this Biblical reference, Acts 16:9, came Massachusetts Bay Colony's seal showing an Indian, labeled, "Come over and help us," for an active part of the plan for an ideal society included the conversion and salvation of the natives. Religious certainty and fervor so filled the settlers that they thought this would be an easy task. Instead, the Iroquois and other native tribes had their own intricate religions, worldview, and long history that they would not readily let go.

In the following years, the family moved to East Haddam, Connecticut from Massachusetts. There, through three generations, they farmed and acquired land, leading in the community and church. Then to Samuel Spencer, Gerard's great-grandson, was born Oliver Lecar Spencer on October 6, 1736. As he grew up, he helped his father to farm their land at East Haddam alongside his brothers. In addition, as the descendant of Puritans, he learned to respect and to obey the adults in his life, and that it was sinful to find fault with his food, clothing, duties, or situation. His duties included courtesy, silence among superiors, and bowing when spoken to by those older, when entering and leaving school, and to every adult, of whatever station, gender, or race on the road.

Oliver L. Spencer's formal education included a study of Latin texts and some Greek, as well as enough geometry and trigonometry to measure land. More important was his religious upbringing. As a Congregationalist, he examined his spiritual state through reading and interpretation of the Bible.

When he turned fourteen soon after the death of his mother, he traveled to Elizabeth-town, New Jersey, the colony's first European settlement and its first capital, with his Uncle Elihu Spencer, a Presbyterian minister assigned to the church there. Shortly before in 1748, when Reverend Spencer was ordained as a missionary to the Oneidas, he'd gone out and wintered on the Susquehanna River, having prepared by studying Indian languages, and while with them, recording a vocabulary of the Oneida language. Blood and marriage tied their family to two other well-known missionaries who did their duty to instruct the Indians, Jonathan Edwards and David Brainerd.

Oliver L. needed to learn a trade or profession. Those with money and inclination could "bleed, plead, or preach;" that is, practice medicine, law, or the ministry. Due to the death of his mother, there were no longer resources to give him a profession, and he became an apprentice in the tannery of Robert Ogden, a member of the New Jersey Assembly. Oliver L. lived as a member of the Ogden family and soon caught the eye of Ogden's daughter Anne. After some years, they married back home at East Haddam and remained there, purchasing land and setting up a tannery. His philosophy, "good wives Deserve good Husbands," shows what sort of husband he was, and soon two children graced their lives, one of whom was Robert. They lived there for several years as a consolation to Oliver L.'s stepmother and siblings, his father Samuel having died of smallpox while a captain in the British Army during the French and Indian War in 1758.

East Haddam was a lovely place dotted with farms, woods, and open pastures; however, it was an unsettling place to live. Local tribes came to the East Haddam area only to placate the evil spirit Habbamock whom they believed lived in Mount Tom. Its native name was Machimoodus, the place of noises, the mountain being near the epicenter of many recorded earthquakes. When asked why there were noises at that place, an old Indian answered, "that the Indian's God was very angry because Englishman's God was come here."

During these years, Oliver L. missed living in Elizabethtown, a place with "enlarged and liberal ideas of prosperity and honor with which his mind had been imbued during his residence" there. After five years, he returned with his young family to Elizabethtown, where "[s]laves, Servants, apprentices, and laborers . . . mixed freely with persons of quality and refinement." Fortune smiled at his return, as his father-in-law took him into partnership and vested in him the absolute management of his tannery. There, Oliver L. most certainly would have been happy to spend his days, but war intervened.

CHAPTER TWO

EARNING A REPUTATION

INHERITING THE SPIRIT of his ancestors, Oliver L. Spencer was among the first to resist the pretentions of Great Britain and to arm in defense of their rights and liberties in the Revolution. When he was thirty-nine, he served as a Major in the New Jersey militia in 1776, and, per General George Washington's orders, harassed British convoys and foraging parties. Washington himself crossed New Jersey on his way to attack the Hessians, mercenaries in the pay of Great Britain, wintering at Trenton.

Spencer's favorite war story was when he was detached with a command to Springfield, occupied by regiments of the enemy within six miles of Elizabethtown. On December 17, 1776, his mounted sentinels spotted 1000 British troops marching toward them and alerted the rest of the patriot forces in the area. Major Spencer prudently abandoned Springfield and retreated towards Chatham. Rejoined with their brigade, they advanced to attack the enemy at Springfield, where the British officers were refreshing themselves at a tavern, and the soldiery was sprawled all over the meadow behind it and in the fields across the street.

Spencer brought up the center of the brigade and restrained his line until within pistol shot of the enemy. Soon into the attack, he had his horse shot from under him, but he remained calm, a pistol in each hand and smiling when he informed his commander that he was on foot due to the death of his horse.

Combat continued about an hour until darkness fell, suspending the contest, and both sides ceased firing.

The brigade fell back that evening only one mile, lighting fires and laying all night on their arms, intending to make a second attack in the morning. The first dawn light revealed the stealthy retreat of the enemy, having silently taken their dead and wounded away in wagons.

This was the first instance in the state of New Jersey in which the British troops turned their backs and fled from those they called rebels. The battle taught the Jersey militia that the foe could be conquered, and Spencer's role in this engagement was the one of which he was most proud in the American Revolution.

A week later, a determined George Washington loaded his force onto boats and crossed the raging, ice-choked Delaware River, taking nine hours to move 2500 men 1000 feet. His well-known victory at Trenton on December 26 followed.

Not one to rest solely on his own laurels, soon after, Washington proudly reported some additional clashes of the New Jersey Militia to Congress, skirmishes in which detachments of militia took prisoners without losses themselves. "The most considerable was on Sunday morning (January 5) when 8 or 10 Waldeckers were killed and wounded and the remainder of the party 39 or 40 made prisoners with [their] officers by a force not superior in number and without receiving the least damage." This significant capture made by a force of militia happened at Connecticut Farms, New Jersey, where Spencer, now a Lieutenant Colonel, commanded the forces.

Then on a wintry January night, a storm had blown a British supply ship, the *Blue Mountain Valley*, off course, and it sheltered in Sandy Hook Bay. Its supplies were for the British soldiers occupying Boston, and now the British were sending an armed vessel as an escort.

Spencer mustered in Elizabethtown as one of the Sons of Liberty, groups of which had sprung up in every colony in the previous ten years in order to fight British oppression, particularly the economic oppression of the Stamp Act. The Elizabethtown Safety Committee was rallying the town's citizens to take the ship. Spencer brought to the expedition a boat and his son Robert, who was still a teenager. Also answering the call were seventy-eight other citizen soldiers of Elizabethtown and thirty soldiers of the Continental Army.

At dawn, they spotted the *Blue Mountain Valley*, which had forty men and twelve guns; and at Spencer's suggestion, all but a few men hid below deck on his boat. Approaching slowly, they had the look of a fishing vessel, and coming alongside, the men swarmed up and charged over the railings of the supply ship. The surprise tactic worked so well that the *Blue Mountain Valley's* captain surrendered without firing a shot. The Elizabethtown militia sailed the supply ship to their home and sold the contents of the hold.

In 1777, Congress added sixteen regiments to those already formed and in response to his success in the militia, gave Spencer command as a colonel of the 16th Additional Regiment, also known as the New Jersey 5th Regiment, and then the 4th after the original's reduction. He commanded this regiment in the battles at Brandywine, Germantown, and Monmouth, and spent an awful winter at Valley Forge.

In addition to this extensive service, Colonel Spencer was one of those assigned to serve on the frontier in 1778. Washington ordered Spencer's Regiment to "repair immediately to Coles Fort, at the Minisink." There, they guarded the sparse settlements in the Minisink Valley, at the headwaters of the Delaware River, from attacks by the natives and Loyalists. Local farmers and businessmen supported them voluntarily with contributions of food and forage. Their presence successfully protected the area, but the settlements in the Cherry and Wyoming Valleys of Pennsylvania were not so fortunate.

In the summer and autumn of 1778, the Mohawk, Seneca, Cayuga, and some of the Onondagas, all Iroquois, joined their longtime allies, the British, to fight the Patriot Americans. Loyalist Americans and Indians began using Fort Niagara as a base for launching raids on the Pennsylvania and New York frontiers. They killed hundreds of combatants, destroyed eight forts and all the mills, burned at least a thousand houses, and drove off the Patriot's cattle, sheep, and hogs. Finally, they overran and defeated the Cherry and Wyoming Valleys.

In response in 1779, General Washington began to plan a strike against the Iroquois, with the purpose of ending the Indians' ability to attack Patriots on the frontier. In the spring, Washington ordered all the western units to the Wyoming valley in Pennsylvania. Malcom's Regiment, another "additional" regiment with companies from Pennsylvania and New York, went to Easton where they were "to apply to the quarter master for such tools as may be necessary for the making or repairing roads." Washington wanted to clear a way for the army to Wyoming, and they had no time to lose.

Colonel Spencer again made himself memorable to George Washington, since his regiment was to join with Malcom's, for in the spring of 1779, Congress had determined to reduce the number of regiments, and they chose to merge Spencer's and Malcom's. The joined units would be over-officered as they stood, and it was a delicate proposition choosing who should lead, Malcom or Spencer. Congress had left it up to General Washington to determine who should become Colonel and Lieutenant Colonel of the new combined unit, but Washington wanted no part in the decision, "where officers of such character and rank are concerned." He threw the choice back to Congress.

Colonel Spencer replied to Washington's order to incorporate with Malcom's Regiment with some poignant observations:

> *Altho I wish to serve my country to the utmost of my ability, I cannot say I'm fond of a soldiers life. indeed, if I were ever so fond, the consideration of a lonely Family, subject to a thousand Difficulties and insults from the more rude sort of mankind must excite some attention at least, as well as compassion, and render the service irksome and Disagreable; Especially when we consider that the money which ought to be equal to gold and silver is so Depreciated, that what was thought to be a little Estate a few years ago, will not now subsist a Family a few months. this, to Officers in the Army, must be truly alarming and Distressing, and those who remain in the service, that have not an independent fortune, must inevitably in a short time reduce themselves and their families to poverty and want, unless something in their favour should soon take place. and therefore that Duty which once called me to the field, now seems as loudly to call me to domestic life.*

He finished his letter with a promise to have his regiment ready to march at any time.

Washington wrote to Malcom, noting Spencer's desire to leave due to "the embarrassed state of his domestic concerns," but pointed out that Spencer would not leave if it did "injury to the service." Malcom decided the affair by declining command of the new corps due to his own circumstances.

When Spencer's Regiment arrived at Easton at the end of April, Colonel Spencer revised the roster of officers of the regiments and made Robert, who was paymaster of the regiment, a supernumerary, an extra. He may have done so in an attempt at fairness, but it also was a good opportunity for his son to go home to help protect the family.

All should have been well; instead, the trouble continued. Colonel Spencer wrote from Easton that Malcom's men "unanimously declared they will not march from this town under my command, which makes me extremely unhappy. Am very loathe to take command of such men, although I am of opinion the riot might have been quelled, but between the officers who were leaving them, and those who were to take command, there seemed to be a difficulty attending rash measures."

Malcom's New York Companies of men wanted to leave the corps and return to New York's State lines. Washington flatly refused, because if he allowed Malcom's officers to do so, it was only fair to allow Spencer's to do the same in the Jersey Regiments. Previous experience with such allowances had only caused "confusion" and "dissatisfaction" from which they were trying to "extricate [them]selves." General Washington was also concerned with the beginnings of a mutiny from Malcom's men, "a spirit, of which the first workings are disagreeable and dangerous." Colonel Spencer was unable to move his regiment on to their next service at Wyoming as the mutinous spirit continued, and Washington urged him to quell it with any necessary measures, writing "the task cannot be pleasing to you, the necessity, I am convinced will make you chearfully execute it." Most gratifyingly, he expressed his opinion of Colonel Spencer thus—"I have the fullest confidence in your exertions; and I doubt not they will be seconded by the officers in general."

Washington also gave Spencer ample ammunition: Tell the officers he was determined to have them settled into one Continental unit. Tell them they were to comply out of a "sense of duty" and fairness. Tell them he would send a force from the army "to compel the obedience of the refractory and punish the instigators," if necessary. Washington wanted it kept secret that he might consider resignations and a re-distribution later. "The first object [was] to teach the disobedient submission."

In addition, Spencer replacing Malcom meant that the responsibility for building the road to Wyoming fell to him. Disciplining the troops had kept him from beginning work on the road, but Washington finally insisted that the work begin, regardless of the difficulties. In mid-May, Spencer's and Cortland's Regiments did begin work on the road. Each day a fatigue party marched at 7 a.m. with axes, shovels, crowbars, and picks. Moving their camp every few days as they worked their way northeast, they widened the old Indian path and built bridges over Tunkhannock and Tobyhanna Creeks.

By the end of May, Colonel Spencer's commander wrote to Washington, "the Road is now Cut the whole Distance & through a Country the most Difficult I ever Saw. It is not possible for a Country to be Thicker with wood among which the Laurels are so thick that a man cannot get through them but on his hands & knees. The number of Sloughs & Creeks are almost Incredible. Notwithstanding all these Difficulties Colo Courtland & Spenser have So Exerted themselves as to have a Road very passable for Coach. They & their men have great merit for their Industry—what now remains is nothing Compared with what they have done."

Spencer's accomplishment was all the more impressive since, as he said, he had "just got acquainted with making the roads," meaning he had just learned how to do so.

Colonel Cortland gave "his most sincere thanks to Colonel Spencer . . . as nothing can make an officer more happy than the orderly behaviour of those under his command." Spencer had resolved the difficulties of joining the two regiments.

Then Washington made the purpose of gathering the troops and the road building clear in a letter to the leader of the expedition: "The expedition . . . is to be directed against the hostile tribes of the six nations of Indians, with their associates and adherents. The immediate objects are the total destruction and devastation of their settlements and the capture of as many prisoners of every age and sex as possible. It will be essential to ruin their crops now in the ground and prevent their planting more."

They set out late in the season, and did just as Washington ordered. An army of several thousand of their best troops marched into the lands of the Iroquois. At the end of the expedition in October, its commander wrote, "The number of towns destroyed by this army amounted to 40 besides scattering houses. The quantity of corn destroyed, at a moderate computation, must amount to 160,000 bushels, with a vast quantity of vegetables of every kind. Every creek and river has been traced, and the whole country explored in search of Indian settlements, and I am well persuaded that, except one town situated near the Allegana, about 50 miles from Genesee there is not a single town left in the country of the Five nations."

Many of the Iroquois fled to the region of Fort Niagara after the Patriots drove them from their country. That winter was a great trial for them. Part of the trouble was that they didn't want to divide into smaller groups and go elsewhere to accept aid, due to a new distrust of the British, having received little support from them during the invasion. The British Indian Agent was able to convince them there had been no bad intentions, but they remained in the region.

They lived in impromptu brush huts, dugouts, and caves, and having fled their homes in the expectation of returning, they had no tools, cooking gear, or winter clothing. Except for some meager hunting, they were entirely dependent on the British for food. Indian bark homes crowded eight miles along the road from Fort Niagara to Lewiston. There followed a severe winter with blizzards in November, January and February, piling snow into eight foot drifts. Hundreds of the homeless Iroquois died. In some of the huts and caves, families froze to death. In the spring, work details made a burying ground by throwing in quicklime and filling the holes. Others starved to death from depravation or died from scurvy caused by eating only salted meat.

When the weather broke, the Iroquois at Niagara were ready for vengeance. With the aid of the British, they so successfully destroyed the Schoharie and Mohawk Valleys, their leader Joseph Brant was able to move his theater of operations west in 1781. From Detroit, Brant led raids into Kentucky. The western tribes welcomed his aid and the natives "in all that Country are very much touched and vexed at the Six Nations Country being run off and destroyed by the Rebels."

The journey west by some of the Iroquois to continue fighting the Patriots was why Wapawaqua, one of Ollie's captors, and the rest of his family would fight so hard for the Ohio Valley. Previous cessions by the Iroquois in the Treaty of Stanwix of 1768 over ten years earlier had caused them to remove to the area from New York, in order to strengthen the Iroquois claim to Ohio. With the influx of their brethren, they knew they had to take a stand now. Wapawaqua meant White Loon, a loon being a bird that sinks and rises again. He was the son of

Cokundiawthah, "a distinguished war chief of the Mohawks," and the medicine woman Coohcoocheeh, meaning grandmother. They had two other sons, Catawawaqua (Black Loon) and Wapunnoo, and a daughter with her own infant girl child.

As for Colonel Spencer, he and his regiment fought their last battle of the revolution when the British again tested the resolve of the Jerseyans at another, larger battle at Springfield in June of 1780. The following month, wounded Colonel Spencer was appointed to "superintend the hospitals in Jersey." On January 1, 1781, near the end of the conflict, he retired from service, and with a spirit of patriotism and optimism, gave up his right to a pension when he and other officers accepted General Israel Shreve's "commen[d]ation in lieu of half pay for life." He was on his own financially.

Like many of his companions in arms, after encountering the dangers and enduring the hardships of a protracted war, Spencer found himself at its close reduced from affluence to comparative poverty. With them, he enjoyed the proud satisfaction of having aided in achieving the independence that laid the foundation of their national greatness and prosperity, and the hope of perpetuating to his children's children the blessings of civil and religious liberty. With impaired health and injured constitution, he again engaged in business, hoping in time to retrieve his losses. After toiling many years with little success, and hearing the flattering accounts then in circulation of the beauty and fertility of the Miami country, he determined to explore it.

CHAPTER THREE

STRUGGLE FOR OHIO

FROM THEIR SERVICE in the Revolution, Colonel Spencer knew Major Benjamin Stites, the first settler to draw attention to the Miami valley in the Ohio country. Originating in New Jersey, Stites had migrated to western Pennsylvania, from where in 1787, he took a flatboat to Kentucky loaded with essential supplies, flour and whiskey. When Indians stole horses from inhabitants there, Stites joined with the militia in pursuing them.

The Indians had rafted with the horses across the Ohio River, and the militia, finding their trace, pursued them to the headwaters of the Little Miami River, nearly to the village Old Chillicothe. They lost the tracks and returned unsuccessful down the valley between the Great and Little Miami Rivers, but the look of the country and fertile soil so took Stites that he determined to make a settlement at the mouth of the Little Miami River.

He must have known there would be contention with the Shawnee tribes, which were still in possession of the soil. The Shawnee, whose name meant Southerners, had lived in the Ohio Valley, including present Ohio and Kentucky, for hundreds, if not thousands of years, until the Iroquois drove them out in the Beaver Wars for furs and captives in the 1600s. The 2500 remaining Shawnee fled and spread throughout the eastern part of North America, trading and inter-marrying with the Creeks, Cherokee, Mingo, Delaware and Miami tribes. They had knowledge of customs and terrain, and they became traders and diplomats. More importantly, they gained blood ties with far-flung peoples. War was a part of

Shawnee life, and they continued to fight, not only to defend themselves, but to gain prestige and spoils.

The Iroquois claimed the Ohio country, especially the hunting and trapping rights, but did not move there, leaving the area open for settlement. By the 1730s, various tribes began to stake claims to regions, the Shawnee to the south, the Wyandot to the northeast, the Delaware the east, and the Mingo, who were the few Iroquois who chose to live in Ohio, the northwest. The Miami tribe even spread into the western Ohio region, extending eastward from their lands in the Indiana country. By 1738, the Shawnee had re-settled at the mouth of the Scioto on the Ohio River, at Lower Shawnee Town, and the Shawnee began a large-scale return to their ancestral home, to land they felt the Great Spirit had given them.

By the time that the Shawnee reoccupied the Ohio country, they already were dependent on trade goods and their life was no longer traditional. They used firearms and utensils they could not create or repair. They paid for these things with furs and pelts, and there was a tendency to overhunt the land to acquire the white men's goods. Like other natives, the Shawnee needed large tracts of land for their hunting life way. Ideally, to acquire these expensive new goods using traditional methods to pay, the natives needed more land, not less.

The French, British, and natives fought over the Ohio country, and to facilitate peace, the King of England attempted to control white settlement west of the Appalachians with his Royal Proclamation of 1763. He declared that colonial Governors could not grant Indian lands and only special royal agents could negotiate for Indian land. Western settlement became illegal except for those who earned Bounty Land Warrants through military service. In addition, no one was to molest the Indians.

Then, the Iroquois used the Shawnee as a bargaining chip. Trying to preserve their homelands, they claimed dominion over the Shawnee and gave up both tribes' rights to land west and south of the Ohio River at the Treaty of Fort Stanwix in 1768, effectively moving the treaty line from the Appalachians to the Ohio. When the Cherokee gave up rights to land in Kentucky that the Shawnee considered their own, the colonists felt that the Ohio country was theirs now for the taking, despite the fact that the Shawnee did not admit that anyone had dominion over them or their lands.

Ignoring the king's wishes, settlers poured in, particularly to rich land in Kentucky, and the Shawnee gave up any claim to it after the Battle of Point Pleasant in 1774. They also pledged to remain neutral at the start of the Revolution, but still eager to fight the Patriots who were encroaching on their land, the young warriors chafed to go to war. Their peace chief Cornstalk was one of the few who took a stand for peace, and making a dramatic gesture, visited the fort at Point Pleasant, giving himself as a hostage to prevent the Shawnee from going to war. Tragedy followed. Cornstalk was drawing a map giving the Americans intelligence when other Indians scouting the region killed and scalped a militiaman who was out hunting. In a rage, his companions entered the fort and killed Cornstalk, his son Elinipsico, and two other visiting natives.

The murder of their peace chief animated the warriors to fight harder against the Big Knives, as the natives called the Americans, during the Revolution, and other outraged tribes joined them. Though the Virginians and Kentuckians responded to the attacks by burning Indian villages and crops, the Shawnee were able to come back repeatedly with aid from the British and gain control of the Ohio Valley.

After the war, imagine the Shawnee's surprise when the British ceded the land in the Ohio country to the Americans in the 1783 Treaty of Paris, with the treaty not mentioning the native occupants at all. The British Indian Agents told the natives that the British could not have ceded land north of the Ohio River because they had never acquired the rights, which was true. The 1768 Treaty of Fort Stanwix had given the British rights only south of the Ohio. Despite this lapse, the Indians preferred the British, as both sides wanted the fur trade to continue. The Indians could continue with their traditional hunting-by-men and farming-by-women lifestyle as long as they had large tracts of land to do so. The British got not only the profitable fur trade from the transaction, but also a buffer area between themselves and the Americans. The hostile tribes would keep American eyes off the Canadian prize.

For its side, the infant U.S. government counted on selling the land to pay its Revolutionary War debts. The Americans wanted time to make their own treaties and survey the land for proper sale, but there was pressure from their own people, American squatters, who created havoc with the native Shawnee and other tribes by simply moving in. In 1786, the land fever was so heavy that the American government had to send a company of soldiers down the river to disperse the frontier people settling on the Indian shore, or northern bank of the Ohio.

The natives attempted to preserve their rights to the land. Mohawk war chief Joseph Brant, educated at Eleazar Wheelock's school for Indians in Lebanon, Connecticut, understanding the big picture, became the center of an alliance in 1783 to have the Iroquois, western, and southern tribes sell land only as allies in a confederation.

To defeat Brant's confederation, the Americans forced piecemeal treaties on small groups of Indians. The

Iroquois, Wyandot, Delaware, and a few Lakes Indians
had ceded any title to land north of the Ohio, and the
Americans now wanted the same from the Shawnee and
so summoned them to Fort Finney, constructed just for
the treaty, at the mouth of the Great Miami in 1786.

Moluntha was now head peace chief of the
Shawnee after the murder of Cornstalk, and he did not

New Jersey Journal, June 3, 1789
To the Inhabitants of New Jersey,
Friends and Fellow Citizens.

IT is with great pleasure I have observed a spirit of enterprise
prevailing among you in emigrating to distant and uninhabited
countries, to the great emolument of certain Gentlemen who
have a particular genius for land-jobbing.

I am however to congratulate you on a late discovery by which
you may keep your own estates that you have honestly earned,
or   them to the best advantage, and be possessed of as much
land as your hearts can wish.

A number speculative gentlemen, well skilled in aerostaticks,
have lately invented a Balloon, capable of carrying 100 people,
in which they have made a visit to the Moon, and have
discovered one of the finest tracts of country that ever man
beheld. The luxuriance and fertility of the soil is beyond
description. All kinds of grain and the most delicious fruits grow
spontaneously. The climate is the most healthful and delightful
that imagination can picture, and what adds to your advantage
in peopling this country, there is no Indian Savage to murder or
scalp you neither on your passage nor when you arrive thither.

The Balloon is to set off the first Monday in every month, from
the top of the Allegheny Mountain, at the rate of three dollars
for every passenger, if they take their own provisions, otherwise
to agree with the proprietors.

For terms, apply to D—H—, Esq. or B—S—, who will give
every possible encouragement.

know what else to do but to make his "X" on the treaty. The American "invitation" to the treaty had been a warning to come and sign, or there would be war. Moluntha had no way of enforcing his endorsement among his tribesmen, and he knew the Shawnee were for war. His actions bought them a little time.

Despite the treaty, the governor of Virginia soon authorized an expedition against the Shawnee because of continuing raids from the Mingo and Cherokee. The settlers felt that the Shawnee were capable of stopping the other tribes and blamed them for the attacks. Seven hundred ninety men left Limestone (Maysville) and advanced north to Mackachack, the Mekoche (a clan of the Shawnee) town in present Logan County. They surrounded the town on November 13, 1787 with orders to "spare the white blood;" that is, spare any white captives or traders who happened to be in the town.

When Moluntha learned they were coming, he raised the American flag in front of his cabin. "Melanthy," an officer wrote, "would not fly, but displayed the thirteen stripes, and held out the articles of the Miami treaty, but all in vain . . ."

The militia rode in and found only old men, women, and children. Moluntha was a prisoner when Colonel Hugh McGary, whose own rash behavior had been the cause of the slaughter of Patriots at the Battle of Blue Licks, asked Moluntha if he had fought there. The old peace chief apparently misunderstood the question, for he answered yes. He had not been there, nor had the Shawnee. McGary tomahawked and killed him on the spot.

The militia burned Mackachack, Wakatomica, Pekowi, McKee's Town, and Blue Jacket's Town, all towns recently made when the Shawnee had been forced north after the Revolution. They also burned the year's food supply, 12,000 to 15,000 bushels of harvested corn. They killed 11 men who made no resistance. "The men were literally murdered," wrote an officer who was present. They took twenty women and children as hostages to Kentucky.

It was soon after this that Benjamin Stites made his way to New Jersey and contacted John Cleves Symmes, a good friend of Colonel Spencer's. From Symmes, Stites learned that the United States claimed ownership of the land northwest of the Ohio River, and nly Congress could provide legal title for the land. Congress was sympathetic to plans to settle the region, as illustrated on July 13, 1787, when it passed the Ordinance of the Northwest Territory, which set rules for governance of the region now covering Ohio, Indiana, Illinois, Michigan, and Wisconsin. The creation of this document disclosed the full intention of the United States to possess those lands.

When Symmes learned of the fertility of the soil and beauty of the land, he became intent on the settlement of the

New Jersey Journal, 5 Sept., 1787
THE subscriber begs leave to inform the public that he has petitioned Congress for all the land between the Great and Little Miami Rivers, adjoining the Ohio, and thinks it probable that the grant thereof will be made to him and his associates. Such gentlemen as hold continental certificates of any denomination, who wish to become purchasers, are desired to signify their pleasure to the subscriber.

Officers and soldiers of the late continental army who choose to have their bounty lands in the abovementioned district of country are desired to send their names and rank to General Dayton at Elizabeth-Town.

JOHN CLEVES SYMMES.

Elizabeth-Town, Sept. 3, 1787.

Northwest to help the United States solidify its claim. Symmes had been a New Jersey militia colonel before resigning to become an Associate Judge of the supreme court of New Jersey from 1778-1785. He also served as a member of the Continental Congress of 1784-85, as Lt. Governor of New Jersey for two years, and as a member of its Council for six. He was now a member of the U.S. Congress, whom he convinced to allow him to buy the land between the Miami Rivers, believed to be one million acres. Stites' finder's fee was ten thousand acres of land at the mouth of the Little Miami, and Stites and Symmes set about recruiting buyers. To increase the number of settlers in this risky arena, Symmes offered to any male who would enter the area, erect a cabin, clear three acres, and remain for three years the title to the land on which he lived.

CHAPTER FOUR

SETTLING COLUMBIA

IN AUGUST OF 1788, a party of sixty volunteer militiamen from Kentucky explored the Miami region under Symmes's command, finding a truly romantic scene. Ancient trees vied for the sun—ash, walnut, hickory, beech, sugar maple, and buckeye made a cool summer retreat on the hills and higher plains; rows of cottonwood and water maple lined the banks of the rivers; bear, deer, raccoon, opossum and wild turkey ranged over the green pasture of the rich bottomlands. But the spell was broken when the party came across a group of defenseless Indians in camp, and Symmes would not allow the militiamen to hurt them. After this, the Kentuckians became unruly. About half of them left Symmes, and the rest wanted to go home.

Undaunted, Symmes soon made another trip up the river with those willing, measuring the distance between the Great and Little Miamis and then returning to Limestone.

Stites, his family, and men in his employ remained behind at Limestone to plan a fort and cut and rive the timber for it. They prepared clapboards and double plank doors with the hinges already attached to make for speedy onsite construction. It was dangerous work even there, for while working in the woods, Stites' nephew Nehemiah and a friend had turned aside to hunt turkeys when a party of Indians fired upon them. Stites was shot clean through the breast and out at the back. His dog stayed with him while his friend fled and hid behind a bank of earth, where he could hear the dog. The Indians, following the sound of the dog, found Nehemiah, scalped him, and then stuck a tomahawk into his head and struck his head against a tree, "where his brains were seen sticking." The dog survived.

Despite this attack, Stites's party continued with their plans, the men loading the prepared wood into boats, leaving Limestone on November 17. Five families and twelve single men, making in all twenty-two men able to fight, floated their boats downriver in the night and pausing, timed their arrival at the Little Miami at dawn.

There had been rumors that the Indians knew they were coming and waited with a force of 500. Five men volunteered to go ahead in a canoe to scout the area, because the women were very much afraid. By the time the scouts gave the all clear, the flatboats had floated a half mile past the mouth of the Little Miami. There they climbed the steep bank and began to clear a thicket of papaw. Placing sentinels, they thanked God for their success, first singing a hymn, and then on their knees in prayer asked for God's continuing protection. They named their settlement Columbia. They quickly set about the construction of their fort and before evening had finished the body of one blockhouse, hanging the door and chinking in the cracks between the logs. Each day thereafter, they posted sentinels and worked on the fort. After a month's hard labor, they finished Fort Miami, which was actually the settlers' cabins aligned to form the outer walls of the fort. A typical blockhouse was two stories high, with the upper story containing loopholes, small openings from which to shoot. The second story was wider and longer than the first, creating an overhang.

In the meantime, a few dozen Shawnee Indians staying with their families in a winter hunting camp spotted the settlers' boats on the shores of the Ohio. They conferred with each other in council at their camp and decided to try a friendly approach with the newcomers. They had too few numbers to repel the invaders, and wanting the advice of their chiefs, seized the opportunity to size up the situation. To this end, they asked a white captive who lived among them, one George, to approach the white settlers. This may have been George Ash, who was taken prisoner near the Falls of the Ohio when he was ten years old. He had light hair and was fair skinned.

While the settlers were working on the blockhouse, George and an Indian approached as closely as they dared. George called out in very good English for the men to come to him. The men believed that he was one of their own and ignored him.

George remained where he was, and after a while, one man called out harshly, why don't you come to us if you want to talk to us?

Unwilling to expose themselves to such danger, George and the Indian retreated to their camp.

Unaware of the proximity of the Shawnee camp, the settlers considered themselves fortunate when Lt. Jacob Kingsbury of the First U.S. Infantry arrived with a small company of soldiers and began building their own fort nearby. Kingsbury had begun as a private from Connecticut in the Revolution and worked his way up through the ranks.

With the assurance of troops in the neighborhood, and blissfully ignorant of having seen Indians, the settlers began planning for the spring crop. Three men sent to select land found a nice piece of bottomland up the Little Miami with only a few small honey locust, hackberry, and box-elder trees and some large sycamores. They named the area Turkey Bottom, reflecting the great number of those fowl found there. As they returned home, a party of Indians surrounded the three explorers. One of the settlers raised his gun. The lead Indian "took off his cap, trail[ed] his gun, and [held] out his right hand," while George said, "Do not shoot, I'm your friend."

A friendly conversation followed, and they agreed to visit each other. The Indians asked about John Cleves Symmes, whom they had heard of when Symmes visited the area the year before. Symmes gesture of peace in preserving the Indian camp was paying off. Now the Indians wanted to go to the fort to meet the white people, but the settlers would allow it only on condition that they leave their weapons behind, "so as not to alarm the women." The Indians agreed to do so and spent some time in the fort, leaving with a pledge of friendship.

The following day two of the settlers reciprocated and visited the Indian camp, east of the Little Miami. They found a friendly family camp with the warriors and their wives and children on their winter hunt. The two settlers spent the day hunting with the Indians and then slept in their camp. They left the next day with a generous gift of fresh venison from the Indians, whom they invited to visit them at the fort again and to bring their wives and children.

The Shawnee did so on the following day and amused themselves with the "many curiosities they saw about the fort," with the Indian women especially fascinated with a newborn baby, Jane Stites, the daughter of Rhoda and Elijah Stites, only two or three days old. The Indians agreed to return in a few days to celebrate Christmas.

On Christmas day the settlers celebrated with Turkey Pot Pie, cooked in two large kettles over a fire made from burning a large sycamore they had felled to build the fort. The Indians arrived, and they all visited peaceably until Lt. Kingsbury arrived from his camp with his soldiers to partake in the dinner. The Indians thought it was an attack, and one of them whistled using his fingers, giving an alarm. They ran, but Major Stites called to them and assured them that all was well. Returning, they dined on the meal prepared for them. Ironically, there was much discussion among them on the peppery flavor of the food, for which they could not account. After all, the settlers called them Indians because Christopher Columbus was certain he had found India in his search for commerce there in spices, particularly black pepper.

The get-together was successful, and throughout the winter, the Indians and settlers maintained almost daily friendly contact.

Right after Christmas, the river flooded and the rising water stranded the soldiers close to the blockhouse they were building. As the water continued to rise, they entered the blockhouse and retreated to the loft. From there, they boarded a boat that they had saved from the crushing winter ice and that the resourceful Kingsbury somehow made available to them. On the last day of December 1788, Kingsbury's force floated down the Ohio in search of dry land, finding a spot some miles down on a naturally terraced site. Here Kingsbury commenced building a new fort, the Picket Fort.

Seven men who had surveyed Symmes' purchase the previous year lived on one of the terraces in a large shanty, having discovered the site from their explorations. They were now laying out a new town, soon named Cincinnati.

It was a difficult winter. In addition to continued flooding, the settlers' stores of flour and salt gave out. Starvation forced the women and children to dig roots found on the Turkey Bottom floodplain. In particular, they boiled, dried, and pounded bear grass roots into an acceptable flour. At least wild game and fish were plentiful.

At the end of January, Stites sent word to Symmes at Limestone that the Indians were impatient to see him.

The Indians had accused Stites of "amusing them with falsehoods," by telling them that Symmes soon would be there and would supply them with the articles of trade they wanted. Wanting to keep his friendly relationship with the Indians, Symmes immediately set out, arrived safely, and spent the remainder of the winter six miles up the Great Miami, living in a lean-to and building a cabin. He named his new settlement North Bend, since it was near the regional northernmost bend of the Ohio River.

Some Shawnee Indians, not those who visited Columbia, came to visit Symmes, first an old man with George as interpreter. Others followed, and they remained with Symmes for a month, living at his expense. They traded hundreds of furs for linen and cloth. They took his leave "in a most friendly manner," promising to return.

The Shawnee Indians at Columbia did not fare so well. Some traders coming down the Ohio sold them whiskey ruined by being frozen in the cask. They also overcharged the Indians for a rifle and for a horse. Then a gunsmith made an Indian leave "two bucks," (two buckskins) to repair his gun for a part worth several cents, and the Indian had to pay another "two bucks" to retrieve the repaired gun. They complained of their treatment bitterly to Symmes before leaving in the spring to go plant crops at their summer camps. In addition to complaining, the Indians retaliated by stealing all of the settlers' horses on their way out.

The loss of the horses and more flooding made for late planting of the settlers' crops. The previous occupation of the area by the Indians, who had cleared around six hundred and forty acres on Turkey Bottom, saved them a great deal of labor, though; and the soil was the most fertile they had ever seen. Stites leased part of his 10,000 acres to the settlers, who worked in groups. The men took turns either planting or keeping armed guard.

Morale grew with the arrival of more families settling at Columbia, Cincinnati, and North Bend. One welcome visitor was Elder Stephen Gano, a Baptist minister from Providence, Rhode Island. The first "church" was a rude log house built on a forest-covered knoll. While armed sentinels stood watch outside, Reverend Gano, "with locks white with years," and "a voice tremulous with age, ably expounded the word of truth and affectionately encouraged penitent sinners to hope in the Divine forgiveness." He preached several times, and then, on the last Saturday in March, organized a church. The members requested Gano to remain in charge of the church, but he declined. Pennsylvanian Elder John Smith eventually became pastor.

Meanwhile, John Cleves Symmes wrote to his business partner, Jonathan Dayton, who at age sixteen in 1776 had been an ensign and Paymaster in his father Elias's 3rd New Jersey Regiment. The graduate of Princeton and practicing attorney was Jersey's representative to the Constitutional Convention and the youngest signer of the Constitution. He bought up vast land holdings around present Dayton, Ohio, but never visited the area. Symmes complained to Dayton of the lack of support by the United States and wrote of the settlement at Marietta, "At Muskingum I believe, from two to three hundred men are stationed, tho that post is not to be named in point of danger with the Miami Settlement." He went on to say that an ensign and seventeen soldiers, "are all the guards that are allowed me at present, for the protection & defense of this Slaughterhouse, as some in this country (Kentucky) are pleased to term the Miami purchase."

Then the attack that Symmes anticipated occurred. Indians attacked the guards posted at North Bend, killing one and wounding four soldiers, with the result that many settlers fled southwest to the closest large settlement, Louisville on the Ohio River. Others planned to follow soon.

WHEN COLONEL SPENCER arrived at North Bend in the summer of 1789, he carried two things. The first was a Bounty Land Warrant for 500 acres from the United States, dated June 11, 1789, based on his service as a Colonel in the New Jersey Line. The second was a letter from Jonathan Dayton to John Cleves Symmes. In it, Dayton stressed what Symmes already knew, that Spencer "sets out tomorrow to view your lands previously to his determining to take out his family & settle there. Very much depends upon what that determination shall be, and upon the report he shall make when he returns here. It is I do assure you, highly your interest to give him every encouragement & satisfaction possible for I scruple not to say that there is not a single person in the state who can induce more settlers to follow him than the Colonel. The affection which the people bear to him & the entire confidence they have in his veracity & integrity, have determined many to wait his return & be governed by his report & decision."

There was an air of excitement at Symmes's place at North Bend, since he had "such a continued throng of people . . . running in and out, that [he] could not think of having any papers exposed, nor could [he] command attention to any subject, when some one or other was unceasingly interrupting [him]."

Colonel Spencer hoped to have a farm on the Ohio River, but Symmes had promised it to others. Spencer was still interested in the region, and he explored the possibilities.

Symmes described the region and its politics:

There are very few hills after one leaves those of the Ohio: but large bodies of meadowland of excellent quality in many places. It is generally very well watered,.. A variety of stone is met with in the purchase: such as mill-stone-rock, limestone, and a gray stone, flat & well formed for building. The timber is in many parts excellent ... As to the ... climate, I am fully of opinion that the climate is an healthy one; there has been no complaint of agues or fevers since the first lodgment was made in November last; very little stagnant water is to be met with; and where the land is a little wet, it may be drained without difficulty. 'Tis true the Indians have hitherto been unexpectedly pacific; but who can vouch for a continuance of peace. They are a subtle enemy, & all their boasted friendship may be only to learn our numbers, and what state of defense we are in. The Shawanoe nation (and they are nearest to us) would not treat with Governor St. Clair at Muskingum; and why should they refuse him peace, and observe it with us?

Symmes must not have known the full story, for the Indians had not refused St. Clair, but rather the opposite. Arthur St. Clair, a Scotsman, then a Pennsylvanian, who attained the rank of Major General in the Continental Army, had studied surgery, been a judge of the Court of Common Pleas and a member of the Pennsylvania Executive Council, and ultimately, the President of the Continental Congress. He was now Governor of the new Northwest Territory, which the Americans created with the Ordinance of the Northwest Territory of 1787, and part of his duty was to treat with the Indians.

His job was complex because the various tribes did not agree on how to respond to the Americans. Joseph Brant believed that they must cede to the Americans the land they had already settled on the north shore of the Ohio, and he had worked tirelessly to convince his fellows of this, sometimes to his own detriment, as some natives questioned his loyalty. Others held to the Ohio River as the ultimate boundary line, as the Shawnee had surrendered Kentucky with an agreement brokered by Cornstalk. Regardless, the local Indians were ready to talk, but when Chippewa "banditti" attacked the American soldiers building the council house for the treaty at the Falls of the Muskingum, St. Clair canceled the treaty. The natives gave the rational response, "From the misconduct of a few individuals who live at a great distance . . . and are little concerned with a union with you, you have extinguished the council fire."

St. Clair's actions became clear from his comments on treaties he negotiated earlier in the year in New York with the Six Nations (except for the Mohawks) and another with the Wyandot, Delaware, Ottawa, Chippewa, Potawatomi and Sac Nations. He wrote to President Washington, "A jealousy subsisted between them which I was not willing to lessen by appearing to consider them as one people. They do not so consider themselves; and I am persuaded their general confederacy is entirely broken. Indeed, it would not be very difficult, if circumstances required it, to set them at deadly variance."

Symmes gave Colonel Spencer a copy of a letter from the Indians to carry to Jonathan Dayton. Isaac Freeman, one of the first settlers of Cincinnati, had transcribed the letter in which they did "promise and flatter sufficiently to be sure." Freeman had accompanied an Indian and translator to the Shawnee towns at the request of Symmes, offering an olive branch. Symmes chose Freeman for his courage, activity, and ability to interact with the natives in a way that pleased them. The Indians had met with him to arrange a prisoner exchange, and while he lodged with Chief Blue Jacket, he learned that the British in Detroit had made delivery of one thousand pounds of gunpowder by packhorse to the Indians. They now waited only for artillery to be sent from Sandusky or Detroit with a British Indian Agent, "to rout these settlers altogether" from the region of the Miami Rivers and at Limestone.

Symmes naturally wanted friendly relations with the Indians, but his settlement north of the Ohio was at the heart of the problem. The Shawnee rightly insisted that there had never been a legitimate purchase of their territories north of the Ohio, and to them, he was an illegal squatter.

Regardless of this, peace and health reigned during Colonel Spencer's visit that summer. He was very pleased with the Miami country and decided that this was where he would bring his family and live out his days. From the Little Miami River's fertile alluvial plain, Turkey Bottom, the land quickly rose into hills. The well-built blockhouse there, as opposed to a badly constructed little blockhouse at North Bend, may have influenced his decision to locate there. Spencer bought land near the base of a large hill set back from the river, close to the settlement of Columbia. He bought several lots, consisting of 428 acres, using the Bounty Land Warrant granted for his military service as payment. He also contracted to have a cabin built for the reception of his family. By mid-July, he was ready to return home. He carried a letter back to New Jersey in which Symmes wrote to Dayton, "I am happy that I have it in my power to inform you that I believe our very worthy friend Col Spencer is accommodated as well as it is possible to do it in this purchase."

When Colonel Spencer returned home by way of North Carolina, his horse became lame, and he stayed for a few days while it healed. At this time, he "providentially" met his elder brother Samuel, a Carolina Supreme Court Judge. This unplanned meeting inspired him to write to another brother. Though he was coping with his losses, his melancholy state was evident. He wrote, "Time is on the wing. We are swiftly passing through life and shall soon reach the end of it; let us consider whether we have, or are taking, the advice which our Lord gave to Martha, to procure the one thing needful (Luke 10:38-42). For let us have ever so much of the things of this world, if we are not possessed of that good past which Mary had acquired, it will avail nothing at the last."

If Colonel Spencer was apprehensive at all about his move to the West, he was reassured upon his return to New Jersey, where he learned that two companies of men from Fort Harmar at Marietta were to build a substantial fort on the Miami Purchase. They chose Cincinnati as the best site and began construction of Fort Washington.

The building of the fort was a little late for some of the settlers at Columbia, who became apprehensive when there were signs of the Indians in the autumn, but they had not come to trade at Fort Miami as they had previously. One day at the end of September, a Mr. Seward sent his two sons, John, aged fifteen, and Obadiah, twenty-one, to fetch some green corn from their cornfield. They took no weapons and didn't return. After an awful night of waiting, at dawn some of the men divided into several search parties and went after the boys. Two men went directly to the cornfield on the usual path and found John a short distance from the field, next to a fallen tree that blocked the path. The boy rested on his elbows and knees, with his forehead resting on the earth. He was scalped, and he'd been tomahawked three times, each stroke piercing his skull and penetrating his brain.

When the Indians scalped a person, the eyebrows fell down over the eyeballs. This gave them a fearful look.

The men couldn't find Obadiah, and they carried the still-living John back to the fort. The boy regained consciousness there and told his story: They were on their way to the cornfield when a party of Indians surrounded them, which frightened them very much. One of the Indians said, "Do not be frightened; you are safe," and used a rope to tie Obadiah. Seeing this, John ran for home, chased by the Indians. He kept ahead of them until he came to the fallen tree, and as he was climbing it, the Indians knocked him down, and he knew nothing more.

John died after suffering for thirty-nine days.

Obadiah's captors took him to Sandusky. After some months, they started with him and other captives to Fort Pitt to ransom them. While driving some packhorses, Obadiah accidentally took the wrong trail. An Indian angered by this shot him dead and cut off his head, sticking it on a stake by the side of the road.

THE UNITED STATES continued to try to settle their difficulties with the natives. During this summer, Henry Knox wrote to President Washington. Knox had been a bookseller who super-intended the conveyance of captured ordnance from Ticonderoga to Cambridge, Massachusetts. He commanded the Continental artillery in the battles of Princeton, Brandywine, Germantown, Monmouth, and at the siege of Yorktown. By 1782, he was a major general and, after the war, in 1786 founded the Society of the Cincinnati for fellowship of the officers and commemoration of the war. He was now Secretary of War and observed of the hostilities on the frontier in a letter to Washington:

> *By information from Brigadier General*
> *Harmar, the commanding officer of the troops on the*
> *frontiers, it appears that several murders have been*
> *lately committed on the inhabitants, by small parties*
> *of Indians, probably from the Wabash country.*
>
> *Some of the said murders having been*
> *perpetrated on the South side of the Ohio, the*
> *inhabitants on the waters of that river are*
> *exceedingly alarmed, for the extent of six or seven*
> *hundred miles along the same.*
>
> *It is to be observed, that the United States*
> *have not formed any treaties with the Wabash*
> *Indians; on the contrary, since the conclusion of the*
> *war with Great Britain, hostilities have almost*
> *constantly existed between the people of Kentucky*
> *and the said Indians. The injuries and murders have*
> *been so reciprocal, that it would be a point of critical*
> *investigation to know on which side they have been*
> *the greatest.*

Knox was concerned that the clashes would grow and include all of the Indians in the region. He believed that the U.S. had two choices, one to "rais[e] an army and extirpat[e] the refractory tribes entirely," or two, "form [illeg.] treaties of peace with them, in which their right and limits should be explicitly defined, and the treaties observed on the part of the United States with the most rigid justice, by punishing the whites, who should violate the same."

In his report Knox pointed out that the "Indians being the prior occupants, possess the right of the soil," and they could be dispossessed by force only in a "just war." He asserted that a nation seeking to establish itself based on justice rejects benefiting itself at the expense of its neighbors, "however contemptible and weak" they may be. It was his opinion that the attacks by the Indians allowed for a just war on the part of the United States, but that they must hear the Indians in a treaty in "order amicably to adjust all differences."

To follow through on this, in the spring of 1790 the Americans sent a Vincennes trader, Antoine Gamelin, with a message and wampum for the Indians living on the Wabash, the Miami tribes and their guests, the Shawnee and Delaware. Gamelin set out from Fort Knox in early April and visited various Miami towns, where the natives received him politely and listened to the American's message in counsel. Gamelin took it upon himself to remove the words "I do now make you the offer of peace; accept it or reject it, as you please," since the first to hear it found it menacing.

On April 23, Gamelin arrived at Kekionga, the capital town of the Miami. The chiefs of the Miami, Shawnee, and Delaware Nations assembled, as well as the French and British traders who lived there. Gamelin delivered the message from the Americans and gave "two branches of wampum" to the peace chiefs of each nation. But who would speak for the Shawnee? Americans had murdered two of the Shawnee head peace chiefs, Cornstalk in 1777, and more recently, Moluntha in 1787. In the end, a couple of days later it was the Shawnee war chief Blue Jacket who invited Gamelin to his home.

Blue Jacket was born in the early 1730's and was a member of the Pekowi clan, which provided the tribal war chiefs. He was probably the half-brother of Red Pole, who was a Mekoche civil chief. Blue Jacket was in the subgroup, the Rabbit clan, and was known as Big Rabbit as a child. His adult name was Waweya-piersenwaw, the Whirlpool, colloquially known as Blue Jacket. He dreamed of the reunification of the Shawnee and was engaged in power struggles with the Mekoche, the peace clan of the Shawnee.

He spoke on behalf of the Shawnee and Delaware and pleaded the need to consult with the British, their "father" at Detroit. He gave back the Shawnee's wampum saying, "From all quarters, we receive speeches from the Americans, and not one is alike. We suppose that they intend to deceive us."

Blue Jacket met with Gamelin again a few days later to ask that he go to Detroit to consult with the British. The following day, Gamelin informed all the chiefs that he was not to go to Detroit; neither he nor the Americans had anything to say to the British.

In a final private meeting at supper, Blue Jacket told Gamelin that the Shawnee did not trust the Americans, who had "first destroyed their lands, put out their fire, and sent away their young men, being a hunting, without a mouthful of meat." He observed, "Moreover, that some other nations were apprehending that offers of peace would, maybe, tend to take away, by degrees, their lands, and would serve them as they did before; a certain proof that they intend to encroach on our lands, is their new settlement (Marietta) on the Ohio. If they don't keep this side clear, there will never be a proper reconcilement with the nations [Shawanoe], Iroquois, Wyandot, and perhaps many others."

Blue Jacket's observations were astute, and since the natives refused to make a peace treaty, the Americans prepared an attack against them.

CHAPTER FIVE

THE FAMILY'S JOURNEY WEST

NEITHER COLONEL SPENCER'S DESCRIPTION of the Miami country, nor the most glowing representations almost daily published of *"the land flowing with milk and honey"* could have prevailed with his wife to abandon the home of her fathers. New Jersey was "her own, her native land." She would not easily leave the early companions of her youth, her faithful and long-tried friends, and above all, some of her own daughters, who had married and settled around her; but she was a most exemplary wife, sensible and intelligent, possessing great resolution and uncommon fortitude, and withal, a woman of deep piety. Being satisfied that the step on which her husband had decided was necessary, she acquiesced in that decision without murmuring.

Anne Ogden Spencer, and her father, the wealthy Robert Ogden, were descendants of John Ogden, a founder of the Colony of New Jersey. Ollie's grandfather had been a lawyer active in Elizabethtown politics. He had worked his way up through various political offices to become speaker of the New Jersey House in 1763. He used that office to oppose the Stamp Act, writing, "The affair is Serious and Greatly Concerns all the Colonies to unite & Exert themselves to the utmost to Keep off the Threatening blow of Imposing Taxes, Duties, etc., so destructive to the Libertys the Colonies hitherto enjoyed." But he had refused to sign a resolution opposing the

Stamp Act sent from Congress to Parliament, believing that each Colony should present its own resolution. For his trouble, people throughout New Jersey burned him in effigy. He subsequently resigned from the Assembly, but continued to criticize British policies, and gradually regained favor.

In 1776, he was Chairman of the Elizabethtown Committee of Safety. His son Matthias, "a swashbuckling youth of enormous strength" was Colonel of the First New Jersey Regiment. Besides Oliver Spencer, another son-in-law Francis Barber was a regimental officer, a Princeton graduate, and Schoolmaster of the Classical School at Elizabethtown. Another son of Robert's, Aaron, had been an instructor at the school, and was an officer in the First New Jersey who eventually advanced to Colonel and commanded General Washington's Life Guard.

Anne and her family thus were deeply involved in public life before and during the Revolution, and she had been through much anxiety in the war years. Her 15-year-old sister Hannah Ogden wrote about the war in Elizabethtown in 1777. Before the British victory at Long Island, they had cannonaded Elizabethtown Point as a diversion from their real intentions, making the locals skittish that an invasion was coming. Hannah wrote to Major Francis Barber, her brother-in-law, of a false report that the enemy was already at the ferry crossing at the Point. "We were almost distracted for we hadn't sent away anything at all not even our clothes and could not bear to leave everything behind us to be burnt as we expected it would be as soon as they came up; we [cached] every one what clothes we could not do without and huddled them into empty barrels, Hogsheads and anything that came first at hand, & kept horses by the door ready to set off as soon as we saw them coming, which we expected every minute. The whole town was in an uproar: Women and Children running out, some on horseback, some on Carts & many on foot."

THE FIRST FEW DAYS of the Spencer family's October 1790 journey to Columbia passed very heavily. There was indeed much that amused and even delighted Ollie, but they had little conversation. His thoughtless whistle and the quaint expressions and occasional humorous sayings of the driver, an old soldier, was all that for hours broke upon the stillness of the lonely woods or varied the dull monotony of their rumbling wheels. Gradually, however, the family became more cheerful. Dwelling less upon the past, they began to think about their present condition and future prospects, and they now found much to interest them and to render their journey agreeable.

From Mendham, a small village in East Jersey and their late post war residence, their route lay through Easton and Harrisburg in Pennsylvania. Passing these towns, they soon reached the formidable Allegheny Mountains, which separated the waters of the Atlantic states from those of the Mississippi valley. Here they had to exert all their fortitude and exercise all their patience.

Emigrants to the west endured fatigue and privations from extremely bad roads and worse accommodations. They traveled, certainly at the risk of limbs and even of life, on an ancient narrow road winding among the trees, now rising, now descending abruptly by steep steps of solid rock. It was scarcely possible that any vehicle ever passed over it. After a day's fatiguing journey over the worst portion of this road, where they were delayed more than an hour in repairing damages to one of their wagons from a disastrous overset, night overtook them in the midst of a dense forest more than two miles from any habitation. This to their family, who had never lacked a comfortable shelter, was a novel and indeed an almost appalling circumstance. Their apprehension increased when the wolves commenced a most hideous howling, and their fruitful imaginations soon added a host of bears, panthers, and robbers.

With the aid of a tinderbox, they soon kindled a large fire. After a small meal of biscuit and cheese, with a little pure water from an adjoining brook, they retired to their wagons and soon in deep sleep forgot their cares and apprehensions. After sleeping perhaps two hours, Ollie awoke around eleven o'clock and discovered that his bedfellow, a nephew a year his elder, had left the wagon. He also was an Oliver, the son of Ollie's deceased brother Robert, and they lived as brothers.

After waiting some time, as he did not return, Ollie called him, and repeating his calls louder and still louder, soon woke the family. The men searched for him in every probable direction, but in vain. Loud calls and the firing of guns received no response, save the louder howling of wolves, which they now confidently believed had torn him to pieces.

In the midst of their alarm and distress, they received the welcome information of his safety from a family who found them by following the sounds of their gunshots. Ollie's nephew had walked in his sleep on a cold night in October, with bare feet and almost naked, to a house about two miles ahead on their road. He had knocked at the door; the family admitted him; but, he did not awake until the screams of its inmates, some of whom were terror stricken, roused him. Recovering himself, he soon convinced them that he was not an apparition, but a real "spirit of health." As it was now late, they kindly accommodated him with a bed for the night.

Before the application of steam to the propulsion of vessels, almost the only conveyance on the western waters was by keel- and flatboats. Families descending the Ohio and Mississippi always sought the latter boat, being cheap, easily built, and intended wholly for conveyance down these rivers. Several places along the Monongahela River built these boats on less expensive terms than at Pittsburgh. Instead of taking the direct road to that city, they went to Jacob's Creek, a branch of the Youghiogheny River, to buy their flatboat. Arriving safely, they waited more than a month for the building of a boat and for a rise of water to carry them down, following which they embarked for Columbia. In company with another family, and numbering together about sixteen souls, they soon found themselves quietly gliding down the beautiful waters of the Ohio River.

WHILE THEY TRAVELED to their new home, the United States sent a military force against the Indians. General Josiah Harmar's army consisted of three battalions of Kentucky militia, one battalion of Pennsylvania militia, and one battalion of Light troops mounted, totaling 1133 men. In addition, there were two battalions of Federal troops numbering 320 men.

The men arriving at Fort Washington in September were not the expected hardy frontiersmen, but only boys and old men, some even infirm, making up the contingency. They were to have brought their own camp equipment, such as kettles and axes, and had none. General Harmar put this in order as well as he could with the supplies available, and the army set out for the Indian towns northwest of them on the last day of September.

On October 13, 1790, a patrol of mounted men captured a Shawnee Indian. He informed them that the natives were evacuating the region, and they would be gone by the time the slow-moving army arrived. When they reached the Indian villages, they did find that the natives and traders were gone and had burned their own houses.

About a hundred Miami Indians ambushed one of Harmar's scouting parties, consisting of thirty regulars of the American Legion and several hundred militiamen.

Most of the militia fled, with a mere nine standing to fight with the army soldiers. Only their commander survived the onslaught. After his last man fell, he ran and hid for several hours in a cold lake. He later said, "My men fought and died hard."

After this, the rest of Harmar's force burned six villages with all of their crops, "corn, beans, pumpkins, stacks of hay, fencing and cabins," as well as, "twenty thousand bushels of corn in ears." They then began the return to Fort Washington.

The night of October 21, General Harmar ordered four hundred "choice" men to return to "the ruins" to see if they could yet take a toll on the lives of the Indians. Once again, the natives surprised them and defeated them. On November 3, the remnants of the army returned safely to Fort Washington with losses equal to, or greater than, those of the Indians.

The people at Columbia listened to the reports of the returning militia and blamed Harmar for the losses, and they feared that the burning of the Indian's villages would only excite them to revenge. Their consolation was the knowledge that so many settlers had arrived that the militia now numbered one hundred and fifty at Columbia and one hundred at Cincinnati.

There were a number of Indian depredations around North Bend and Columbia in consequence of the lost battle. Symmes wrote to Dayton:

I hope sir you will do your endeavour to
dissipate the fears which some intended emigrants
in Jersey may imbibe on our late losses. I pledge
myself to them that they may be perfectly safe here
as to their wives & children all men to be sure are

and must be more or less exposed when abroad.
Last week in attempting to go from Northbend to
Capt Ludlow's station I got lost and was two days in
the woods alone, and at last found myself near
Dunlap's station on big Miami, the weather was very
dark & rainy all the while, and yet I escaped the
Indians, tho the wolves had nearly devoured me in
the night as I could make no fire. I expect this
incident will give a fresh occasion to some to report
that the Indians had got me, as some people went
from this for Lexington while I was Missing.

Sure enough, the *New Jersey Journal* falsely reported Symmes death soon after; however, the mode was creative.

Despite his protestations and declaration of safety for women

> *New Jersey Journal,*
> December 22, 1790
> WE hear that the Honorable John C. Symmes, Esquire, one of the Judges of the Western Territory, was drowned in that district some time since.

and children, and despite Symmes long friendship with Colonel Spencer, he wrote, "I expect that the panic running through this country will reach Jersey and deter Many—I wish Col Spencer may be set out before the bad news reaches him."

Symmes was truly undeterred. He also offered, "It [is] impossible to describe the lands over which the army passed in their way to the Indian towns, I am told that they are inviting to a charm—"

THERE WAS A MELANCHOLY PLEASURE in viewing the unbroken wilderness, its solitude undisturbed save by the howl of the wolf or the terrific scream of the panther. The Spencers beheld the varied scenery of the west in all its loveliness and in all its primeval grandeur. The unbroken banks of the beautiful Ohio on one side first gently sloped from the pebbled shore, fringed with willows. It gradually ascended several yards, covered with cottonwood, linden, and soft maple, and then with steep ascent rose to the summit, crowned with elm and sycamore. In other places, the river bounded the ample bottom where the stately beech and poplar, the noble ash and walnut, the tall hickory and the majestic oak had withstood the storms of ages. Here too one could see the flowering buckeye; the guarded honey tree, dropping its sweets; the fragrant spicewood and sassafras, both affording tea; and the maple, yielding sugar to the early settlers.

On the other side, bounding these fertile bottoms, were hills forming a vast amphitheater, sometimes breaking abruptly in huge masses of rock interspersed with cedar, creating an unyielding barrier to the stream. Lofty trees covered the precipitous descent quite down to the water's edge. Blended with the beauty and lovely scenery of the Ohio, inspiring pleasure, was wildness and solitude, striking the beholder with mingled fear and awe.

Such were their sensations as they descended the Ohio. Indeed, there was with them a prevailing sense of loneliness—a feeling of apprehension—which after they left Pittsburgh was interrupted only as they passed by Wheeling, Marietta, Kanawha, Gallipolis, Limestone (now Maysville), and a few other settlements to their place of destination. Although they were sometimes alarmed and often feared an attack from the Indians, they saw none, nor but few signs of any during their passage, and they arrived safely at Columbia early in December 1790.

CHAPTER SIX

BURNING ABNER HUNT

THE BROAD AND EXTENSIVE PLAIN stretching along the
Ohio, from Crawfish Creek to its mouth and for three
miles up the Little Miami, was the ancient site of
Columbia. Its original proprietor, Major Benjamin Stites,
had the town surveyed and expected it to become a large
city, the great capital of the west. He divided the ground
into blocks, each containing eight lots of half an acre,
bounded by streets intersecting at right angles. He laid
out the rest of the plain into lots of four and five acres for
the accommodation of the town. On the Spencer family's
arrival, they found scattered over this plain about fifty
cabins, flanked by the small stockade, Fort Miami, nearly
half a mile below the mouth of the Miami. More families
had arrived in the past year, and more were arriving daily,
so that the little fort had several families living in each
apartment; and it served as both church and school.

There were also a few blockhouses for the
protection of the inhabitants at suitable distances along
the bank of the Ohio.

To the east, Turkey Bottom lay along the Little
Miami for one and a half miles, divided into five-acre
plots, the whole surrounded by one community fence.

The Spencer's first humble shelter had narrow
doors of thick oak planking, which turned on stout
wooden hinges. When secured with strong bars braced
with timber from the floor, the doors formed a safe barrier
at the entrance below. Above on every side were portholes,
or small embrasures, from which they might see and fire

upon the enemy. Of windows, they had but two, containing only four panes of glass in each, with openings so small that any attempt to enter them by force must have proved fatal to an assailant.

They had occupied their new habitation about a month, adding greatly to its accommodation and supplying many conveniences around them. Indeed, they began to submit to the inconveniences, privations, hardships, and dangers common to the pioneers of the west without much complaining. They were quite well off compared to those around them.

Those women already settled in were soon accustomed to seeing their children clothed in dirt and rags. As their things wore out, there were no shoemakers or tailors to replace them, no weavers, or blacksmiths. As for the dirt, even soap was at a premium. For those accustomed to wealth, it was especially trying, for they were unused to making do.

Before their arrival that summer many, while planting and tending their crops, were confined wholly to boiled corn as a substitute for bread, and sometimes destitute even of that, used in its stead a sweet bulbous root called bear grass, which they ground by hand and boiled.

Although corn was now abundant, there was but one mill, Wickerham's floating mill on the Little Miami. Built in a small flatboat tied to the bank, its wheel turned slowly with the natural current running between the flat and a small pirogue anchored in the stream, on which one end of its shaft rested. Since it had only one pair of small grinding stones, it was, at best, barely sufficient to supply meal for the inhabitants of Columbia and the neighboring families. Sometimes from low water and other unfavorable circumstances, it was of little use, so that they were obliged to supply the deficiency from hand mills, a most laborious mode of grinding.

The boys began school upon their arrival. Mr. John Reily, a young Virginian and veteran of the Revolution, had opened an English school on June 21, 1790. The girls, protected from the rudeness of the world, learned at home with writing, arithmetic, and some music and dancing as the necessary topics.

The Spencer family attended the Columbia Baptist Church, established in January of 1790, and held at settler Benjamin Davis's cabin; but being Presbyterians, they were not members.

Colonel Spencer became head of the Hamilton County militia and a judge of the county probate court. Serving on the boards of several court-martials while in the military had given him the necessary experience for the latter.

There were plenty of visits from the local military. With Colonel Spencer's role in the Revolution, and with some of his daughters of marriageable age, officers of the army began regular visits to their home. Having heard of no disturbances by Indians in their immediate neighborhood for some time previously, they felt little apprehension of danger.

WHILE THEY WERE SETTLING in at Columbia, in late December of 1790 three hundred warriors set out in dugout canoes from the headwaters of the Maumee. They had defeated Harmar and now they would press their advantage. The Indians carried ample supplies, planning for a siege. The party divided and some went east to a settlement on the Muskingum River, Big Bottom, where they surprised the settlers, burned their buildings, and killed fourteen.

The remaining two hundred warriors followed the Shawnee war chief Blue Jacket. Two Loyalist interpreters, Simon Girty and his brother George, helped lead this expedition against Dunlap's Station, an outpost about twelve miles up the Great Miami River. Their goal was to drive out the most advanced settlement on the Great Miami and then eventually to push back those upon the Ohio, to push the Big Knives out of their lands. They divided themselves into small groups to scout.

Meanwhile, on the evening of January 7, 1791, four surveyors were camping near Dunlap's Station, exploring the floodplain of the Great Miami. The river at this spot curved and nearly enclosed 1000 acres of fertile land.

The surveyors were Mr. Cunningham, John Sloan, John Wallace, and Abner Hunt. Abner Hunt, probably of Hunterdon Co., New Jersey, had arrived at North Bend and purchased land in 1789. Along with his father William he was a resident of Cincinnati, and his brother Captain Ralph Hunt dealt with John Cleves Symmes as an agent for men in New Jersey, trading cattle, iron, and farms on the Monongahela River in exchange for land in Ohio. Abner was also associated with Symmes, perhaps as a surveyor. In addition to this, he may have been privately surveying land in a scheme with his family, in an attempt to get a jump on Symmes's claim. A member of the Hunt family reasoned, "It was impossible for [Congress] to have the land surveyed without sending an army out to protect the Surveyor while he was doing it— this they would not go to the expense of in less than two or three years . . . all which times . . . [the Hunts] were to have the land surveyed to [them]."

In the summer and autumn of 1786 and 1787, a team of surveyors appointed by Congress had partially surveyed the region. The Indians frequently stole their horses, slowing the work. This raised the question: why did the Hunts believe that while the Congressional surveyors needed protection, they themselves could survey with impunity?

The Hunts wanted to sell the land as improved farms on credit and so buy the land before the U.S. could legitimize Symmes's claim.

Symmes knew of the scheme and said, "I despise such low cun[n]ing from my soul." Symmes wanted to get a jump on other's claims; however, he had higher motives than only personal gain. He was trying to get the land settled in order to claim it for the United States.

Early in the morning of Saturday, January 8, 1791, a group of eight warriors from Blue Jacket's war party tossed their packs aside. The braves were on cold rations for stealth's sake, and they smelled roasting venison. They approached the scent on the west bank of the Great Miami but were disappointed by the empty site. Motion to the north must have given them heart again. Four white men trotted away on horses.

The warriors ran to within range and fired their muskets. They killed Cunningham instantly. Lucky man. The startled horses threw off Hunt and Wallace. Sloan was bleeding but kept his seat and fled. One of the horses followed him.

The warriors rushed forward and took Hunt prisoner. Wallace recovered himself instantly and fled on foot.

Two warriors pursued the running man, who fled in the direction of his still-mounted companion.

They chased him at top speed, but he managed to increase the distance between them. The Indians loaded their guns while running and after the first mile, one got off a shot. Wallace fell and the two Indians joyously raised the scalp shout, Wah Hoo!

But Wallace was only tangled in his leggings, which had become loose, coincidentally causing his fall at the time of the shot. He tied them, rose unwounded, and fled again. He sprinted for his life and approached the mounted man, who held back from full flight and had possession of the reins of the horse that had followed him.

The second Indian got off a shot, but missed. Wallace escaped by catching up with his friend Sloan and mounting the horse. The two crossed the Great Miami beyond the range of the guns.

Sloan had to stuff his shirt into the hole from his wound to stop the blood loss. He and Wallace initially set out for Fort Washington but turned back a short time later to warn the people at Dunlap's Station. In addition, Sloan was too weak to reach the bigger fort.

The eight warriors rejoined forces. They had gained one scalp, two horses, and one tightly bound prisoner.

Blue Jacket and Simon Girty were pleased with the proceedings. They met in council and made their plans as the reports of the warriors came in.

On the east bank of the Great Miami, Dunlap's Station was a small cluster of rudely built cabins and a blockhouse surrounded on three sides by pickets and open on the side fronting the river. The cabins were half-faced cabins, with shed roofs and the lowest part of the roof on the outside of the ring of buildings. The intention was for rainwater to flow out of the station, but the low roofs provided a dangerous point of entry.

The station had garrisoned there eighteen men, commanded by Lieutenant Kingsbury, who had built the Picket Fort at Cincinnati at about the time of Stites's arrival. Six families had built cabins outside of the station. Of these, eight or ten men were capable of handling arms.

The warriors held back from attack and observed the inhabitants, unaware of the presence of Indians, working the fields that day. That evening, all the settlers took inside everything of value that they could manage, as was their habit, and they sealed the gate of the tiny fort.

That night it rained, then froze, and snow fell to a depth of four inches.

Sometime during this period, Sloan and Wallace arrived safely at the station. Lt. Kingsbury gave up his narrow quarters to the wounded Sloan.

The following day, the settlers did not leave the fort and the chiefs surmised that the two escapees had warned them. With this unpleasant development, the Indians held a council and revised their strategy.

The next day was Sunday, the day of rest and for the most part, the settlers stayed inside. Wallace and a party of five or six men left the station and buried Cunningham with great stealth. They saw no sign of the Indians.

Attackers would not surprise Kingsbury. He posted sentinels and stayed awake most of the night, telling stories in the troops' quarters. As he headed to bed just before dawn on Monday the tenth, a barking dog alerted him to danger. He awakened his sentinels by clapping his hands and calling out, "The Indians!"

The native force had not yet reached the gates, and at the alarm, they set up a constant volley. The half-dressed soldiers quickly manned their stations and returned fire.

Kingsbury's eighteen-year-old orderly sergeant ran to the millhouse, which had no chinking, to get a good look at the attacking force. He had never seen an Indian, and, "[t]o his unaccustomed vision, the whole face of the earth appeared at first to be covered with them, and their peculiar head gearing of feathers and pigment, and the horrid jingling of the deer hoofs and horns, tied around their knees, presented a spectacle of great interest, so much so as to make him forget, for the moment, that they were enemies."

Then soon, not having made a total surprise, the war party put forth a white rag on a pole and pushed the pinioned prisoner Abner Hunt forward as intermediary. Simon Girty, who had a bounty of $800 on his head, sat protected from gunfire behind a tree next to the prisoner and directed the events. He held a rope tied to Mr. Hunt.

Lt. Kingsbury showed himself a little behind the pickets, the white plume from his hat shining brightly in the sun.

Mr. Hunt introduced himself as mediator and demanded the surrender of the garrison, on the promise that the Indians would respect their life and property.

Lieutenant Kingsbury, not to be taken in, declared that they were "happy to see them, that [they had] plenty of men, arms, ammunition, and provisions, and had been waiting impatiently for them for several days."

Simon Girty scoffed and declared this untrue. He ordered Mr. Hunt to give that reply, as well as announce they were laying a siege.

Kingsbury countered with a claim that he'd sent a messenger to Judge Symmes, and all the settlement on the Ohio would soon come to their relief.

Girty replied that this too was a lie. They knew Judge Symmes was in New Jersey. Girty was bluffing, as Symmes was in residence at North Bend all that winter.

Hunt and the lieutenant parleyed for an hour, the officer leaning out over the pickets on the east side of the fort to better hear Mr. Hunt giving the terms of surrender, including threats to lay a siege and starve them out or to attack and set fire to the station.

The attacking force also declared that they had a force of 500, with 300 warriors in the area of the station blocking any escape to Fort Washington.

During the parley, the soldiers on the west side of the fort tried to pick off any Indian who peeped from behind the logs lying in the vicinity.

After a number of shots from their muskets, Simon Girty asked through Mr. Hunt, "What sort of a treaty is this, where you keep up a constant fire pending the parley?"

The lieutenant swore and loudly threatened death to the next person who fired, but quietly added, "Kill the rascals, if you can!"

Finally, Hunt insisted that the fort surrender.

The lieutenant shouted, "I would not surrender if surrounded by five hundred devils!"

Then a shot took off the plume of his hat as he leaped from the pickets. The Indians fired volley after volley.

In the meantime, a Mr. Cox had been out hunting to stock his family's larder. He had headed up the Great Miami and was waiting for game to come down to the river for a drink when he heard the cracks of distant musket fire, intermittent, as if someone had come across a herd or flock. He was a cautious man so he set aside his own hunting task and crept toward the shooter.

Suddenly, a storm of shots came from up the river, and Cox surmised he must turn and run for Fort Washington with all his might.

The firing went on for a couple of hours. Hunt had been withdrawn during the engagement, but now the shots ended and the natives sent him out again. He said only that they would return in the evening to carry all by storm.

The Indians hoped that the resulting tension would unnerve the inhabitants, but the men and women of the station alternately waved their hats over the tops of the pickets, and then popped up, exposing themselves to mock the Indians. Before the appointed evening engagement, the young warriors became impatient at the provocation and resumed firing their muskets. They also lighted arrows and launched flaming brands over the pickets, but each time the soldiers and settlers within scurried to douse the flames.

Finally, as evening came on, Abner Hunt begged the lieutenant to surrender, for the station's sake as well as his. If they did not, Hunt would be tortured to death, and when the Indians overran the station, the inhabitants would likewise be tortured. The warriors continued harrying the station throughout the evening, and periodically, Hunt begged for his life.

As ammunition became short in the station, the women began melting down pewter plates and spoons and pouring the hot metal into bullet molds.

Late that night a messenger from General Harmar at Fort Washington galloped into Columbia. Hearing cries of, "Turn out, for the Indians are coming," the men of the village rushed into the open area inside Fort Miami.

Mr. Cox had run all day from the Dunlap's Station area and warned that it was under heavy attack. The commander at Fort Washington called on the militia at Columbia to send a force to join with the regulars from the fort and the Cincinnati militia.

Someone suggested that the attack was a feint by the Indians to draw the militia away from Columbia in order to strike a harsher blow there. They soon decided, however, that there could be no delay if they were to save Dunlap's Station. All but the most aged joined in the expedition, and those men remained behind to protect the fort.

Their townsmen were happy to have the most experienced man, Colonel Spencer, remain behind to guard their village, though he commanded the county militia.

All the boys of the village, including Ollie and Oliver, watched the force of twenty men prepare. The men were dressed in hunting shirts, armed with rifles, knives, and a few with tomahawks, and they set out for Fort Washington. They saw their townsman prancing away on their horses single file like Indians, under the command of General John S. Gano, the head of the Columbia militia.

At midnight, the warriors pulled Hunt out of firing range within two hundred yards of the garrison, and quite within hearing, stripped him naked and pinioned him tightly by his wrists and ankles, spread-eagled on the ground.

Hunt begged for mercy, but this was an affront to the warriors who prided themselves in enduring pain. There was a protocol for being tortured to death, and not even their women would behave so.

They built a fire next to his body, and with fierce and exultant yells, the warriors circled around him with the Warriors' Dance. The extreme heat caused Hunt to call out for water, which they answered by applying live coals to his body.

The warriors took turns with this torture. Those who had the death of a friend or family member to avenge were the ones who ran up to the task yelling with pleasure.

Hunt cried out in his agony and the Indians prolonged this phase of the torture through half the night. If only he had answered them with insults, someone likely would have hastened his death.

The people in the station could hear it all quite clearly.

Then, as Hunt's skin became numb to the pain, the warriors slit open his arms and legs and inserted more flaming coals.

The warriors cried out with delight at his fresh shrieks, and as Hunt's cries faded to groans as he neared death, they kindled a fire on his abdomen, renewing his agony as the coals sank through his bowels.

Toward dawn, the moans ended. The warriors carefully set a pair of crossed war clubs on Abner Hunt's chest. Thus was war declared.

Back at Fort Washington, a force of about fifty mounted men, including the men from Columbia, set out before dawn. Captain Trueman of the Legion, who had served in the Revolution in the Maryland line, commanded them. Schoolmaster John Reily and another man scouted in advance of the force on white horses.

About six miles out they met eighteen-year-old William Wiseman and John S. Wallace, the member of Abner Hunt's party who through his great exertion outran the Indians and warned Dunlap's Station. These two had snuck from the Station around three a.m. while Hunt was being tortured, crossed the Great Miami by canoe, and run for help. They now accompanied the soldiers back to the station.

At dawn, excited by the night's violence, the Indian force renewed their attack, setting up a constant fire from the two hundred warriors, while some shot flaming arrows at the buildings' roofs. They did not catch due to the frantic efforts of the station.

The all-out attack had gone on for half an hour when one of the braves rushed from the woods with a flaming brand. He streaked across the clearing under the cover of heavy fire to the station before the settlers shot him down.

Firing suddenly ceased under orders from the chiefs. The scouts had come in with news of a mounted force on its way. The Indians divided their force in two and retreated to their canoes.

Around ten a.m., the force from Fort Washington crested the hill overlooking the still-whole station. When the inhabitants of the station came out they found that the Indians had killed most of their cattle and burned all of the out buildings and any corn stored within.

Only two of the soldiers and no settlers were wounded, and twelve to fifteen Indians were wounded or killed. Kingsbury sent to General Harmar the scalps of the dead Indians that their fellows could not carry off, and promised that if he found any more dead, he would "send [him] their heads, unless they are damaged; [he would] then send their scalps..."

Soon after, Ollie learned firsthand the shocking details of Hunt's death from John Wallace, the rescuer of the station.

THEY WERE ABLE to forget their troubles for a time. To celebrate George Washington's birthday on February 22, 1791, Colonel Spencer took his family to a ball, splendid by local standards, at Fort Washington in Cincinnati. Few who now behold Cincinnati have any correct idea of what it was when first settled. When Ollie first saw it, it contained not more than forty dwellings, all log cabins, and not exceeding two hundred and fifty inhabitants. Many of the first settlers lived on so-called donation lots won in Symmes lottery, on which they built cabins and were endeavoring to remain and bring in crops for three years.

Just below on the first bank, between the mouth of Deer Creek and Lawrence Street, were scattered among the trees four or five more cabins. Between Eastern Row (a narrow street now enlarged into Broadway) and Main Street on Front and Columbia Streets, there were about twenty log houses. On Sycamore and Main, principally on the second bank or hill, as they called it, there were scattered about fifteen cabins more. At the foot of this bank, extending across Broadway and Main, were large ponds on which boys skated.

All the ground from the foot of the second bank to the river between Lawrence Street and Broadway, in use by the fort, was an open space on which, although the army left no trees standing, they left the large trunks lying. On the top about eighty feet distant from the brow of the second bank stood Fort Washington, facing the river, and occupying nearly all the ground between Third, Fourth, Ludlow and Broadway streets. This fort, of nearly a square form, was simply a wooden fortification. The army constructed its four walls of hewed logs, each side about one hundred and eighty feet long, and erected barracks two stories high, connected by high pickets. The corner bastions or blockhouses, also of hewed logs, projected about ten feet in front of each side of the fort so that the artillerymen could use the cannon within them to rake its walls. Through the center of the south side or front of the fort was the principal gateway. This passage through this line of barracks was about twelve feet wide and ten feet high and secured by strong wooden doors of the same dimensions. Appended to the fort on its north side, and enclosed with high palisades extending from its northeast and northwest corners to a blockhouse, was a small triangular space in which the army constructed shops for the accommodation of the craftsmen. Extending along the whole front of the fort was a fine esplanade about eighty feet wide, enclosed with a handsome picket fence on the brow of the bank. The descent from it to the lower bottom was sloping, about thirty feet. The workers whitewashed the front and sides of the fort, and at a small distance it presented a handsome and imposing appearance. On the eastern side were the officers' gardens, finely cultivated, ornamented with beautiful summerhouses, and yielding in their season an abundance of vegetables.

There were a dozen participants in the ball, composed of the officers and ladies of Columbia and Cincinnati. All were able to enjoy it when, to mark the celebration, soldiers fired the cannon and set off rockets and other various fireworks. The occasion included riding and visiting, dancing and other amusements of the winter. The officers soon forgot their wounds and the dangers of their late disastrous campaign.

JUST A WEEK LATER, prowling Indians stole the Spencer family's two horses from a shed adjoining their cabin. A few days after that on March 4, they narrowly escaped the total massacre of their family. They had just ended their evening meal and were about to rise from their table when one of Ollie's sisters, hearing, she believed, the almost noiseless tread of approaching footsteps, cast her eyes upon the door. She saw the latch gently rising. Springing up, she seized it and held it down until the others barred the doors.

They immediately prepared to defend themselves, instantly extinguishing their lights, and the females of their family sought safety by covering themselves with the feather beds. The three men, with a rifle and two muskets, manned the portholes above. By frequently moving to the different sides of the house, they endeavored to impress the Indians with an idea of their strength. They all now clearly heard the tread of the Indians, and the men saw the forms of two or three of them gliding indistinctly through the darkness. Their intention no doubt had been to take them by surprise by opening the back door silently, firing upon them, rushing into the house, and with their tomahawks completing the work of destruction. Failing in this, being too few to take them by assault, seeing no opportunity to injure them, and not wishing to alarm the town without first affecting some mischief, they soon stole off and disappeared. They never fired a shot.

The Indians crept over to the next cabin on the hillside a short distance to the west of them, probably attracted by the light that glowed through the gaps in the never-chinked cabin of the Bowman family, who burned a large fire to keep the cabin warm. The Indians stealthily peered through the gaps between the logs.

Mrs. Bowman sat on a bench by the fire, suckling a child, and Mr. Jonas Bowman rested after a day of hunting turkeys on the Licking River in Kentucky.

An Indian fired, and Mrs. Bowman seized a bucket of water next to her on the hearth and doused the fire.

Mr. Bowman grabbed his rifle and ran outside to fire at the retreating Indians.

Three musket shots in quick succession soon sounded the alarm, and in ten minutes about thirty men assembled at the cabin of Ensign Bowman. They found the family in great consternation. Mrs. Bowman found a flattened bullet in the bosom of her dress. Fortunately, the bullet had ricocheted off a log before striking her.

At sunrise of the following day, a small party pursued the trail of the Indians, whose number probably did not exceed six. Toward noon, the search party found their tracks quite fresh, and judging that they were now almost in view of the enemy, the men moved cautiously, half bent, and straining their eyes as if they would look through every tree before them. Suddenly, at the sharp crack of one of their own rifles, as by one impulse each sprang behind a tree and waited a few moments in breathless suspense for the appearance of the Indians. At this moment, a huge bear was seen bounding off some yards from their left, and the disappointed marksman muttered curses on his rifle for deceiving his expectations. The rest of the party held strong doubts of his courage and believed he had taken this opportunity to avoid an encounter with the enemy. They were deeply incensed. With difficulty could they be prevented from summary punishment on the culprit who in one unlucky moment, as they confidently believed, had deprived them of the certain spoils of victory.

Then at Columbia a few weeks later on March 27, as the boys just left school for dinner, one of them spied a boat on the Ohio, calling out, "Yonder comes a flat-boat," Another added, "She must have run the gauntlet to get here; let us go and see."

They ran to the river's edge and saw its boards riven and shattered with bullets and splattered with blood. The boat's owner, Mr. William Plasket, with his family, reported that he had been coming down the river with two other families by the name of Greathouse, who carried with them as sightseers several passengers. Their two boats were half a mile in front of his as they approached the mouth of the Scioto River.

Plasket witnessed canoes loaded with Indians going out and taking possession of the boats in front, with no resistance. He could see no escape, the current being too strong for him to retreat, and any landing place was within easy reach of the Indians' canoes. He saw his choices as "shall we fight or die?" for being taken prisoner by the Indians often led to death.

He prepared for action by making sure that all nine guns on board were loaded and by splitting off the top of a board on the cabin to make a place from which to shoot. He had one son lie down in the bottom of the boat with the task of loading the guns as soon as they fired them. He had his wife and other children lie in hiding, with orders "not to stir or make any noise on any consideration." He placed the men in a row to fire, with instructions each to choose a different Indian as target and with strict instructions to wait for his orders.

When they were opposite the mouth of the Scioto, three canoes with three Indians in each paddled out to them. Mr. Plasket waited until they must have believed he was making no resistance, for he allowed them to put down their paddles and reach out to grasp at his boat before he gave the order to fire. Six Indians dropped and the other three veered off and made for shore.

As many as five hundred Indians appeared on the shore and fired at them while giving chase.

Mr. Plasket had his men put all their effort into rowing, and by extreme exertion, they passed a tributary stream downriver, which hindered the Indians so much that they gave up the chase. Upon taking stock, they found that the Indians had wounded two and killed two, and all the horses and cows were dead. They threw the livestock overboard, and at some quiet place, landed and buried the dead.

CHAPTER SEVEN

THE LARGEST DEFEAT

AT COLUMBIA, THE SETTLERS believed that these fright-ening events would stop the flow of immigration. Indeed, John Cleves Symmes declared in his letter to business associate Jonathan Dayton, "The Indians kill people so frequently that none dare stir into the woods to view the country, and people will not purchase at a venture as formerly."

In response to these attacks and others, Brigadier General Charles Scott, who had had two sons killed by Indians, and General James Wilkinson, Maryland born and commander at Fort Washington, mounted an attack on the Indians on the Wabash. In the attack, they captured women and children, some the family of Little Turtle, a war chief of the Miami, and brought them back as hostages. They imprisoned them in the small Picket Fort, but the raid and capture had little effect on the tribes north of them, whose boldness and daring remained unchecked.

Soon after the failure of General Harmar's expedition, the government determined to send a more powerful force against the Indians, sufficient at once to reduce them to subjection. Troops were arriving daily at Cincinnati, so that in September 1791 a large force, consisting of regulars, levies, and militia under the command of General St. Clair, then governor of the Northwest Territory, was ready to march against the enemy. From the known experience and distinguished reputation of the general as a soldier and the character of the officers under his command, the greater part of whom had "seen service," everyone confidently anticipated complete success. In the full expectation that the Indians would soon be humbled into submission, and feeling no danger while a force so formidable guarded their frontiers, the inhabitants of the Miami valley enjoyed tranquility and repose for some weeks.

St. Clair's army consisted of 1500 regulars and militia, a number of non-military wagon men and pack-horse handlers, and almost two hundred women, primarily camp followers who did washing and cooking.

While the Army regulars were ready, the men of the militia lacked the stamina needed of soldiers, many being libertines accustomed to idleness and vice, recruited from cities and large towns. In addition, the army had not the funds or organization to properly clothe, feed, or pay them.

There was great pressure to act from the public and from the government, so despite these difficulties, they marched in September. From Cincinnati, General St. Clair's army marched in a direction a little west of north past Fort Hamilton, which they had previously built on the site of the present town of Hamilton. They crossed the Great Miami, advancing about twenty-six miles. After building Fort St. Clair, near the present town of Eaton, they marched twenty-two miles farther north and erected Fort Jefferson.

Unavoidably, their progress was slow, not only from the delay of building forts, but from the nature of the ground over which they passed, where much labor was required in opening and making a road for the passage of their artillery and baggage wagons. They had suffered some delay, too, from the lack of supplies, sometimes failing due to the neglect of contractors, and at others, the enemy interrupting or cutting them off. Pursuing a direct course to the Indian villages on the Maumee River, they had on November 3 advanced about thirty miles northwest of Fort Jefferson, ninety-seven miles from Fort Washington, and were within forty-five miles of the nearest town of the enemy.

It was snowing on the afternoon of November 3 when the main body of the army, principally regulars and levies, encamped on the south side of a branch of the Wabash, in two lines distant from each other seventy or eighty yards. They were fronting the stream within a few hundred feet of it and extending along it about three hundred and fifty yards. They guarded the artillery in the center on a beautiful hillock. On the north side of the stream, a quarter of a mile in advance of the main army, Colonel Oldham had his militia posted. Beyond them at a suitable distance, Captain Slough placed his advance guard of a company of regulars. They were in open woods where were found the remnants of countless Indian camps, both ancient and new.

Indeed, they did not realize that a native force as large as their own had gathered, comprised of Shawnees led by Blue Jacket, Miamis led by Little Turtle, and Delawares led by Buckongahelas.

The night of the third, the natives prepared. Their medicine men armed the warriors outside St. Clair's encampment with their sacred protection, and all waited for dawn and the order to attack. It was after dark and snowing when Blue Jacket spoke to all the chiefs, "Our fathers used to do as we now do. Our tribe used to fight other tribes—they could trust to their own strength and their numbers. But in this conflict, we have no such reliance. Our power and our numbers bear no comparison to those of our enemy, and we can do nothing, unless assisted by our Great Father above. I pray now that he will be with us tonight, and that tomorrow he will cause the sun to shine out clear upon us, and we will take it as a token of good and we shall conquer."

Sometime before light of the ensuing day, the approach of a considerable number of Indians compelled the guard of St. Clair's army to fall back upon the militia, and the guard reported this fact to Major General Richard Butler.

General Butler was second in command of St. Clair's expedition and had served well in the Revolution as a Lieutenant Colonel, commanding the First Pennsylvania Regiment, following Anthony Wayne in a forced march into Virginia, where they had a desperate encounter against John Graves Simcoe, then against Cornwallis. Butler had also been a trader, living with the Shawnee before the Revolution. His wife was Shawnee.

Now Butler responded to the reports of Indians lurking at the edge of St. Clair's camp by sending out a party to investigate. A captain, two subalterns, and thirty men paraded at Butler's tent for instructions. They were to stop the roving bands of Indians from stealing the horses that were grazing outside the guarded lines.

Major Denny and a few other officers stayed with the General until late. Sometime after that, the captain returned from reconnoitering and reported that Indians had surrounded the detachment, and they escaped only under the cover of night. General Butler did not pass the report on, although an officer advised him that the Indians would certainly attack the army that morning. The general seemed either to have regarded the information "as an idle tale," or to have relied so confidently in the strength of the army as to have considered it invincible.

During the night, the sentinels fired their guns frequently, disturbing the camp. The guards reported many Indians were scouting and spying around them, but no one expected an attack, believing that as usual the Indians were trying only to steal horses. The constant firing of the sentinels did alert General St. Clair to some danger, and he ordered the men "should lay upon their arms with all their accoutrements on."

Before dawn, the Indian army approached to within sight of the fires of the Americans, and Blue Jacket began to sing a prayer to the Great Spirit.

Meanwhile, the shrill fife and rolling drum sounded the army's cheerful reveille. The troops, as was their daily practice, manned their lines and stood under arms in battle array until after the sun rose. When no enemy appeared, they retired, some to prepare their breakfasts or perform various other duties, and not a few to lounge in their tents.

Friday, November 4, 1791 dawned with a moderate northwest wind, a serene atmosphere, and blue skies. The Indians surely took the sun shining clear as a good omen.

Suddenly, a large force of yelling Indians, making the "damnedest noise imaginable...sounding like ten thousand cowbells around [them]," along with the sharp crack of their rifles, announced but too certainly that a great force of the enemy attacked the militia that camped three hundred yards in front. The regulars instantly took their positions, but the routed militia, sprinting in terror, retreated through the regulars, throwing them into confusion. The Indians advanced, scalping the fallen as they went, dead or living.

The drums of the encampment instantly beat to arms, and the soldiers hastened to their posts.

The Indians chased the militia almost into the camp, but when they spotted the Federal troops in battle lines with fixed bayonets, they suddenly found cover behind trees and bushes, seventy yards away. The regulars began a constant volley, aiming and hitting their targets, forcing the Indians to fall back.

The artillery manned the cannons, firing a great deal of canister (a tin cylinder loaded with iron shot) and some cannon balls at the hidden Indians, to little effect, their high ground causing their gunshots and cannon fire to strike above their enemies' heads, sometimes as much as thirty feet. More Indians arrived, totaling at least a thousand, and surrounded the army that was only a little larger than the attacking force.

The Indians had a strategy. After their initial terrifying yells, they became silent, and while some of the natives retreated from one side of the camp before the charge of the bayonet, others rushed in on the opposite side or on the flanks, killing and scalping the wounded. They repeated these charges several times, always with great loss to the troops. Indeed, it seemed as if the Indians fled at first before their charge as if to draw the soldiers out some distance from their lines, and then they would turn upon them suddenly and compel them to retreat, leaving their wounded to certain destruction.

There was tremendous noise with the firing, and with the cover of the smoke and unusual silence, the Indians were able to advance from trees, logs, and stumps. The left flank of the army gave way first, with the Indians taking part of the camp, but because of the nature of the ground, General St. Clair on foot led a party to the right and forced them back.

From the rear, the battalions charged and forced the Indians from cover, but the lightly equipped Indians skipped beyond the reach of the bayonets and turned, chased, and fired on the fleeing Americans with impunity. They again disappeared into the cover of the shaded woods to pick off the wounded left on the perimeter.

They continued to repeat this until dead Americans littered the ground, a disproportionate number of them officers, singled out. St. Clair ordered that any of the wounded who could be reached to be taken to the center of camp. The women and uninjured but fearful militia also sought safety there. The women rousted out the lurking militia from their hiding places under the wagons with firebrands and anything else at hand.

General St. Clair and other officers rallied these men from the center two separate times and took them out to the lines. In particular, General Butler's battalion on the left charged the enemy with spirit. In one of these forays, the attackers mildly wounded him. With his coat off and his arm in a sling, he walked close to the lines, shouting encouragement to the men.

During the course of this action, the Indians wounded General Butler again, this time more severely in his side, but still a flesh wound. This forced him to retire to the center, where he sat propped by knapsacks. Here the Indian's shots now concentrated, taking the general's servant and two of his horses.

General St. Clair sent his aide-de-camp, Major Ebenezer Denny, who was the acting Adjutant-General of the Army, "with his compliments," to seek Butler's status. Denny reported that Butler was calm, and that he shook with laughter when a young man from Virginia cried in alarm when a ball at the end of its velocity nicked him on his kneecap.

The Indians killed all the officers of the artillery except Captain Mahlon Ford, who ordered his men to spike the cannon (driving a piece of iron into the vent to make them unusable) and to retreat. The Indians gained possession of the damaged pieces.

All the while, the Indians scalped and mangled the bodies of the living and the dead. They cut the bodies of women in two, and along with a number of the officers, threw them onto the campfires.

After two hours of fighting, the remaining men abandoned the lines and in despair, crowded into the center. They ignored the exhortations of the remaining officers and began to fall in the crossfire of the tightening circle of Indians, the groans, cries, and calls of the wounded adding to the horror.

Captain Ford became severely wounded and disabled, and his men placed him against a large tree opposite to the side from which the Indians were charging.

The rifles of the enemy were still dealing death, and their tomahawks and scalping knives were completing the work of destruction. The Indians had killed nearly half the soldiery and more than three-fourths of the officers when General St. Clair, satisfied that further resistance would be hopeless, determined on a retreat as the only means of saving the remnant of the army. He repeatedly ordered a retreat, but the men were so dazed that they did not at first understand it. Colonel Darke formed the remaining troops, and they vigorously charged the Indians, who gave way on their right and left. The troops gained the road and commenced a retreat, which soon increased to a flight, with some throwing away their arms.

General St. Clair mounted one of the few surviving horses, and along with Major Denny, waited until the rear of the army was ahead of them. As Denny retreated, a woman caught hold of his horse's tail and hung on until he took her up behind him.

They abandoned the artillery and baggage. Each struggling for his own preservation thought not of the safety of others, leaving even the wounded to their fate, with very few exceptions. One of Captain Ford's devoted men saved his life by placing him upon a horse, which bore him safely from the battleground. Dr. Richard Allison, senior surgeon of the army, also rescued several from the battlefield. Few were more brave, humane, and benevolent than he. Mounted on his own powerful and spirited horse, with his manservant seated behind him, he brought off Captain Shaylor and three others from the field. By laying hold of the mane and tail of the noble powerful animal, they escaped the pursuit of the enemy.

Had the Indians pursued their advantage, they easily might have cut off the whole remnant of the troops, but having soundly defeated the army and satiated for a time their thirst for carnage, the greater part of them remained to plunder the camp. Those who pursued the flying troops to cut off the stragglers and scalp the wounded followed them about four miles, but the Indians fearing they would not obtain their share of the spoil suddenly gave over the pursuit and returned to the encampment. Fortunately for the army, later in the day "spirits" visited Little Turtle's warriors and told them they would fail if they pursued the army at all.

Of about fifteen hundred men who engaged in battle on that fatal morning, the enemy killed six hundred and thirty, including thirty-seven officers, and wounded two hundred and forty-four, including thirty officers. Besides these, a number of pack-horsemen, wagon drivers, and others attached to the army died in the engagement. Finally, of nearly two hundred women, principally its followers, only three escaped; the natives killed about fifty of them and made the rest prisoners. All of the private baggage, military stores, artillery, and horses were a prize to the Indians, and they left a living general on the field. This is the largest defeat of the American army ever by a native force.

Major General Richard Butler probably could have survived his wounds, but Major Denny speculated that Butler ordered his aide-de-camp to abandon him and save himself. Butler's men had placed him in his tent, and he waited with his loaded pistols. Two Indians raced for him and the General killed the first. The second Indian killed the General with a skillful throw of his tomahawk, and so took his scalp and plundered his person and tent.

After plundering and stripping the dead, securing everything that they could individually appropriate to themselves, and after being gorged with feasting, principally on slaughtered cattle, the victors began to drink and carouse. Some became stupid; others grew more ferocious as they felt the influence of the "fire water," rending the air with their hideous war whoops, acting over their savage feats. They cut and mangled the dead bodies, and finding many not yet dead from their wounds, tore out the hearts of some and threw others into the fire, terminating their sufferings. A few Indians less ferocious dressed themselves in the uniforms of the dead officers and strutted about the encampment.

Several brave and experienced chiefs had led the Indians, and besides the infamous renegade Girty and the notorious Colonel Elliott, Captain McKee of the Royal Americans and several British officers were in the battle.

All the while, the inhabitants of the Miami settlements, who had heard almost daily of the progress of the army and who confidently anticipated their complete success, anxiously expected to hear soon that they had achieved a glorious and decisive victory. Inexpressible was their disappointment, and deep was their consternation, when on the evening of November 6, a ragged and dirty man appeared out of the woods, saying he was, "nearly starving with hunger," and believing he might be the only survivor of the destruction of St. Clair's army. He related the tale of the three-hour battle in which the Indians had rushed upon them and slain most of St. Clair's men. His story spread like lightning, and woodsmen, known as Indian hunters, questioned him, believing him to be a deserter. Then other men began coming in from the woods from St. Clair's army with similar tales.

Fear and chaos followed, with wailing mothers and wives, for most of the families had some member in the campaign, a husband, father, brother, or child. Instead, the grief ended quickly enough, as by sundown all that had gone to war from Columbia returned, with the exception of James Bailey and Isaac Morris. These two died in the battle. The people of Columbia believed that they had nothing to depend upon now but their own personal resources and that the Indians would attack them in such numbers that they would be forced to flee.

The defeat hit the town of Cincinnati harder. About half of the able-bodied men in the village had gone on the expedition, and many of them died.

THOSE DISASTROUS CONSEQUENCES that the settlers at first anticipated did not follow the defeat of General St. Clair. Strong garrisons kept up at Hamilton, St. Clair, and Fort Jefferson afforded to the inhabitants of the Miami settlements great protection. In Fort Washington, several companies of troops, more than were necessary for its defense, provided constant security to the citizens of Cincinnati, giving the means of repelling any inroads of the enemy and of extending aid in case of attack to other villages.

Even so, there was a great deal of dismay throughout the region with the military losses and Indian attacks, and about twenty families fled to Kentucky. John Cleves Symmes worked to persuade many others to remain, fearing that all the other inhabitants of the Miami region would flee, deserting his purchase.

Of those remaining, each man furnished himself with "a good gun, one pound of powder, sixty bullets or one pound of lead, and six flints." They met twice a week to drill and parade, and a gun fired after sundown required the men to instantly rendezvous, ready to do battle.

Colonel Spencer, in charge of the militia, gave the order for the men to meet in parade on Sunday mornings fully armed and equipped. Along with their families, they marched to a cabin, stacked their guns in a corner, and attended a church service.

On March 9, 1792, Winthrop Sargent, of Gloucester, Massachusetts and a major in Henry Knox's artillery in the Revolution, now acting governor of the Northwest Territory, ordered Colonel Spencer to call out sixty men of his militia to establish some fortifications for the protection of the inhabitants of Hamilton County. They were to rendezvous at Fort Hamilton on March 12, for a service of fifteen days.

The following day Colonel Spencer acknowledged the order, but said that fifteen Indians had stolen a hog from the neighborhood, and they still were expecting much worse from such a large party. In addition, they were cut off from the surrounding area due to a flood. The men were reluctant to turn out, "alleging that we ourselves are in danger," and Spencer concurred, writing that I "cannot in the least [imagine] but you will readily excuse us."

On March 11, Sargent replied that he couldn't excuse the militia of Columbia from service "without manifest injustice to the other settlements of the County." He insisted that the natives would disperse when the force marched from Fort Washington and allowed another day for the preparation of the men. Sargent also reminded Spencer of a previous letter in which he instructed him to make certain preparations, and warned that if it were not done, Columbia "will be greatly exposed some weeks hence."

That same day, Colonel Spencer replied that about sixty men from the surrounding area had gathered, high water limiting the number, and their purpose was to send out a scouting party and to build more blockhouses for their defense. The skulking of the enemy on last Saturday had "alarmed their fears to that degree that they are now willing to perform the work." Spencer used the opportunity to read Sargent's order to them and demand compliance. He believed that the men would go to Fort Washington on the thirteenth, but Spencer replied that it was "with the utmost reluctance that a single man turns out; for there is no man of common sense but what is sensible of the defenseless state in which he must leave his Family behind on this Occasion." The Colonel also made the point that they had been unable to complete their blockhouses because of the frequent drafts of the militia, and the Indians continued to be more active in the area than ever in capturing settlers.

In one incident, Benjamin Alcott, James Newell and Henry Ball were out touring east of the Little Miami to locate some of the better lands of the Virginia Military District. They set out late in the evening in order to pass the most dangerous place on the narrows of the river at night. After briskly trotting three miles with Newell's dog running along with them, Indians fired on them from a ravine as they passed on the ridge above. Alcott took a shot to the arm but kept his seat and wheeled around. Newell fell from his horse, slightly wounded. The girth of Ball's saddle broke, and he fell with it. Both their horses followed Alcott.

The Indians saw that they had wounded Newell and ignored him while they tied Ball, during which time Newell slipped away.

The Indians searched around for him in the fading light and passed a tree where Newell's dog sat. The Indians moved on a short distance, when one of them stopped and said, "The white man must be up that tree, or the dog would not be there whining."

They went back, found Newell, and made him come down, whereupon they decided he was in no condition to travel and promptly tomahawked and scalped him.

Meanwhile, Alcott raced home with the party's horses. The man passed a group of playing boys and called out, "Run home, the Indians are coming; I am wounded, and Newell and Ball are taken prisoners."

In the morning, the militia went out to search for Newell and Ball. They found Newell still alive, "but most horribly and barbarously mangled," and took him home to his widowed mother. A physician brought in said he could not possibly survive his wound, as the tomahawk had pierced his brain. Newell died by evening without gaining consciousness.

CHAPTER EIGHT

THE CAPTURE

THE UNITED STATES tried again to affect a peace with the Indians, and to do so they sent separately a number of emissaries with speeches and wampum. One emissary was Captain Alexander Trueman, who had led the force that rescued Dunlap's Station. Secretary of War Henry Knox wrote to him, "You will observe that the speech is designed to effect a peace with the hostile Indians, on the terms of humanity and justice; your language must all, therefore, be to the same effect." He also wanted chiefs of the tribes to visit Philadelphia so that they could see firsthand the power behind America, with her large population and "improvements of all sorts." There they would see the futility of resistance.

In the speech, the United States asserted that they did not want to take the natives' lands and drive them out of their country. Rather, they wanted to teach them to live a civilized life with farming, raising livestock, building comfortable houses, and educating their children. They also warned that a war against America would "prove ruinous" for the Indians.

AN EARLY AND DELIGHTFUL SPRING followed the winter of 1791-2. On the last of February, some of the trees were putting forth their foliage. In March, redbud, hawthorn, and dogwood in full bloom checkered the hills, displaying their beautiful colors of rose and lily. In April, mayapple, bloodroot, ginseng, violets, and a great variety of herbs and flowers covered the ground. They saw flocks of Carolina Parakeets (now extinct), decked in their rich plumage of green and gold. Birds of various species and of every hue flitted from tree to tree, and the beautiful redbird, the untaught songster of the west, made the woods vocal with their melody. Now and again, they heard the plaintive wail of the dove, the rumbling drum of the partridge, or the loud gobble of the turkey. Here they saw the clumsy bear, doggedly moving off, or urged by pursuit into a laboring gallop, retreating to its citadel in the top of some lofty tree, or approached suddenly, rising erect in the attitude of defense, facing its enemy and waiting its approach. There was the timid deer, watchfully resting, or cautiously feeding, or aroused from its thicket, gracefully bounding off, then stopping, erecting its stately head and for a moment gazing around or snuffing the air to ascertain its enemy, then instantly springing off, clearing logs and bushes at a bound, and soon distancing its pursuers.

With a few exceptions, it seemed an earthly paradise. The wily copperhead lay silently coiled among the leaves or beneath the plants, waiting to strike its victim. The horrid rattlesnake, with head erect amidst its ample folds, preparing to dart upon its foe, more chivalrously with the loud noise of its rattle apprised its victim of danger. The still more fearful and insidious savage, crawling upon the ground or noiselessly approaching behind trees and thickets, sped the deadly shaft or fatal bullet. Except for these, you might have fancied you were in the confines of Eden or the borders of Elysium.

The inhabitants of Columbia village went forth to their labor, enclosing their fields that the spring flood had opened, tilling their ground, and planting their corn for their next year's sustenance; "went forth" for their principal cornfield was distant from Columbia about one and a half miles east, adjoining the extensive plain on which the town stood. Columbia's surveyor had divided that large tract of alluvial ground, still known by the name of Turkey Bottom, into lots of five acres each. It lay about fifteen feet below the adjoining plain, flooded annually, and was very fertile. Each family possessed one or more lots, and to save labor, they had enclosed it with one fence. Here the men generally worked in companies, exchanging labor or working in adjoining fields with their firearms near them, that in case of an attack they might be ready to unite for their common defense.

Their usual annual crop of corn, from ground very ordinarily cultivated, was eighty bushels per acre. Some well-tilled lots produced a hundred, and in very favorable seasons, a hundred and ten bushels to the acre. In hills four feet apart were four or five stalks, each one and a half inches in diameter, fifteen feet in height, and bearing two or three ears of corn. Some ears were so far from the ground that to pull them an ordinary man was obliged to stand on tiptoe.

Small as Ollie then was, he drove the oxen while his father guided the plow between the rows, followed by the corn planters. Having lost their horses, they were obliged to substitute cattle connected by a long yoke having the draft near to one of them, which permitted each to walk in a separate row. This setup fully supplied the place of a horse.

Ollie performed his labor with alacrity on the promise of his father that he would spend the approaching Fourth of July at Fort Washington. With gaiety and high expectations of coming pleasure he left home to realize those expectations. He set out on the afternoon of July 3, 1792 in company with his sisters, Sophia, age twenty-two, Sarah, age nineteen, Dorothea, age thirteen, several ladies of Columbia, and some officers who had arrived there on the morning of that day for the express purpose of conveying them to Fort Washington. They were to partake of a dinner given by the officers, followed with a ball on the evening of the Fourth. Ollie had made his own arrangements to go to Fort Washington with some of the officers, and his father gave him strict instructions to return from the fort with his sisters.

They left the shore south of Colonel Spencer's dwelling in a fine barge rowed by eight soldiers, and were soon descending with the rapid current of the river at the rate of six miles an hour. The scenery of the Ohio between Columbia and Cincinnati was in those days truly romantic. Scarcely had settlers cut a tree on either side between the mouth of Crawfish and that of Deer Creek, a distance of more than four miles. In this stretch there was a small island between which and the Kentucky shore was a narrow channel with sufficient depth of water for the passage of boats. Embracing about four acres, the upper and lower points of this island were bare, but small cottonwood covered its center and willows extended along its sides almost down to the water's edge.

The right bank of the river was crowned with lofty hills, now gradually ascending, and now rising abruptly to their summits, extending down about two miles from Columbia. Covered with trees quite down to the beach, it was very steep and formed a vast amphitheater. From thence nearly opposite the foot of the island, its ascent became more gradual, and for two miles farther down bordering the tall trees that covered it was a thick growth of willows, difficult to penetrate. Below this, the beach was wide and stony with only here and there a small tuft of willows, while the wood on the side and on the top of the bank was more open.

Not far from this bank was a narrow road from Columbia to Cincinnati, just wide enough for the passage of a wagon. It wound round the point of the hill above Deer Creek, descended northwardly about four hundred feet, crossed that creek and in a southerly direction ascended its western bank, gradually leading along the ground directly toward Fort Washington. Diverging at the intersection of Lawrence Street to the right and left of the fort, the road entered the town.

Scarcely an hour enlivened by conversation had elapsed from the time they left Columbia before they landed on the shore in front of the garrison. Ascending the bank, in a few minutes they entered Fort Washington.

They did not know at the time that messengers had arrived from Vincennes with the news that Indians likely had murdered three peace messengers, Captain Trueman and two others, since spies had seen their speeches and belts of wampum in the Indian towns without the deliverers.

In addition, General Rufus Putnam, another peace emissary sent by the Secretary of War, had arrived at Fort Washington. He informed Knox:

Soon after my arrival Genl Wilkinson returned from a Tour to Fort Jefferson with the Disagreable News that on the 25th ult[imo] about 100 Indians made an attack [on] a party of men Cutting hay near Fort Jefferson. That 16 of our people were Killed and Missing, that four Dead bodies only had been found on whom was marks [of] the greatest enmity and cruelty practiced. A War Club also with a very extraordinary Spike in the head of it. That the Indians had three horses with them. One man was dressed in a Scarlet Suit and the whole (or at least a great part) appeared in white Shirts. [A trader] returned with News that four men going from Some of our Forts with Flag had been Fired on by a party of Indians. Three of the men were killed, the man with the Flag and papers was taken, that after keeping him one day they killed him also. That the Indians took the papers to Some white man who could read and that they contained a long and good Talk from a Great Chief which when the Indians understood they were Sorry for what they had done.

— If this account be true there is little reason to doubt but Colonel Har[din] and Major Truman have fallen a Sacrifice and that Soon after they left Fort Washington as it was intended that they Should not Travel far together.

The man in the "Scarlet Suit" would have been a British officer, and natives wearing white shirts meant that the shirts were new, rewards from the British to their allies.

The now reluctant Putnam was to make a treaty with the hostile tribes of Indians and to return the captives already taken in raids. He informed Wilkinson, "all the Women and Children belonging to those tribes with whom [we have] made peace are to be well clad and released from their Captivity — the women to have Some of the Silver ornaments presented to them."

THE DAY AFTER OLLIE ARRIVED at Fort Washington, cannon fire awakened him at dawn. There were fifteen rounds from a six-pound cannon, one for each of the original colonies and the two new states, Vermont and Kentucky. At noon, the artillery fired another fifteen rounds, and he watched as the troops under arms performed various evolutions, engaging in marching drills. At dinner, as usual, the discharge of artillery followed the toasts. At dusk there was a brilliant exhibition of fireworks, and at night, if not a splendid, yet in the opinion of those present, a very agreeable and sprightly ball.

Ollie spent the next two days playing with some boys that he fell in company with, the sons of officers, doctors, merchants, artisans, lawyers, farmers, hunters, and the soldiers.

Cincinnati was an interesting and raucous village. In fact, there were more than thirty stores, the town now filled with merchants and awash in goods. The inhabitants at that time have been described as "the class that congregates around military encampments," "a bunch of Sodomites." It was reputed that when the law was well established, these people would leave for Kentucky, and perhaps eventually make their way to Orleans.

When Ollie exhausted his various amusements and grew tired of play, he became restless and uneasy. He knew his sisters had decided upon Saturday July 7 to return home and the appointed time had passed.

He arrived at the meeting place and found that his sisters had already gone. They had anxiously waited for him but felt compelled to set out early in the afternoon without him so that their bargemen could return to the fort before dark.

Determining to return home, with all the inconsiderateness of childhood, for he was not yet eleven years old, he secretly left the garrison, whose first knowledge of his absence was the report of his capture.

Reaching the bank in front of the fort about three o'clock on the afternoon of the seventh, he found a canoe with four persons bound for Columbia, just about to push off from the shore. Discovering one of them to be an acquaintance, he hailed them, requesting them to take him onboard. After a few moments' consultation, they complied.

The canoe, which was small, narrow, and quite unsteady, proceeded only a few dozen yards above the mouth of Deer Creek when one of the men, much intoxicated, made several lurches on both sides and tumbled overboard, nearly oversetting them. After a few awkward flounces, he reached the shore. Being afraid to continue in the canoe since he did not know how to swim, Ollie prevailed with the remaining men to set him on shore. Leaving the drunken man sitting on the bank, after a few minutes they continued toward Columbia.

Mr. Jacob Light stood in the bow of the canoe, propelling with a pole. In the stern a stranger to Ollie, a swarthy athletic man with thick black bushy hair, sat with a paddle that he sometimes used as an oar and at others as a rudder. In the bottom of its center sat Mrs. Coleman, then an old woman of sixty. Ollie walked along the beach a little below the canoe, now listening to the merry conversation of his companions, and now amusing himself by skimming small flat stones over the surface of the water. About a mile above the mouth of Deer Creek a canoe descending the middle of the river passed them. They had discovered it sometime before, and onboard were some market people and a woman whose child cried loudly and incessantly. This elicited from Mrs. Coleman, as is common in such cases, some remarks on the government of children.

They rounded the point of a small cove less than a mile below the foot of the island and proceeded a few hundred yards along the close willows, here bordering the beach at about ten yards' distance from the water. The stranger in the stern of the canoe, looking back and discovering the drunken man staggering along the shore nearly a mile below them, remarked with an oath that he would be "bait for the Indians," or "food for the Indians."

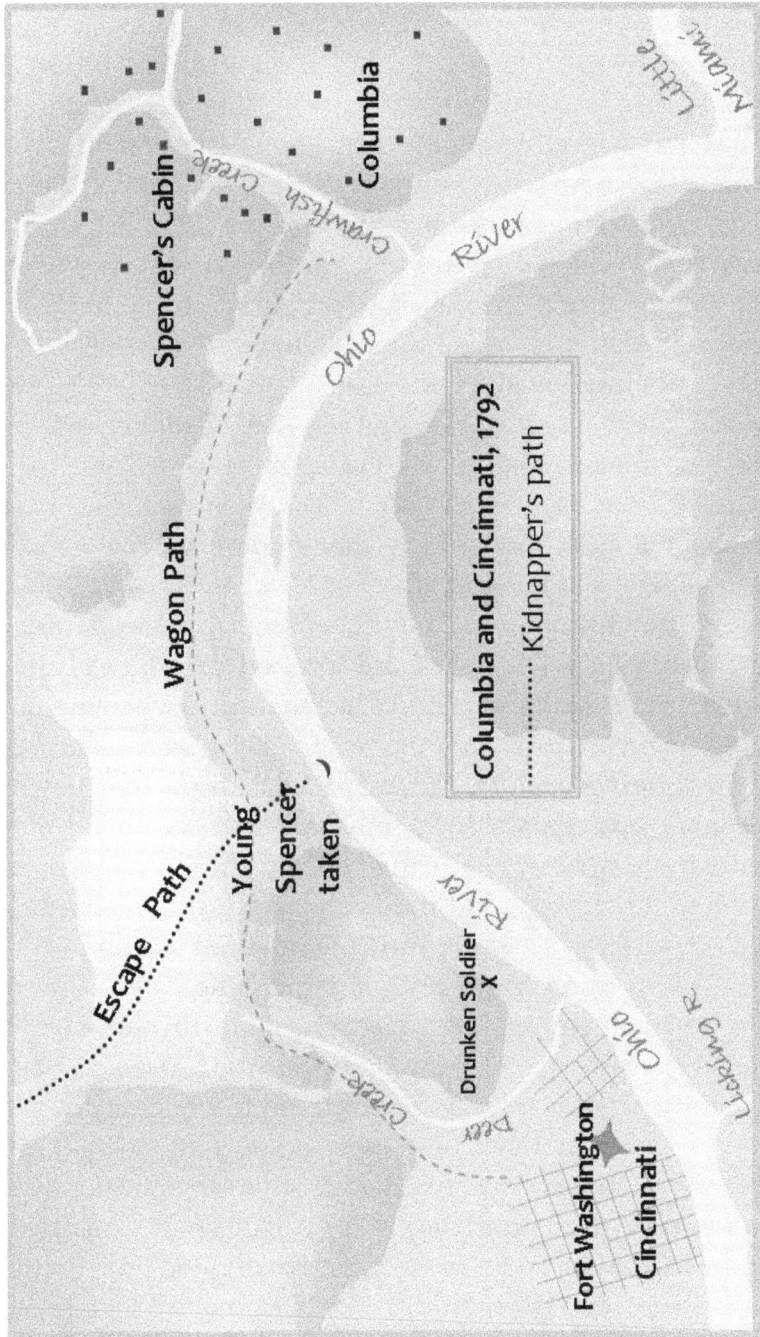

Columbia and Cincinnati, 1792
·········· Kidnapper's path

Columbia

Little Miami

Ohio River

Crawfish Creek

Spencer's Cabin

Wagon Path

Escape Path

Young Spencer taken

Drunken Soldier X

Deer Creek

River

Fort Washington

Cincinnati

Ohio

Licking R.

Scarcely had he spoken and resumed his labor, for a few moments suspended, when turning his eyes from the drunken man to the men in the canoe, Ollie saw Mr. Light spring suddenly into the river and the stranger at the stern falling over toward the shore. In the next moment, he heard the sharp crack of two rifles in instant succession, the sound lagging the bullets, and looked toward the willows about ten yards above him. He saw through the thick smoke of their guns two Indians with faces painted black as midnight (a symbol they were ready to die), rushing toward the canoe.

Never would Ollie forget his feelings at that moment. For an instant he stood motionless, and then he involuntarily drew down his head between his shoulders. His brief reflection was, I have made some narrow escapes, but now death is inevitable.

One Indian, Wapawaqua, was now within ten feet of him. In his right hand was the uplifted tomahawk, and in his left, the naked scalping knife. Instantly wheeling, Ollie ran toward the water, hoping to reach the canoe and push out into the river. The Indian passed above him down to the shore and struck his tomahawk into the head of the unfortunate stranger. Seizing him by the hair, he passed his knife quickly around the scalp and tore it violently off, holding it up for a moment with fiendish exultation.

Finding he could not gain the canoe which by this time had got out into the current, Ollie turned from the heart-sickening sight of the mangled man. Dreading every moment a similar fate, he next attempted to run down the river in the vain hope of escaping. He had not gone ten steps when discovering his design, the other Indian easily headed him. Instead, however, of seizing him violently, he approached within a few feet and extended his hand in token of peace. Ollie took it. Feeling assured of present safety from what he had heard of the character and customs of Indians, he became at once calm. The whole of these events occupied no more than thirty seconds.

One of these Indians later told him that while on the hill in quest of horses, they had heard the loud crying of the child in the canoe that had passed them about ten minutes before. They came down to the bank of the river, thinking they might have an opportunity to affect some mischief.

Arriving too late to injure those in that canoe, and discovering theirs about a quarter of a mile below, the Indians determined to wait their approach. They planned to kill the men and woman and take him a prisoner, and so concealed themselves behind a large log among the willows. From there as they came nearly opposite they made their attack.

Ollie had time only to cast a brief glance at the shocking scene before him. Mr. Light, although wounded in the left arm, was with his right swimming out into the river about a hundred yards from the shore. The dead body of the stranger was lying just in the edge of the water. Mrs. Coleman was floating about ten yards out in the river, her clothes spread over the water with her head near its surface. The desolate canoe slowly descended with the current.

The Indian who had taken him prisoner still held his hand as he led him off. His companion followed with his tomahawk extended almost over his head. They soon began to climb the high hill bordering the Ohio. Crossing the road a short distance, they stopped a few moments on the hill's side, the Indians casting their keen glances around them and listening intently as if hearing some sound indicative of danger. Apparently satisfied that they were undiscovered, they resumed their retreat and quickly gained the top of the hill. They ran off in a northerly direction at the height of Ollie's speed, one of them still holding him by his hand, the other following with his uplifted tomahawk.

They ran about four miles. His conductor, whom Ollie now regarded as his master, noticed his bare feet, for soon after leaving Cincinnati he had thrown his shoes into the canoe. The Indian supplied him with a pair of moccasins and seemed much pleased when in return for them the boy gave him his pocket-handkerchief, which he received as a mark of gratitude. The other Indian had now put his tomahawk in his belt, and fearing he might have excited his jealousy, Ollie presented to him his hat. The man dashed it on the ground at first as worthless; but instantly picking it up with the thought that it might direct pursuit, he carried it in his hand until evening, when he burned it.

Relaxing their speed, although the long strides of the Indians kept Ollie in a continual trot, and still pursuing a northerly course, about an hour before sunset they descended a high hill. They reached a small stream running in a westerly direction (the rivulet and the hill adjoining the present Sharon). Entering this stream, they waded up it about half a mile with the leading Indian directing him to step in his track, while the other followed treading in his. Then leaving it and traveling about a mile farther north, they encamped at sunset on a low point of thick underwood, near a rivulet.

Here, while one Indian kindled a fire, the other went in pursuit of game. He soon returned with a raccoon that he had killed with his rifle and proceeded to dress it by singeing off the hair. He then divided it and broiled it on the fire. The Indians ate voraciously, but Ollie was exceedingly weary and could eat very little.

Besides, he had just witnessed a most sickening scene, calculated to destroy all relish for food for a time. While his captor was dressing the raccoon for supper, he had seen Wapawaqua draw from its sheath his large brass-handled knife and cut off the limb of a small tree.

Spencer, D.M., Carleton & Lanahan.

He then took from his bullet pouch the black scalp recently torn from the head of the unfortunate white man. Cutting a small hole near its edge and hanging it on the stump of the severed branch, he deliberately and carefully scraped off the thick fat. Then forming with the limb a small hoop about six inches in diameter, with a thread of deer's sinew he stretched the scalp within it, as if he had been preparing to dry the skin of an animal.

Having finished their meal, the Indians prepared for rest. First tying the middle of a cord around Ollie's neck and extending its ends around his wrists separately, they spread a blanket on the ground and ordered him to lie down. Then lying down on each side of him, passing the ends of the cord under their bodies and covering themselves with the remaining blanket, they soon sank into a profound sleep.

For some time Ollie lay ruminating on the sad events of the day. His mind now filled with fearful apprehensions of the future, and then he was "stung with the thought of home," to which he feared he would never return. As he thought of his beloved parents and affectionate sisters, and felt for the moment that he would never again behold them, tears of bitter regret flowed plentifully, and scarcely could he repress his sobs. Then, as for a moment, a ray of hope shone through the gloom. His soul became more tranquil, and he began to explore in his mind the means and the probabilities of escape. Overcome at length with fatigue, in deep sleep he soon forgot all his sorrows.

MR. LIGHT HAD SWUM TO SHORE after seeing the Indians retreat. He reported the first news of Ollie's capture at Fort Washington and received treatment from the Army surgeon. General Wilkinson immediately dispatched an express to Colonel Spencer, announcing the painful occurrence and proposing to send out a small force of regulars.

While the news was spreading, a number of the inhabitants of Columbia soon assembled, anxious to pursue the Indians. Colonel Spencer, understanding that the Indians would instantly kill Ollie if they found themselves pursued and unable to carry him off, returned by the express a request that the military should send no troops after them. Dissuading his neighbors from their purposed pursuit with some difficulty, he obtained their promise that they would go no farther than the spot where the dead man still lay and where the Indians took Ollie prisoner. Colonel Spencer was distressed, but quite composed. He told his neighbors, "If they have determined to keep him prisoner, he may some day return; but if pursued and overtaken, their first object will be to kill him, then run."

Mrs. Coleman did not struggle in the water. Her dress had many layers, including a stuffed quilted petticoat, which did not absorb the water and served to buoy her on the surface of the river. The current carried her about two miles before she decided to make for the shore at the mouth of Deer Creek, where she hauled herself out with the aid of some overhanging willows. From there she walked to the home of a friend at Cincinnati, where she stayed and rested a few days.

People all around were shocked and alarmed. The Spencer family was well-known and well-liked, and the Colonel was a successful military man. If this could happen to them, it could happen to anyone. In addition, until now, the Indians had captured hunters and explorers in outlying areas. The settlers had begun to feel safe due to the number of soldiers in the vicinity, but now were surprised that Indians would come so close to guarded settlements in broad daylight.

A letter writing campaign to rescue Ollie began. General Wilkinson wrote to inform the captain at Fort Hamilton, about twenty miles north:

> *I send to apprize you that, this day about noon, a party of savages fired on a party consisting of two men, a woman and Col. Spencer's son—about one and a half miles above this, and on this side of the river—one man killed, the other wounded but not mortally, and poor little Spencer carried off a prisoner. I sent out a party who fell in with their trail in Gen. Harmar's trace about six miles from this, and followed it on the path about two miles farther, when the men failing with fatigue, the Sergeant was obliged to return—master Spencer's trail was upon the path—this is a farther answer to the pacific overtures.*

To describe the feelings of Ollie's parents when the news of his captivity reached them would be impossible. In a once numerous family of whom but six were living, to be bereaved of an only son would by death under ordinary circumstances have been a severe affliction. Had rescuers found him dead, inhumanly scalped and mangled on the beach by the side of his unfortunate companion, the shock, though powerful, would have gradually subsided and the violence of grief with time would have abated. That he had been carried away captive by the Indians, the cruel barbarous savages, was to his parents, and especially to his mother, almost insupportable.

Often when she thought of him, she fancied she saw him fainting with fatigue, famishing, or pining with disease. Sometimes her terrified imagination represented him falling by the knife, sinking under the stroke of the tomahawk, or expiring at the stake in the flames under the cruelest tortures. Only her faith gave her some relief, and she prayed constantly for his protection.

CHAPTER NINE

ESCAPE!

WITH THE DAWNING of July 8, the Indians awoke, and untying the cord with which they had bound Ollie, they all arose. They soon made their scanty breakfast from the remains of the raccoon that had furnished their supper. They examined the priming of their rifles and shouldered their baggage, consisting of two blankets, a bridle, a cord, and a scalp. Before the sun rose, they were marching in single file, Ollie's master in front, he in the center, and Wapawaqua bringing up the rear in the direct course of the Shawnee villages.

The morning of this day was very pleasant. The sky was clear, the air balmy and refreshing. The verdure-covered ground was less broken and hilly. The tall woods through which they passed were beautiful, and except for Ollie's condition, a captive whose every step bore him farther from friends and home, he would have been delighted. As it was, however, his mind by degrees became more cheerful, and his spirits began to resume their native elasticity.

THAT SUNDAY MORNING in Columbia as people gathered before church, they gave the Spencer family their sympathy. Colonel Spencer admitted to a great deal of anxiety for Ollie and remarked on his brother Robert, "My oldest son left home, leaving . . . one infant son behind, to make a voyage at sea, and we never heard from him again; and now my youngest and only remaining son is either slain or captive among the savages. It would be some relief to know what his fate has been."

Anne Spencer told her associates that she was glad it not her grandson, but her son, who the Indians had taken, "for she knew he was so good natured they wouldn't hurt him."

GENERAL PUTNAM WROTE to the Secretary of War, Henry Knox:

> *Yesterday a canoe going up the Ohio with two men, a woman and a boy was attacked by the Indians, one of the men was killed, the other wounded, the boy taken, and the woman escaped unhurt. This is another circumstance against my hearing from [another of the peace emissaries] in the way proposed, and with some conclusive evidence that the grand Council is broke up with a determination of continuing the war; but I doubt this, for there has not been time for the chiefs that were at Philadelphia to council at buffalo Creek and arrive at the [Ot]Tawa River by this time.*

He was correct, as the council he referred to would take place at the end of September. Indians were now gathering for it from an extensive region.

ABOUT NOON THIS DAY, passing along the east side of a hill beyond which there appeared to be a large opening, the Indians moved cautiously, half bent, and with trailed rifles. Proceeding about half a mile, they halted in a deep ravine. Wapawaqua, taking the bridle and pursuing a westerly course down the hollow, soon disappeared. In about ten minutes, however, he returned mounted on a fine cream-colored horse, which he had just stolen. Taking

Ollie up behind him, they trotted off several miles, the other Indian following until coming to thick undergrowth, where they slackened their pace into a brisk walk. Here they found a faint trace, which they pursued a few miles until it led them into a plain path, the Indians' warpath.

The Indians seemed highly pleased with their late acquisition, riding by turns the spirited animal, and occasionally taking Ollie behind them, relieving him from fatigue. Alas, how uncertain are the comforts of this world! About the middle of the afternoon, the horse suddenly became dull and seemingly sullen, so that with difficulty could they urge it forward. At length it stopped short, when in vain did Wapawaqua, on foot, apply the hickory. The horse only stood and kicked. In vain did the other Indian, dismounting, endeavor to lead it forward. It would proceed no farther. It had a violent attack of either bots (a parasite), or colic, and suddenly lying down, began to roll and groan, sometimes struggling with every limb, and sometimes dashing its head against the ground. The Indians stood over it, now beating it severely, and now talking to it in Indian as if arguing with it or threatening it with vengeance in the case of its remaining stubborn. At length, Ollie's master, seizing his rifle as if to shoot it, began in broken English to curse it, and after loading the poor animal with all the abusive epithets that he could think of, left it lying in the path.

They encamped this evening about sunset in a low rich bottom near a beautiful stream. Having made a fire and roasted part of a young fawn, which Wapawaqua a few minutes before had killed, they ate a very hearty supper, though without salt or bread, neither of which did they taste until they arrived at the Indian villages. After supper, Wapawaqua took a small piece of tobacco and cut it fine by passing the edge of his knife between his forefinger and thumb, receiving it as thus prepared into the palm of his left hand. With great solemnity and

apparent devotion, he sprinkled a few grains of it on the
coals and moved his lips as if uttering some petition, an
offering to the Great Spirit. He believed the powerful
tobacco was a "Truth-Bearer" which carried prayer to the
Creator. Then mingling the residue with some dried sumac
leaves that he drew from his bullet pouch, and filling the
bowl of his tomahawk, which also served as a pipe, he first
smoked a few whiffs. After which, he handed the pipe to
his companion who also smoked a few moments and then
returned it. The Indians thus alternately puffed until the
tobacco was consumed, frequently filling their mouths
with smoke and forcing it through their nostrils, closing
their brief use of the pipe with a peculiar suck of the
breath and slight grinding of the teeth.

The companion of Wapawaqua then surprised Ollie.
When he was captured, his roundabout and pantaloons
were of plain summer wear with covered molded buttons,
but his vest was of blue silk, double-breasted, with two
rows of small, plated sugar-loaf buttons, which attracting
their attention, the Indians had several times examined,
supposing them to be silver. The Indian took his vest, cut
off both rows of buttons, including a strip of two inches of
the silk on each side. He carefully folded them up and put
them in his bullet pouch. Unable to form any idea of his
motive in spoiling his vest, Ollie thought savage malignity
only made him act.

The day had been remarkably fine. They had
traveled with short intermissions from early dawn until
sunset a distance of at least forty miles. Very weary, lying
down before their fire under a spreading beech, they soon
fell into a profound sleep.

They slept only a few hours when the roar of a
tremendous tornado awakened them by passing only a few
dozen yards north of them, prostrating the trees with a
terrible crash and carrying devastation in its broad track.
Over their heads, thunder broke with deafening peals, and
the lightning seemed a constant sheet of flame. From the

black dense cloud that was furiously sweeping eastward, it sent its vivid bolts athwart and onward; the storm passed with the rapidity of thought. Ollie sprang from the ground, and gazing on the awful scene, stood motionless with terror. He feared that the "great day of God's wrath is come," and he felt that he was not "able to stand." He vowed to God that if he would spare him, he would dedicate to him his future life. Alas! No sooner had the fury of the storm passed and the now distant thunder ceased to terrify him, than he forgot his vows to God and banished thoughts of the great white throne.

Expecting every moment to perish, for some minutes he stood unconscious of the presence of human beings. His terror subsiding a little, he looked at the Indians standing near him and saw them perfectly calm, apparently insensible of danger, and gazing with a sort of delighted wonder. Frequently, as from the dense cloud shot some more vivid bolt, with more deafening peal, they expressed their admiration with their customary exclamation, *"Wawhaugh! waugh!"*

ON JULY 9, 1792, General James Wilkinson wrote to Henry Knox:

> On the 7th instant a canoe ascending the river to the neighbouring settlement of Columbia, navigated by two men, and having on board a woman and the only son of Colonel Spencer, was fired upon by two savages from their shore about three miles above this post. The woman jumped out of the canoe and being buoyant floated with safety. One of the men was killed, the other dangerously wounded, and the ill-fated child was carried off a prisoner.

The family of Col Spencer are in deep distress for the loss of an only son, a fine boy, about nine or ten years of age, and the colonel has conjured me to interest you in his behalf - The child is no doubt a prisoner and will be conveyed to some Indian town, as his tract has been discovered more than sixteen miles from this post, with those of the enemy, on general Harmar's trace - The commanding officer of the British garrison of Detroit could readily find and redeem this child - The colonel is a respectable citizen, and a good man, he relies much on your friendship, and the patronage of the President of the United States in this case - Pardon Sir this interposition - I have sons, and all the feelings of the father are excited into the warmest sympathy.

THE SUN ROSE BRIGHTLY above the cloudless horizon and shone upon a sky as clear and beautiful as if clouds and tempests had never touched it. Except for bent treetops above them, fallen branches around them, and widespread devastation before them, one would scarcely have believed that in the heavens now so bright and tranquil desolation and terror had so lately held their empire.

They breakfasted early and pursued their journey. Their progress for the first half hour was slow and very difficult, since they sometimes had to climb over the large bodies of the fallen trees, to wind around their up torn roots, and to creep through their tops now interwoven with the under-wood.

One who has never seen the effects of a tornado can have but a faint idea of its power and operation. For at least a quarter of a mile in width and many miles in length, not a tree had been able to withstand its force. Not only were the largest trees torn up by the roots, but many one and even two feet in diameter were twisted off, some near to the ground and others ten or twenty feet from it, apparently with as much ease as a man would break off a slender twig.

Passing at length the fallen trees and traveling on for a few hours, when hearing the sound of a bell, they halted not far from a small opening on their left. Wapawaqua left them, again taking a westerly direction, and in about half an hour returned with an old black horse, probably a pack horse belonging to the army that had given out and afterward strayed off. Suspended from its neck by a broad leather strap was a large bell, which Wapawaqua had stuffed with grass to prevent its tinkling. Ollie esteemed this horse, though inferior to the one they had lost, a valuable acquisition, for his feet had now become sore from walking, and he was delighted with the opportunity of relief which riding it afforded. Mounted upon the old horse, a natural pacer, he now rode very pleasantly, able to enjoy the comfort thus accidentally afforded him without interruption, for the Indians seemed not at all disposed to share it with him.

Halting at noon and taking some refreshment, they traveled on until about six o'clock. When passing along the side of a ridge into a low bottom, they stopped on the south bank of a beautiful stream (Buck Creek). They were in the edge of a grove covering both banks of the stream, skirting on one side a small natural meadow of a few acres and on the other a large prairie extending a mile or two north and west. Determining to remain here until the next day, the Indians hobbled the horse, unstopped its bell, and turned it out to graze. Next, intending to secure Ollie, they ordered him to sit down with his back against a small tree. They took their cord, and tying it first to the tree, passed it around his neck. They then knotted it around his wrists separately, extending his arms obliquely on each side, and fastened one end of it to a stake driven into the ground and the other to a root in the bank of the stream. After placing a large piece of bark over him to shelter him from the sun, they went out to hunt.

Left alone, thinking alternately of tender recollections of his home, with a painful consciousness of his wretched condition, sometimes revolving in his mind the probability of escape, then rejecting the thought as chimerical, an hour passed away. He now began to think seriously of making his escape, and after a few minutes, determined if possible to affect it. Being a firm believer in an overruling Providence and in the concern of God for the welfare of his creatures, he first addressed himself to him, and never did he utter a more sincere and fervent prayer supplicating his mercy and imploring his aid. He promised that if he would deliver him from the hands of the savages and restore him to his beloved parents, he would serve him the residue of his days "in truth with all his heart." Believing too, in the use of means, he immediately began to exert his own powers.

Seizing the cord with which they had bound him, he first pulled it violently with his right hand, attempting to break it or detach it from the root. Failing in this effort, he next laid hold of it with his left, endeavoring to pull down the stake on the other side. While trying to affect this, looking at the stake over his left hand, he discovered that they had tied the cord on the outside of the cuff of his sleeve, and making the effort, he succeeded in drawing his arm through it. Then with the aid of his left, disengaging his right hand in the same way, he soon set himself entirely free.

Picking up the bridle, and also thrusting in his bosom a small piece of flyblown deer meat as provision for his journey, he quickly found, bridled, and un-hobbled the old horse. Mounting on its back and using the hobbles (a cord of twisted bark) in place of a whip, he set off for home.

From the report of their rifles, which he had heard only a few minutes before he judged that the Indians were about a mile off in a southwesterly direction and that he could easily return along the path they had traveled, unperceived. As considerate for a child as he might have been, the thoughts of home so engrossed his mind that the probability and even certainty of pursuit did not enter into his calculations. He thought if he could only get a few miles from the camp undiscovered, he should be safe. Unfortunately, as it then seemed, he could not urge the horse beyond a moderate pace. Whipping it with the hobbles until he was tired, he threw the cord down in the path and supplied its place with a switch, but with all his exertions, striking with his heels, jerking with the bridle, and applying the switch simultaneously, he could not force the horse into a trot.

The sun when Ollie left the camp was about an hour high, and as he traveled steadily until sunset, he had probably proceeded three or four miles before concluding to halt for the night. He dismounted from the horse, and bending a small twig by the side of the path in a direction toward home, he led the animal a few hundred yards directly off from the trace up a gentle slope of woodland into a very close thicket of small sassafras. Securing it with the bridle, he went in search of a lodging place.

About sixty yards south of the thicket, finding a large fallen tree facing the path and having near its roots a hollow forming a shelter, he determined to lodge under it. Being very hungry and having no provision for his journey, saving the small piece of meat that he thought he would more need on the morrow, he concluded to make his evening's meal on raspberries, which grew here in great abundance. Straying from bush to bush, eagerly picking and eating to satisfy his hunger, he paid little attention to his course. When having eaten sufficiently, he turned as he thought toward his lodging place, but found after walking some time that he was completely lost. He now felt greatly alarmed. He ran about in every direction, seeking the thicket where he had tied the horse. Terrified at the thought of perishing in the wilderness, he regretted for a moment his attempt to escape. Happily, however, after wandering about for some time, he found the log. Lying down under it, pillowing his head on some leaves which he scraped together and covered with his jacket, and devoutly thanking God for saving him from the horror of getting lost and starving in the wilderness and for all his kindness thus far, he composed himself to rest.

CHAPTER TEN

PUNISHMENT

THE SUN SET with the promise of a fair morrow. Evening, mild and calm, followed. The soft twilight, gradually deepening, was fast merging into night. The birds chanted their vesper hymn and a deep and universal stillness reigned. Ollie felt that he was alone in the midst of a vast wilderness, exposed to prowling wolves and deadly panthers. His heart for a moment sank within him from a sense of his utter helplessness and of his inability to oppose even the barrier of a fire between him and destruction. Then the thought of home and the hope of reaching it in safety banished his fears and inspired him with fresh courage.

He had lain thus but a few minutes, now closing his eyes to sleep and now opening them upon the spreading tree tops or stars faintly glimmering through their branches, when he was suddenly roused by the crackling of bushes and a noise like that from quick strokes on the ground. Looking toward the path, he saw a herd of deer bounding through the woods, swiftly approaching him. Presently, one of them sprang over the log under which he lay. The others, leaping between him and the thicket where he had tied the horse, were in the next moment out of sight. Scarcely had he lain down again, when hearing a rustling among the bushes at a short distance from him, he raised himself upon his elbow to ascertain the cause. Words cannot express his feelings, nor describe his consternation and dismay, when he looked through an opening between the roots of the fallen tree under which he was lying and saw the two Indians whom he had left enter the thicket.

Advancing immediately to the horse and laying hold of his bridle, they stood a few moments in the last light looking in different directions from the small opening in the thicket facing his retreat, evidently endeavoring to discover him. Ollie had by this time partially recovered his self-possession and feared that if he waited for them to find him, they would tomahawk him where he lay. He determined at once to return to them. Instantly springing up and putting on his jacket, he ran to the thicket. With the mingled fear of deserved punishment, and the slight hope of impunity, he uttered the truly childlike excuse, "I have been out picking raspberries."

Ollie's captor ground his teeth with rage, and with a look of fiendish malice that almost froze his blood, raised his rifle to his shoulder intending to shoot him.

At that moment, the generous Wapawaqua interposed by throwing up the muzzle of the nearly leveled rifle, saving his life. A brief altercation and then a few moments' earnest conversation ensued, after which, setting down their rifles and cutting large switches from the thicket, they beat him severely on his head and shoulders until their whips were literally "used up." He bore their beating, however, with the firmness of an Indian, never once complaining nor entreating remission, and not daring to make further resistance than to throw up his arms to protect his head. Fortunately, there were none other than sassafras bushes near. Had the Indians thus beaten him with hickory or oak, they would certainly have killed him. After wearying themselves in punishing him and having told him by clear gestures that if he should try to escape again, they would certainly kill and scalp him, they set out for their camp.

Wapawaqua was in front, leading him by the hand through the barely visible thicket, and the other Indian followed on the horse until they reached the path, which they proceeded along in single file. If at any time Ollie flagged a little, falling too far behind the leading Indian, the cruel savage behind him goaded him with a stick or strove to ride over him. After proceeding about two miles, discovering in the path the bark hobbles Ollie had thrown down, he sprang from the horse and picking them up, inflicted many severe blows upon the boy's head and shoulders with them.

Weary and faint, Ollie rejoiced when at last they reached the camp. His satisfaction was momentary only, for without stopping even to secure the horse, the Indians tied him. Passing a cord around his elbows, they drew them together behind his back so closely as almost to dislocate his shoulders. Then tying his wrists so tightly as nearly to prevent the circulation of the blood in his hands, they fastened the ends of the cord to a forked stake driven into the ground. His sufferings this night were extreme. He could not lie down and to sleep was impossible. His head, bruised and swollen, pained him exceedingly, but this was trivial when compared with the torture he suffered from the violent straining of his arms behind his back. His ribs seemed every moment as though they would tear from his breast, and his shoulder blades felt as if they would separate from his body.

Forgetting the late signal instances of Divine intervention, he murmured against God, and in the bitterness of his soul longed for death.

NIGHT SEEMED AS IF IT would never end, but at length the day dawned, and gratefully did he hail the cheerful sunrise, when the Indians, having eaten their breakfast and being ready to march, unbound and relieved him from the severity of suffering. They immediately forded Buck Creek (the eastern branch of Mad River), here about thirty feet wide and swelled by the late rain, rising above his waist. They passed on about a mile and a half in a northwesterly direction through the eastern side of a prairie near a high woodland. Crossing Mad River (an important branch of the Great Miami) at a broad ford sixty feet wide, they ascended a high bank matted with blue-grass, covered with raspberry bushes and plum trees, and exhibiting the appearance of having been once the site of an Indian village. Here the Indians stopped a few minutes to adjust their blankets and make a pair of bark stirrups. He availed himself of the opportunity to breakfast on the raspberries, which were very abundant. Traveling on in a northwest course through open woods over high rolling ground, about noon they descended into a rich bottom and halted on the bank of a small creek near a fine spring.

Some yards distant from this spot was a very large sycamore, hollow at the bottom, and having on the side facing them an opening about six feet high, barricaded below with logs covered with brush. The Indians immediately went to this tree, removed the brush from before it, looked into its hollow for a moment, and then returned to the spring. Making a fire and roasting some squirrels, which they had killed in the morning, they made their dinner. Ollie had eaten nothing but raspberries for the last twenty-four hours; he was very hungry, yet the Indians offered him no food. He thought of their late cruel treatment of him and of their continued inhumanity.

He looked at the opening of the hollow sycamore, which appeared black within as if it had been burned, and he suddenly was afraid that they there intended to burn him.

Weak and faint from want of rest and food and from the debilitating effects of severe dysentery which had seized him in the morning, stiff and sore from the beating and confinement, his feet swollen from walking, and his legs torn with briars, he was truly an object of pity.

He sat with his back toward the Indians, ruminating on his wretched condition and gloomy prospects, now begging for death to release him from his sufferings, and now shrinking from the thought of its pains, its terrors, and above all, from that eternity beyond it, for which he felt that he was wholly unprepared. Soon, however, he found relief in a flood of tears, which he carefully concealed from the Indians. Then washing his face and bathing his throbbing temples at the brook, he strove to assume the semblance of cheerfulness.

The Indians now led the horse out to the hollow sycamore and removed the logs from before its opening. Ollie soon discovered the cause of their late haste to examine it and with that discovery dismissed his foolish apprehensions.

In their villages the Indians used neither bolts nor locks. When they left their cabins either empty or with any articles in them for a time, a log placed against its door afforded ample protection to its contents and abundant evidence of the right of possession in its owner. Even by the most worthless among them, this right was seldom, if ever, violated. They paid the same respect, even in the wilderness, to property known or believed to belong to Indians of the same tribe, or to those of other tribes at peace with them.

If discovered, their property here had remained inviolate. The Indians now took from within the hollow tree an old blanket and packsaddle and fastened them upon the horse's back. They next brought out two large packs of deerskins of equal size, neatly folded and firmly tied together. Connecting them with tugs of rawhide and placing them on the saddle so that they hung about halfway down its sides, they made them fast with a cord. They secured between the packs a small brass kettle, made to contain about two gallons, completing the contents of the tree. They took up their line of march.

Providing Ollie with a switch and placing him next to the horse, Wapawaqua followed, ordering him to urge it forward. Whenever the horse lagged, Wapawaqua touched him with his whipping stick and, pointing to the lazy animal, cried, "*Howh caucheeh*," meaning that the boy should quicken its gait. This employment gave him a little excitement and helped to rouse him from a lethargy produced by sickness and weariness, but from which nothing could have effectually quickened him save the certain expectation of death the moment that from any cause he should be unable to proceed.

From the conduct of the Indians, Ollie suspected what he afterwards found to be fact: That after his late attempt to escape from them he became the property of Wapawaqua by purchase from the other Indian, who now exercised no control over him. This gave him some comfort as his former master, a Shawnee, besides being an ugly looking fellow and having something sinister in his countenance, evidenced a very cruel and savage disposition, and withal great meanness and selfishness. Indeed, to Ollie he seemed destitute of every manly feeling.

Wapawaqua, the son of a Mohawk chief, now united with the Shawnees, though in battle fierce and brave, was at other times, humane and benevolent. His person, a little above the middle size, was well formed, combining activity with strength. His face was fine, his countenance open and intelligent, and his bearing noble and manly. True, like all Indians under deep wrongs, he was vindictive, but while some of his nation deserted its ranks and fought on the side of its oppressors, he disdained to aid his natural enemies to crush the remnant of his race.

Having traveled since morning about thirty miles, two hours before sunset they forded a large stream, then to Ollie waist high, to which Wapawaqua pointed and said, "*Miami.*" From its course here, a little north of west, and from its long rapids and the appearance of the banks on both sides, they crossed about two miles above Sidney. They encamped in the evening about six miles beyond the Miami at a small creek, where for the first time in thirty-six hours Ollie ate a hearty meal and then slept quietly through the night.

He awoke in the morning greatly refreshed. In the course of a few hours' traveling this morning, crossing a great many small branches running in various directions and then passing through a very extensive prairie, they came to a stream running northwardly. Following its course until noon, they halted by the side of a small rivulet. Having no provisions, Wapawaqua went to hunt some but soon returned unsuccessful.

Just at this time, a large hawk flew over their heads with a snake in its talons. Alighting on a tree a short distance from them, Wapawaqua brought it down with his rifle. The Indians prepared it by plucking the larger feathers, singeing the smaller, and boiling it in their brass kettle with a quantity of milkweed. They were furnished a dinner of flesh, soup, and greens, but even the Indians ate sparingly. Ollie, though hungry, found the hawk so tough and strong that he could eat but a few mouthfuls. As for the soup and greens, without salt the taste was not only insipid but also sickening.

About the middle of the afternoon, they met a small company of Indian hunters, the first human beings they had seen since they left the Ohio. Here resting awhile, after making various inquiries about their own families, Wapawaqua related all the particulars of their late expedition. He described by the most significant gestures their ambush, their approach, their firing, the fall of one man and the escape of the other by swimming, their taking Ollie prisoner, and finally, exhibiting the scalp as a trophy of their exploit. The hunters listened with profound attention, interrupting only at suitable times with proper expressions of wonder or praise.

After purchasing from them a few pieces of dried venison in exchange for a small silver brooch, they resumed their journey. They traveled near the bank of the same stream, the Auglaize, until sunset, then supping on boiled venison, lay down to rest.

Still traveling down the Auglaize about three hours after sunrise on the morning of July 12, they came in sight of an Indian village. Ollie felt not a little chagrined and indignant, when just before entering the first Indian village, he saw Wapawaqua's friend fasten the spoils of his vest around his legs as garters. The strips of blue silk with silver buttons contrasted strangely with the greasy leather leggings.

Meanwhile, Wapawaqua cut a long pole, and tying the scalp to the end of it and elevating it over his head, raised the scalp-halloo, a shrill whoop. Both Indians repeated this frequently until they entered the town. Here they found all its inhabitants assembled, more than fifty men, women, and children collected in front of the nearest cabin. As soon as the first salutations by the principal men ended, they seated themselves, some on logs and some on the ground, and listened with deep attention.

Wapawaqua, with that gravity of manner and those intonations of voice peculiar to Indian chiefs and warriors, again told the story of Ollie's capture. He was describing at last the act of tomahawking and scalping the unfortunate white man when a little old Indian suddenly sprang upon him. Throwing him down with violence, he gave a loud shout, accompanied with many extravagant and furious gesticulations, and vociferating, as Wapawaqua later told him, that he had vanquished his enemy. Immediately, all the women began to scream, and the children, down to the smallest papoose, set up a long shrill war whoop, gathering around him. Ollie clung to Wapawaqua; but young as he was, he would have been compelled to run the gauntlet through the women and infant warriors, had he not from great debility occasioned by dysentery been scarcely able to move faster than a walk.

Not far from there eleven years before, eight-year-old Jonathan Alder had run the gauntlet. Jonathan and his brother David had been out hunting for a lost horse in Wythe County, Virginia in May of 1781 when several Indians and a white man confronted them. David ran off but the men brought him back after spearing him. They led Jonathan away, and soon one of the men came up shaking the blood from David's scalp.

Alder's kidnappers traveled with him for two weeks or more to reach the Ohio country and then spent the summer hunting bear, deer, and buffalo in various areas. During this time, they treated Jonathan well enough, and he later believed that they treated him with a certain amount of preference because he had black hair and resembled them.

Alder's captors then sent messengers to a Mingo village on the Mad River to tell them that they were bringing in a prisoner. On the afternoon of Jonathan's arrival, all the people gathered for a gauntlet. On a smooth level patch of ground about 400 yards long, rising to a hill at the end, the men, women, and children formed two lines about thirty feet apart, facing each other. Six boys smaller than Jonathan were selected and placed another thirty feet behind him. These boys all eagerly brandished switches.

The white man pointed out an Indian woman who was at the end of the gauntlet on the hill. He instructed Jonathan: "When the word is given to run, run as fast as you can, for your life, right to that woman. These boys behind you will run after, and if they catch you [they] will whip you as much as they please. Now be sure and run right to the woman, and start just as quick as you hear the word."

Jonathan was encouraged that his pursuers were smaller than he and decided to give it his all. When he heard the word "run," he sprinted with all of his strength. The Indians lined up did not try to strike him, but as Jonathan passed them, they gave a shrill whoop at the top of their voices. Because they waited until he passed them, the noise, including the cries of the pursuing boys, was all behind him, and had the effect of cheering him on.

Jonathan reached the woman on the hill and glanced back. He had gained on the boys a little. The woman grasped his hand and ran with him to the council house; the boys followed them, dropping their switches and going in, as well. They all seated themselves.

For an hour and a half, the Indians related the story of Jonathan's captivity and their travels about the country afterwards, and the boy could understand little of it. They then took him to his new family.

THEY PARTED FROM the Shawnee village and about noon that day arrived at another village on the Auglaize. Here also the inhabitants flocked out to meet them and in like manner were entertained with an account of the late expedition of the Indians and the story of Ollie's captivity. Although the women and children manifested a great deal of curiosity, examining his dress and scanning him from head to feet, none of them offered him any rudeness. An elderly noble-looking Indian, whom he took to be the village chief, now led them to his cabin. There his wife, who appeared to be a very mild and humane woman, gave them first some boiled hominy, and then a little corn cake and boiled venison. This to him, at that time more than half starved, was a most delicious repast. He ate very heartily. Then rising from his seat and handing his kind hostess the bowl out of which he had eaten, bowing low, he gratefully thanked her. She smiled, and only said, "*Enee*," that is right, you are welcome, or as if wishing to lessen the sense of the favor conferred, "It is nothing."

From this village they traveled leisurely on, occasionally passing an Indian hut, and toward evening stopped at the cabin of Wapunnoo, a tall stout warrior and a brother of Wapawaqua. His wife was quite a handsome woman, delicately formed, and much fairer than the generality of Indian women. She seemed to possess withal a very amiable disposition and bore the churlish treatment of her husband with a meekness and patience that would adorn a Christian, although it was evident she felt mortified that others witnessed his unkind conduct.

This night, for the first time since his captivity, Ollie slept under a shelter. Lying on a deerskin with a blanket over him, he rested comfortably. The next morning they breakfasted early, and a little before noon of July 13, after a journey of nearly six days and traveling about one hundred and eighty miles, they arrived at The Point, a wedge of land at the confluence of the Auglaize and Maumee Rivers. Here the Indians disposed of their deerskins to a British Indian trader, and they crossed over the Maumee to a small bark cabin near its bank, directly opposite The Point. They left him in the charge of its occupant, an old widow who was the mother of Wapawaqua, and departed for their homes, a village on the river about one mile below.

CHAPTER ELEVEN

A NEW MOTHER

COOHCOOCHEEH, THE OLD WOMAN in whose charge Wapawaqua had left Ollie, was in that advanced stage of life in which we seek rest and quiet. Believing, no doubt, from the boy's squalid appearance and diseased state in an increase of her cares and labors, she at first received him with reluctance. She surveyed him. His emaciated form, his scratched and festered limbs, his swollen feet retaining when pressed the print of the finger, and his toes, from the friction of the sand collected in his moccasins in frequently fording creeks, raw and worn almost to the bone, excited her pity. Some of the dormant feelings of the mother awakened, and she soon began to apply herself to his relief. This was fortunate for him, for if she had rejected him, he may have been condemned to die.

She first affected at the river a complete cleansing of his person, and this simple act was his adoption. She scrubbed away his old life and family, in this way making him her son and Wapawaqua's adopted brother.

Wapawaqua made an interesting choice in bringing him to his mother. If he had adopted him as his own son, he would stay with his wife if she chose to divorce him, when acting according to Shawnee custom. Perhaps Wapawaqua merely felt that his aged mother needed a helper, but he made Ollie his brother forever.

Coohcoocheeh proceeded to wash his clothes, in the meantime compelling him to lie on a blanket for three or four hours under the scorching sun until his back was one entire blister. Then boiling a strong decoction of red oak, wild cherry bark, and dewberry root, of which he drank frequently and in which he occasionally soaked his feet for several days, she affected in a short time a perfect cure.

She began calling him Meecheway, not a proper name, meaning "Eating Again," reflecting her feelings at having another mouth to feed.

Her family consisted of a dark Indian girl, two years Ollie's elder, and a half-Indian boy about a year younger than him. They were both her grandchildren by her widowed daughter, now the wife of George Ironside, a British Indian trader living at the trading station on the high point directly opposite her cabin, a few hundred yards above the mouth of the Auglaize. The boy, reputed to be the son of the famous, or rather infamous, renegade Simon Girty, was very sprightly but withal passionate and willful, a perfectly spoiled child. His mother gave him the Mohawk name of Ked-zaw-saw, while his grandmother called him Simo-ne. The girl, rather homely, but cheerful and good-natured with bright, laughing eyes, her mother named So-tone-goo, but the old woman called her Quasay.

Coohcoocheeh was a princess of the Wolf tribe of the Iroquois, formerly living on the Sorrel River (Richelieu River, a tributary of the St. Lawrence). Her person, about the ordinary stature, was stout and clumsy. Her features were rather homely, and her expression generally harsh and repulsive. When she withdrew her thoughts from the deep and weightier matters of her visions, or when no longer conversing with the spirits of other worlds, and when she felt that she was an inhabitant of this and resumed her interest in its concerns, she was at times cheerful. She was also occasionally quite sociable, relating many pleasant stories and amusing incidents of her early life. She was besides a sort of priestess to whom the

Indians applied before going on any important war expedition, inquiring whether they should be successful. They generally received answers framed in such obscure and ambiguous terms as to confirm and increase her reputation even when an expedition proved most disastrous.

They also esteemed Coohcoocheeh as a very great medicine woman, eminently skillful in the preparation of specifics believed to be of great efficacy, but they attributed her medicines' extraordinary virtues to her powerful incantations and her influence with the good spirits, with whom she professed to converse daily.

Her husband had been a Mohawk warrior, part of the Iroquois, a nation formerly occupying the country along the St. Lawrence as far as Lake Ontario and bordering on Lakes George and Champlain. The Iroquois were related tribes in the New York region who called themselves the Haudenosaunee, or People of the Longhouse. According to their traditional stories, their mode of living encouraged sharing among themselves. The metaphor extended to the Iroquois League, for they thought of the five tribes, the Mohawk, Oneida, Onondaga, Cayuga, and Seneca, all related linguistically, as extending across the New York area in one great Longhouse. When the Tuscarora later joined them, they became the Six Nations. They conquered most of the native tribes southward and west of them and claimed the territory as far west as the Mississippi and southward to the Cherokee, or Tennessee River. Possessing superior bravery and consummate skill in war, they destroyed some nations of whom no vestige now remains, and incorporated others whom they had vanquished, forming a powerful confederacy.

Early Iroquoians had migrated along the upper tributaries of the Susquehanna. Their cultural system, with men moving to women's homes after marriage, women dominating village life, and men roving the forest in trade and hunting, allowed them to dominate the tribes already present. At first, their villages were small and unprotected, but as their numbers grew, palisades turned their homes into fortresses. Two or three ranks of twelve to twenty foot tall palisades surrounded their hilltop homes of 2000 residents. Carved figures of human heads, topped with the real scalps of enemies, guarded either side of the main gate. Inside the town, bark cabins from 40 to 200 feet long filled the space.

If one could hear the voices of the residents, likely they would be mainly the voices of women and children. The town and surrounding farm fields were the domains of women. Women built the longhouses and raised the crops of corn, beans, and squash. The men would be away hunting, trading, warring, or practicing diplomacy up to nine months of the year. The hunting aspect of their way of life called for large tracts of land in which wild animals roamed.

The Longhouses were communal dwellings, with a cooking fire every twenty feet down the center of the building. Two families shared each fire, living and sleeping across from each other. This arrangement reflected their version of the creation of the world. The virgin births of good and evil twins guided their thinking that the world was a balance of power between good and evil, with good usually having the upper hand. Caring and right-thinking neighbors could influence those who did wrong to do good, just as good people could be brought down by bad influences.

There were not just the Five Nations of the Iroquois, but the five nations of the Huron confederacy, the five nations of the Neutral confederacy, three nations of Erie and the nations of Petun, Wenro, and Susquehannock who were of Iroquoian origins. In the sixteenth century, there were perhaps 90,000 Iroquoians. As they became more numerous, they battled each other for resources, and the warring followed a pattern.

For the natives, Man and the natural world vibrated with spiritual power; all beings and things were alive with spirit. The supernatural caused deaths and injuries; nothing was accidental, and an individual's death reduced the spiritual power of the group. When the evil side was in ascendance, a person was no longer in control of himself. Worse, the tribe must avenge evil acts. If elaborate and lengthy mourning rituals, in which a successor received the power of the deceased, did not sooth the bereaved, then the women would ask the men to conduct a raid for captives. Those captured might fulfill their function of spiritual replenishment by incorporation into the group as a family member, or they might be tortured and their bodies consumed in a literal consumption of power.

Captured warriors marked for death were given a feast, where they recited their war honors. Afterward, they placed them on a platform, tied them to a stake, and applied flaming brands to their bodies. Those who did not cry out were the bravest, and sometimes they hastened death with an ax blow if the warrior was particularly good at insulting his captors. They then cut apart, cooked and shared his body as food by all in the town.

Of course, an act such as this caused great sorrow to the warrior's kin and must be avenged and mourned. Thus was the "Mourning War."

This internal warring lasted for up to two centuries for the Iroquois, until the Mohawk warrior Hiawatha, whose three daughters had been killed in war, ran into the forest insane with grief. There, the supernatural being Deganawida interceded with condolences of the Requickening Address to wipe his tears, unstop his ears, clear his throat, and dispel the darkness. Deganawida brought Hiawatha back to sanity, and he taught him the Condolence Ritual to take back to the Mohawk people. Hiawatha did so, and he also brought a formal system of leadership, giving the clans of the Five Nations hereditary chieftainships of peace and diplomacy. This formal system was the Iroquois League, which was primarily a method for keeping the "Mourning Peace."

After 1550, disease caught from the French, famine from a cold snap, and attacks from other tribes temporarily drove the Iroquois out of their towns on the St. Lawrence. After that, their homeland lay in western New York. Being upriver of everywhere, they were at the end of a long trading line centered on the Mississippi and Ohio valleys. Their new location cut off access to the marine shells they used to make sacred wampum for rituals and burials. They also coveted European goods such as iron hatchets and brass kettles, which were useful not only as kettles but as a source of material to make arrowheads greatly superior to the stone tools to which they were accustomed.

Meanwhile, the Iroquois had fought their way back to the St. Lawrence to obtain the goods they desired, but the arrival of the Dutch on the Hudson River at Fort Orange changed the scene entirely. The Mohawks took furs to trade there, but in 1633, the apparent fortuitous trade with the Dutch took an ugly turn with the accidental introduction of smallpox. The natives had no immunity and, devastated by the disease, their populations fell *by more than half.*

The survivors believed that witchcraft caused the deaths, and they must avenge them. The war that followed had as its causes rage at these smallpox deaths and the desire to control the fur trade. In the Beaver Wars, the Iroquois fought for lands still rich in beaver pelts, and they fought against other tribes of Indians, battling the Huron, the Susquehannock, the Erie, and they drove the

Algonquian tribe of Shawnee from the Ohio Valley. In doing so, the warriors were pursuing their traditional path to prestige and power.

After nearly a century of warfare, the majority of the Mohawks were drawn into the French sphere and emigrated to Canada as Catholics. The remnants of the Iroquoian tribes in the Ohio region regrouped as the Wyandot. The remaining Mohawks and other Iroquois allied themselves with the English with the new Covenant Chain, a gift exchange and condolence ritual that maintained the peace, similar to the previous Mourning Peace, but this time including the fur trade with the English in its sphere. They remained firm allies of the British and maintained their supremacy over the northern tribes until the 1768 Treaty of Fort Stanwix, in which they traded any rights to "western" territory for a homeland in western New York.

Then the Americans, including Colonel Spencer, attacked the Iroquois during the Revolution for their attachment to Great Britain, burning their towns and crops in 1779. The colonists totally defeated them then. The Iroquois lost their ascendancy, yielded their claim of paramount authority, and reduced and scattered were in turn incorporated with other Indian nations over whom they had once ruled.

After this signal defeat and loss of the Mohawks, Coohcoocheeh's husband Cokundiawthah and his three sons resolved to make a stand for Ohio with their Shawnee associates. In the victory of the Indians over part of General Harmar's army under Hardin and Willis in October 1790, in a furious charge made against the regulars, while in the act of tomahawking a soldier, Cokundiawthah received a mortal wound from a bayonet. He died on his way home, and his sons buried him on the bank of the Maumee, about twenty miles from the battleground.

Soon after his death, his widow chose her residence and erected her bark cabin on the spot now occupied by her. Only a few months before at the feast of the dead, with pious affection she removed the remains of her late husband from their first resting place and interred them only a few dozen yards above her dwelling, near to the warpath. She did this so that she might not only enjoy the happiness of conversing with him, but that his own spirit might be refreshed from viewing the warriors as they crossed the Maumee on their war expeditions. His spirit would remain until, having ended his probation and being prepared for his journey, he would travel to the final abode of good spirits in a far west land, abounding with game, and enjoy all those sensual delights which, in the native view, constituted heaven.

Buried in a sitting posture facing the west, by his side had been placed his rifle, tomahawk, knife, blanket, moccasins, and everything necessary for a hunter and a warrior, and his friends had besides thrown many little articles as presents into his grave. At its head, they placed a post about four feet high, painted red, and having near its top the image of a rudely carved face. Below were the scalps he had taken in battle, scalps of all colors, of hair of all lengths, which on some great occasions one might see streaming in the wind suspended from a high pole bending over his grave. Ollie once counted nineteen torn from the heads of his unfortunate countrymen.

To those who have never seen the dwelling of an Indian priestess, a description of the bark cabin of Coohcoocheeh may perhaps be worth the reading. Covering an area of fourteen by twenty-eight feet, its frame was constructed of small poles, of which some planted upright in the ground served as posts and studs supporting the ridgepoles and eve bearers, while others firmly tied to these by thongs of hickory bark formed girders, braces, laths, and rafters. Covering this frame were large pieces of elm bark, seven or eight feet long, and three or four feet wide, pressed flat and well dried to prevent their curling. These, fastened to the poles by thongs of bark, formed the weatherboarding and roof of the cabin. At its western end was a narrow doorway about six feet high, closed when necessary by a single piece of bark placed beside it and fastened by a brace, set within or outside as occasion required. Within, separated by a bark partition, were two apartments. The old woman used the inner one variously as a pantry, a spare bedroom, and as a sanctuary where she at times performed her incantations. The other room had on each side a low frame covered with bark and overspread with deerskins, serving for both seats and bedsteads, and was in common use by the family for lodging, sitting, cooking, and eating.

The fire was on the ground in the center of this apartment, and over it, suspended from the ridgepole in the middle of an aperture left for the passage of the smoke, was a wooden trammel, or long hook, for the convenience of cooking.

The site of this cabin was truly pleasant. Shaded by an enormous old apple tree planted by the French, it stood a few dozen yards from the northern bank of the Maumee, with its side fronting that river on an elevated spot. From it, the ground first gently descended about one hundred yards northward, thence gradually ascended to the top of the tableland bounding the narrow bottom, extending about two miles above and the same distance below. The high ground was a beautiful open wood, principally of oak and hickory. The bottom, with the exception of about five acres above the cabin, was cultivated with corn. Bushes covered a small spot around it, interspersed with saplings and a few blue ash, white ash, and elm trees.

Both banks of the Maumee above the Auglaize were steep, high, and willow covered. The opposite bank, down to the point, here slightly curved northeastwardly as it mingled with the waters of its tributary stream, and the current sweeping it made it entirely bare.

Immediately below the point, the Auglaize ran from the southwest. It bent northeastwardly near its mouth, washing the eastern side of the point, entering obliquely and mingling its current with the Maumee, and occasioning in freshets a whirl and roiling of the water in the center and strong eddies on both sides of the river. In a low stage, the water below the point and for some distance up each river was perfectly still. The Maumee above the point was about one hundred and twenty yards wide, directly below it a hundred and seventy. It was here in its center in the lowest stage of water about seven feet deep, although its depth where it had a current was ordinarily not more than three.

It abounded with excellent fish, which the Indians generally took with a gig, or shot with arrows, and sometimes with rifle balls. In this latter method of taking them, requiring great judgment and a practiced eye, they were rarely successful, particularly where the water was deep and very clear. The fish seemed to be within a few inches of the surface when it was at the same time so far below it that the ball flattened and did not reach it.

On the south side of the Maumee for some distance below the mouth and extending more than a mile up the Auglaize to an Indian village, the low rich bottom, about three quarters of a mile in width, was one entire field covered with corn, and when in tassel presented a beautiful appearance. The tribe en mass owned the land and assigned plots to women, who cultivated portions of the same field, the portions separated from each other only by spaces of a few feet, and varying in size according to the number and strength of their families. The native men did the work of clearing fields of trees and heavy brush, after which, the women took over the hoeing, planting and harvesting, and all produce was theirs.

It was customary that Indians seldom raised corn as an article of commerce, but raised it for their own subsistence. Around these large fields, they made no enclosures, nor indeed having no cattle, hogs, nor sheep, were fences necessary. As for their few horses, they either drove them out into the woods or secured them near their cabins. It was the boys' duty, by turns while amusing themselves with their bows and arrows, to protect the fields from the horses; the boys had only to listen for the horse's bell.

Ollie had lived in his new habitation about a week and had given up hope of escaping. Even if he could somehow cross the river alone, an unpleasant prospect with his fear of the water, the vast acreage of corn hinted that Indians, any of whom would stop him if they saw him, surrounded him. In addition, the land outside of the beaten trails was swamp forest, which became sticky muck after a rain. He was in the midst of the great Black Swamp, which had about the same area as the state of Connecticut, being 120 miles long and averaging 40 miles wide. More important than any other consideration, though, was the warning by Wapawaqua—attempt to escape again and he would tomahawk and scalp him.

Ollie began to regard his life with the Indians as his future home. True, the home from which he had been torn and the beloved parents from whom he feared that he was forever separated were seldom from his thoughts, yet he strove to be cheerful. By his ready obedience, he ingratiated himself with Coohcoocheeh, for whose kindness he felt grateful, and who, with the blessing of

Divine Providence, had restored him to health. She now took some pains to comfort and amuse him.

Her son-in-law, a respectable Indian trader, supplied her occasionally with a few necessities. From the Indians who consulted her on most important matters, she received presents of venison, skins, and silver brooches, the common circulating medium among them. Her household furniture consisted of a large brass kettle for washing and sugar-making; a deep, close-covered, copper hominy kettle; a few knives, tin cups, pewter and horn spoons, sieves, wooden bowls, and baskets of various sizes; and a hominy block. In addition, she had four beds and bedding, comprising each a few deerskins and two blankets, so that altogether her circumstances were quite comfortable.

Her dress, like that of the old Indian women in general, was very plain and simple. It consisted of a calico shirt extending about six inches below the waist and fastened at the bosom with a silver brooch. She wore a stroud or petticoat, simply a yard and a half of six-quarter blue cloth with white selvage, wrapped around her waist and confined with a girdle. Then extending a little below the knee was a pair of leggings, or Indian stockings, of the same cloth, sewn to fit the leg, leaving a border of two inches projecting from the outside and extending to the instep. She also wore a pair of plain moccasins.

The form of the dress was the same among the Indian women of all ranks and ages, varying only in its quality and in the richness and variety with which they adorned it. Rank or station did not regulate its ornaments; the ability of the wearer did. All the young and middle aged among the women were passionately fond of finery. The young belles particularly had the tops of their moccasins curiously wrought with beads, ribbons, and

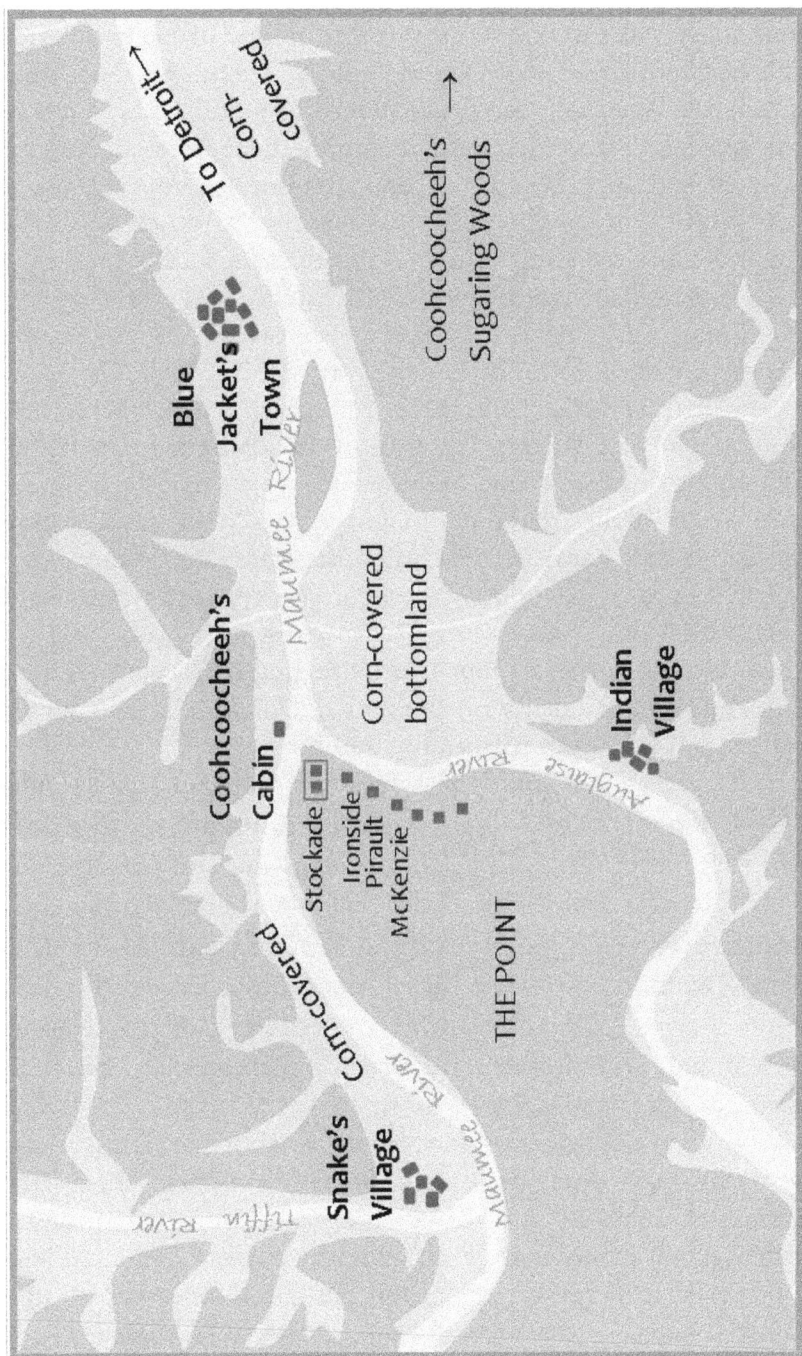

porcupine quills. They tastefully bound the borders of their leggings and the bottoms and edges of their strouds with beaded ribbons of various colors. Frequently, on their moccasins and their leggings they had small tufts of deer's hair dyed red and confined in small pieces of tin, rattling as they walked. Besides these ornaments, according to their ability, they covered the bosoms, shoulders, sides, and bottoms of their shirts (sometimes made of cross-barred silk handkerchiefs) with large and small silver brooches, and wore on their wrists and arms silver bracelets from one to four inches in width.

Nor was the fondness for show confined to the women. On the contrary, it was even stronger in the men, who in addition to the ornaments worn by the women, wore large silver medals and gorgets (a decorative collar) on the breast and silver rings in the nose. They wore heavy pieces of silver in the ears, the rims of which they separated from the cartilage by cutting and then weighed down two or three inches from the head. Remember also Wapawaqua's friend, who despoiled Ollie's silk vest for its rows of silver plate buttons for use as garters.

It was now about July 21, and being a leisure time with Coohcoocheeh, principally perhaps to indulge her own inclination and partly to amuse Ollie, she took him on a visit to the Shawnee village, below them. Wapawaqua kindly received them. His wife, a very pleasant and rather pretty woman of twenty-five, according to custom set before them some refreshment, consisting of dried green corn boiled with beans and dried pumpkins. It made, as Ollie thought, an excellent dish.

After spending a few hours with this family, they went to pay their respects to the village chief, the celebrated Blue Jacket. This chief was the most noble in appearance of any Indian Ollie ever saw. His person, about six feet high, was finely proportioned, stout and muscular. His eyes were large, bright, and piercing; his forehead high and broad; his nose aquiline; his mouth rather wide; and his countenance open, intelligent, and expressive of firmness and decision. The natives considered him one of the bravest and most accomplished of the Indian chiefs, second only to Little Turtle of the Miami and Buckongahelas of the Delaware. He had distinguished himself on many occasions, particularly in the defeats of Colonel Hardin and General St. Clair. He held, as someone told him, the commission, and received the half pay, of a brigadier general from the British crown. Blue Jacket was dressed in a scarlet frock coat, richly laced with gold, confined around his waist with a parti-colored sash, in red leggings, and in moccasins, ornamented in the highest style of Indian fashion. On his shoulders, he wore a pair of gold epaulettes and on his arms broad silver bracelets, while from his neck hung a massive silver gorget and a large medallion of His Majesty George III.

Rifles, war clubs, bows and arrows, and other implements of war hung around his lodge. Deer, bear, panther, and otter, spoils of the chase, furnished skins for pouches for tobacco, or mats for seats and beds.

His wife was a remarkably fine-looking woman. His daughters, much fairer than the generality of Indian women, were quite handsome, and his two sons, about eighteen and twenty years old, educated by the British, were very intelligent.

On this day, he received a visit from the Snake, chief of a neighboring Shawnee village, and from Simon Girty. The Snake was a plain grave chief of sage appearance. Simon Girty, whether it was from prejudice, associating with his look the fact that he was a renegade, or not, seemed to Ollie the very picture of a villain. He was the murderer of his own countrymen, racking his diabolic invention to inflict new and more excruciating tortures. Ollie remembered his dark shaggy hair, his low forehead, his brows contracting and meeting above his short flat nose, his gray sunken eyes averting the ingenuous gaze, his lips thin and compressed, and the dark and sinister expression of his countenance. He wore the Indian costume, but without any ornament. His silk handkerchief, supplying the place of a hat, hid an unsightly wound in his forehead. On each side in his belt was stuck a silver-mounted pistol, and at his left hung a short broad dirk, serving occasionally the uses of a knife.

At first, Girty had been on the American side. White accounts claim that in 1755, Girty, the son of white parents, at age fourteen was kidnapped by the Seneca, or Wyandot as they were known when inhabiting the Ohio country, remaining with them for three years. He saw his stepfather burned by the Indians.

Oral accounts by the natives tell a different story, claiming Girty was half-native by birth, and descriptions of Girty would tend to confirm the native's version, with black hair, piercing dark eyes, and a round and full face. Girty's mother, Mary Newton Girty, had had "lusty" relations with a Seneca man by the name of Fish, possibly Simon's father, and subsequently, during a drunken revel, Fish and Mary's husband, Indian agent Simon Girty, Sr., quarreled over the woman, with Fish killing Girty senior. Fish lived as Mary's husband until the settler John Turner murdered him in 1753. Mary then took up with Turner.

Turner was second in command of a company of enlisted men in the pay of Pennsylvania, and he had Mary and her sons with him at Fort Granville on the frontier. In 1755, a party of French and Indians attacked and devastated the fort. The Seneca took the whole family, including Simon's four brothers, to their village, where they recognized Turner as the man who had killed Fish in order to possess Mary. They burned him at the stake to avenge Fish's death.

When Katepakomen, as the Seneca called Girty, arrived in the Seneca village, he was already a member of the Seneca tribe and spoke, or learned to speak, several native languages. In 1774, the British Army commissioned him as a second Lieutenant. Two years later, the British government made him an interpreter to the British Middle Indian Department at Fort Pitt. In 1777, the British passed him over for promotion, and he resigned his commission. Girty then chose the American side.

In February of 1778, he was with General Hand, who was then trying to raise a militia on the Pennsylvania frontier. Hand wrote, "The English have lodged a quantity of arms, ammunition, provision and clothing at a small Indian town about 100 miles from Fort Pitt, to support the savages in their excursions against the inhabitants of this and the adjacent counties." His object was to destroy the arms and ammunition, and he assured the volunteers that "everything they are able to bring away shall be sold at public vendue for the sole benefit of the captors, & the money equally distributed."

Girty was one of the party's scouts when Hand set out with 400 or 500 men of the Westmoreland Militia for Cuyahoga to seize the food and weapons believed to be cached there. They discovered Indian tracks and intelligence of a camp of fifty or sixty Indians believed to be the warriors who were attacking the settlements. The militia surrounded the Indian town and found only one man called Captain Pipe, and a few women. The militia behaved with barbarity, chasing and shooting at a woman who turned out to be the mother of Captain Pipe. An officer managed to stop the firing, and they found that even with all the bullets flying, she had only lost the end of a little finger. Evidently, there were no marksmen among them. The mayhem continued with an officer shooting an old woman and wounding her in the leg, mistaking her for a warrior, then one soldier tomahawked and another shot her.

Captain Pipe fought back, shooting an officer in the arm, and while loading his gun again, a soldier shot him and another tomahawked and killed him. This raised the militia into a frenzy of yelling and shooting, which the officers could not quell. The rest of Pipe's family escaped, and the Patriots eventually came away with a small amount of plunder.

That afternoon some of the men went several miles up the Mahoning to a place called the Salt Licks, guided by Girty. They found a winter hunting camp with a few women, the men absent hunting. The party killed a small Indian boy out shooting birds, and a number of them claimed the "honor." To avoid argument, they asked Girty to decide whose bullet had found the target, as he had not been involved.

The bad conduct of the men and the badness of the weather prevented General Hand from continuing the expedition, known as the Squaw Campaign.

Within days of returning from that pathetic attack on women and children, Girty defected to the British, after falling in with some friends ready to choose the Loyalist side, who persuaded him to go with them. Having been a scout and interpreter for the British before the war, to return to them seemed the right thing at the time, but Girty later described his defection to the British as a "too hasty step." Girty arrived at Detroit in June where the British hired him at $2 a day as interpreter for the Six Nations, twice as much as the Americans paid. He went to live among the Wyandot and established his own town, Solomon's town, in a Mingo village. It was three miles north of present Huntsville and nine miles north of Bellefontaine, Ohio.

His heart against the Americans was not at first hardened. He met in council an old friend, the captive Simon Kenton. Kenton was so beaten up from running the gauntlet repeatedly that Girty didn't recognize him.

Kenton described the meeting:

He was good to me. When he came up to me, after the Indians had painted me black, I knew him at once. He asked me a good many questions, but I thought it best not to be too forward, and I held back from telling him my name; but, when I did tell him, oh! He was very glad to see me. He flung his arms around me, and cried like a child. I never did see one man so glad to see another. He made a speech to the Indians—he could speak the Indian tongue, and knew how to speak—and told them, if they meant to do him a favor, they must do it now, and save my life. Girty afterward, when we were together, cried to me like a child often, and told me he was sorry for the part he had taken against his countrymen; that he was too hasty. But he was good to me; and it was no wonder. When we see our fellow-creatures every day, we don't care for them; but it is different when you meet a man all alone in the woods—the wild, lonely woods.

Girty obviously succeeded in saving Kenton. By the following year in 1779, the female league elders, the Gantowisas, recognized Girty's leadership abilities and promoted him. As a league warrior, he led the Wyandot Indians on a number of attacks against Americans on the frontier. Hatred of him rose.

On one raid, Girty captured the letters of an old friend, American Colonel Gibson, who wrote "Mr. Girty has not yet made his appearance; I hope, if he does, to prevent his taking my scalp." He wrote to another, "I hope, if Mr. Girty comes to pay a visit, I shall be able to trepan him," that is, to bore a hole into his skull.

This statement reverberated with Girty, bringing home to him the hatred leveled against him. He became fearful and turned whole-heartedly to his task as Indian leader and interpreter, continuing as an interpreter with the Wyandot after the war, and his loyalties lay with them.

While living in the Sandusky region, Girty met the family of Wapawaqua and with Coohcoocheeh's daughter had his son Simo-ne. Girty's relationship with Coohcoocheeh's daughter was in addition to two other wives in succession in his life, the first a "half breed" and the second a Canadian white woman.

During their meeting, Girty made many inquiries of Ollie, some about his family and the particulars of his captivity, but more of the strength of the different garrisons, the number of American troops at Fort Washington, and whether the president intended soon to send another army against the Indians. He spoke of the wrongs he had received at the hands of his countrymen, and with fiendish exultation, of the revenge he had taken, including the burning of Abner Hunt. He boasted of his exploits, of the number of his victories, and of his personal prowess. He then raised his handkerchief and exhibited the deep wound in his forehead, which Ollie afterwards learned came from the tomahawk of the celebrated Indian chief Brant, in a drunken frolic. Girty said it was a saber cut which he received in battle at St. Clair's defeat. He added with an oath that he had "sent the damned Yankee officer" that gave it, "to hell." He ended by telling him that he would never see home, but if he should "turn out to be a good hunter and a brave warrior, [he] might one day be a chief." His presence and conversation rendered Ollie's situation painful, and he was not a little relieved when a few hours after, ending their visit, they returned to their quiet lodge on the bank of the Maumee.

CHAPTER TWELVE

WILLIAM MOORE AND THE GREEN CORN FESTIVAL

A FEW DAYS AFTER OLLIE'S VISIT to Blue Jacket's Town, he accompanied Coohcoocheeh to The Point, the residence of her daughter. On this high ground, extending from the Maumee a quarter of a mile up the Auglaize and about two hundred yards in width, was an open space on the west and south, on which were oak woods with hazel undergrowth. Within this opening, a few hundred yards above the confluence on the steep high bank of the Auglaize, were five or six cabins and log houses inhabited principally by Indian traders. George Ironside occupied the most northerly, a large hewed log house divided below into three apartments, warehouse, store, and dwelling. Mr. Ironside was the most wealthy and influential of the traders on The Point.

George Ironside was a native of Aberdeenshire, Scotland. An unlikely candidate to find in the wilderness, he had graduated with a Master of Arts from King's College (the present University of Aberdeen) in Scotland on Feb 22, 1781. The curriculum included Latin and Greek, Mathematics, Natural and Civil History, and Philosophy, including "Philosophy of the human mind and the sciences that depend upon it." Whether due to a harsh financial situation in Scotland, personal difficulties, or a desire for adventure, he arrived in Canada shortly after the Revolution.

Mr. Ironside used to live in Miamitown, an outpost of the fur trade across the St. Joseph River from Kekionga (where present day Fort Wayne, Indiana lies), the Miami Indian tribe's capital, but as the American Army under Harmar approached it in 1790, the Indians and traders affected their retreat and burned their homes themselves.

There had been a prodigious trade at Miamitown. In the spring as many as four or five hundred natives would bring their peltries there to sell or trade. British and French traders lived peaceably and shared the commerce, but in the slack time in the winter, the trading was highly competitive. Henry Hay visited Miamitown in 1789 and wrote, "I cannot say much indeed for the Trade of this Place. There's but few skins comes in, and almost every individual is an Indian trader, everyone tries to get what he can either by foul play or otherwise—that is by traducing one another's characters and merchandise. For instance by saying such a one has no Blankets another no strouds or is damned bad or he'll cheat you & so on—in short I cannot term it in a better manner than calling it a Rascally Scrambling Trade."

While waiting for the Indians to come in, the traders openly got along well and passed their time in eating, dancing, making music, playing cards, playing practical jokes, entertaining chiefs, and attending church. Three small French boys announced the latter by running through the town ringing cowbells, making a racket.

To pass the long winter nights they drank heavily and played cards, to the point that as one trader wrote, "Mr. A— gave me his daughter Betsy over the bottle. Damnation sick this morning."

Some of their mischief was more innocent. Mrs. Adamher, one of the trader's wives, was a person fond of practical jokes, constantly playing some trick. Her numerous victims decided to reciprocate and planned a prank for several weeks. The joke was to steal a pig that the woman planned to slaughter the following day, a deed sure to madden her because the previous year at about the same time someone had stolen a pig of hers which she never recovered. The pranksters hid the pig, and the justice of the peace satisfied her by giving a couple of the traders a warrant to search the village. They did so and even searched the affected woman's house before undeceiving her and the justice. Mr. Ironside was included in these shenanigans, helping to search the woman's house.

Next to Mr. Ironside at The Point were the houses of Pirault (Pero), a French baker, and McKenzie, a Scot, who in addition to merchandizing followed the occupation of silversmith. He exchanged with the Indians his brooches, eardrops, and other silver ornaments for skins and furs at an enormous profit. Still farther up were several other families of French and English, and two American prisoners.

Indians had captured Polly Meadows, employed by the army, at St. Clair's defeat. She lived as a wife to Henry Ball, who was taken at the time Newell was killed outside Columbia. Their masters allowed them to live here and by labor to pay the price of their ransom, he by boating to the rapids of the Maumee, and she by washing and sewing. Fronting the house of Ironside and about fifty yards from the river bank was a small stockade enclosing two hewed log houses, one of which was occupied by James Girty (brother of Simon), the other by McKee and Elliott, British Indian Agents living at Detroit who visited only occasionally. McKee had duties that kept him in Detroit or at the Rapids of the Maumee, where the British Indian Department kept a storehouse. The agents dispensed British gifts to the Indians from this location, built in 1780 to prepare for the British and Indian raids against Kentucky.

James Girty was a year-round occupant at The Point. The Seneca had given him to the Shawnee at the same time that Simon had gone to live with the Seneca. When a missionary visited the Shawnee in 1772, he referred to James as one "who was well acquainted with their language, but a stranger to religion; neither had he any inclination to engage in such solemn matters, so contrary to the tenor of his life, having little or no fear of God before his eyes."

From this station on The Point Ollie had a fine view of a large village more than a mile south on the east side of the Auglaize, also of Blue Jacket's Town, of the Maumee River for several miles below, and of the extensive prairie covered with corn directly opposite. These formed together a very handsome landscape.

Ollie spent this day very pleasantly among the traders, dining with Mr. Ironside, who treated him with great kindness. The boy found him a very sociable and intelligent man, humane and benevolent. The trader seemed much interested in the story of his captivity and appeared to sympathize with him. He gave him some useful advice and direction for the regulation of his conduct and a great deal of information relative to the Indians—their history, customs, and manners.

MEANWHILE, COLONEL SPENCER'S friends continued to work for Ollie's freedom. General Anthony Wayne, now heading a new western campaign, had been a general of the Pennsylvania Line in the Revolution, with the reputation of being prepared and bold. He wrote from Pittsburgh on August 3, updating Secretary of War Knox on the attack at Fort Jefferson and the boy's capture "within three miles of the Fort Washington." He continued on the topic of the killing of the American peace emissaries, "Would it not stamp disgrace upon the American character in the eye of the World were such enormities permitted with impunity. These reports, and they bear but too strong marks of authenticity leaves little ground to hope for an honorable or lasting peace; should the event be war, by Heavens the Savages shall experience its keenest effects."

Henry Knox wrote on August 8 to Winthrop Sargent, Lieutenant Governor of the Northwest Territory. It took around three weeks for a letter to arrive from Cincinnati. "I have received your favor of the 9th ultimo relative to the son of Colonel Spencer. You may depend upon it I shall take all the steps which individually I may do upon the subject."

The next day, Colonel John Francis Hamtramck, a Canadian who joined the American side in the Revolution, now commanding at Vincennes, wrote to Sargent, "I condole with Colonel Spencer. It is a great misfortune and you can assure Colonel Spencer that I will write to Detroit the first opportunity and do everything that can be done to get the Boy."

ON THE FOLLOWING DAY, Ollie was highly gratified in seeing at their cabin his townsman William Moore, who had likely arrived in Columbia with a group of Baptist families from Pennsylvania. Moore had just returned from a trip to the rapids about sixty miles below. He was a stout, sinewy, muscular man, six feet two inches high, active, bold, and daring. Combining the qualities and peculiarities of the western boatman and hunter, he was one who in Kentucky, in former years, would have been termed "half horse, half alligator." He was a practiced marksman who at fifty steps with his rifle "offhand" often "drove the center" and seldom failed to "cut the black." On the keelboat, he pushed the first pole, and in running, jumping, wrestling, and other athletic exercises, he had few superiors. Fearless and lawless, only his own sense of propriety and right governed him. He was naturally good-humored and obliging, but when roused he was a perfect savage. Bold and powerful must have been the man that would encounter and overcome him.

Moore told Ollie how he came to live among the Indians. Wapawaqua, his brother Catawa-waqua, and three other Indians had taken Moore prisoner a few months preceding Ollie's capture. About five miles north of Columbia on the waters of Mill Creek, Moore had just killed a fine doe, lashed it over his shoulders, and begun a few steps on his return home. The Indians, watching his movements, waited until his load encumbered him and fired upon him from his right. One of their balls grazed his right shoulder blade; another passed through the carpus, or compact bones of the wrist, and rendered powerless his left hand.

Instantly springing forward, for the first hundred yards, even with his load, he outran the Indians. Meanwhile, he placed his rifle on his left shoulder and threw his wounded hand over it. With his right, he cut the lashings, disencumbering himself of his burden, and distanced in a few minutes all but two of his pursuers. He gained the top of a ridge and looked back upon the first Indians, the foremost of whom was several dozen yards behind him. Deridingly slapping his thigh and giving a loud whoop, he bounded off like a deer to the foot of the hill.

Here he failed in the attempt to leap a creek, with his feet slipping on the edge of the opposite bank. He fell backward into the water. By the time he had risen to his feet and recovered his rifle, which had fallen into the water, Wapawaqua overtook him. The Indian leaped down the bank and twice snapped his pistol at him. Moore, meantime leveling his rifle, also twice attempted to shoot Wapawaqua, but unfortunately, its priming was wet, and he had no opportunity to renew it. Clubbing his gun, he next attempted to strike down his adversary, but his left hand being powerless, Wapawaqua easily parried his stroke. He now threw down his rifle and drew his knife. He was just about to close in deadly strife, when at that moment the brother of Wapawaqua reached the spot and interfered. Becoming faint from the loss of blood, seeing the remaining Indians close at hand, and considering further resistance or attempt to escape useless, Moore picked up his rifle and surrendered it to Wapawaqua who extended his hand and received him as his prisoner.

On his arrival at Blue Jacket's Town, a council did not judge Moore, who was a private prisoner to one whose family had then no ancestral spirits to appease or blood to avenge, Wapawaqua probably having avenged his father's death at the burning of Abner Hunt. Custom immemorial required that as a man and a warrior Moore would run the gauntlet, and an early day was fixed for the interesting exhibition. That day soon arrived, and men, women, and children invited from the neighboring village flocked to the capital of the Shawnees, anticipating as much pleasure as we would expect at the celebration of our nation's anniversary.

They gratified their curiosity in examining the prisoner; and then armed with clubs, switches, and other instruments of punishment, they arranged themselves facing each other in two rows about seven feet apart. Numbering more than two hundred persons standing four or five feet from each other, they extended three hundred yards along the level space between the village and the Maumee River. The chiefs and principal warriors stood at the head of the lines within a few dozen yards of the cabin selected as the goal, while the rest of the men, women, and youths intermingled, occupying the other parts.

They now led Moore out stripped to the waist. The Indians, aware of his strength and activity, tied together his wrists for the purposes of hindering his speed and preventing him from retaliating against his tormentors, yet allowing him the means to protect his face. Starting a short distance from the head of the lines, he soon bounded through them. Most of their blows, instead of falling on his back, fell clattering on each other's sticks. Breathing for a few moments, he returned with the same speed and reached the middle of his course. The Indians, fearing that from his fleetness he would run through with little injury, half closed their ranks and attempted to obstruct his progress.

Appealing in vain to their sense of honor and justice, he frequently cried, as he told Ollie, "Honor, bright," and "Fair play." Finding that they would probably beat him severely, he undertook himself to redress his wrongs. So effectually did he use his feet, head, and right fist, kicking some, striking down others, and with his head overturning a number, the rest readily made way and opened for him an ample passage. Amidst the shouts of the warriors, he soon reached the goal. Having passed the ordinary trial, they now congratulated him as a brave man; and some applauded him for his late resistance. All but the sufferers were highly diverted at his successful expedient to rid himself of a severe beating.

Moore was a great favorite of Coohcoocheeh, to whose comfort and accommodation he had largely contributed. A short time before Ollie's arrival, to her solitary room he had added an additional cabin—her sanctuary and storeroom. Now preparatory to the feast of green corn, he was building a bark shed for her. Closed at the back and facing their cabin a few dozen yards distant on the west, it was elevated about three feet from the ground for the accommodation of her more aged guests.

Unable to take any active part, they might here witness the exercises and sports of the day.

It was on a pleasant morning about the middle of August, when the ears of corn were grown to full size and still in that soft milky state in which they are good for roasting. The three sons of Coohcoocheeh, with their wives, her daughter with her husband Mr. Ironside, Captain Walker, some other Shawnee warriors with their wives, and a few old women assembled.

Captain Walker and some of the other warriors were recounting their actions in the Battle of St. Clair. Walker wore the dress coat of an infantry field officer with silver epaulets, and had a pocket watch hanging from each ear. He grasped the facing of his appropriated coat and declared in broken English to Ollie, "'Me kill um . . .'" He then struck his own breast and said, "'Captain Walker! Great man me!'"

In compliance with Coohcoocheeh's invitation, the guests were there to celebrate the feast of *green corn*. The festival was said to be similar to that of "*first fruits*" among the Jews (and by some, used as an argument to prove that the aborigines of America were descendants of that nation). The more wealthy and influential among the Indians of the same tribe, apparently to show their gratitude to the Great Spirit for his many mercies, invited the members and relatives of their respective families to a feast principally of green corn, variously cooked. They then entertained themselves with different games and sports, usually crowning their festivities with copious draughts of "fire water"—either rum or whiskey.

After the usual salutations at meeting, all assembled and sat on the grass. They passed the pipe, according to custom, several times round the circle. A venerable Indian then arose, and with much solemnity of tone and earnestness of manner addressed them. He spoke, as Mr. Ironside afterward informed Ollie, of the distinguishing favor of the Great Spirit to his red children, who were the first and most honorable of the human race. The Great Spirit had given them the vast country stretching from the sun's rising place far to the east, to where it sets in the great waters beyond the Rocky Mountains, from the frozen sea of the north, to the boundless salt waters of the south. The land yielded abundantly corn for bread; supplied meat and clothing for their families from buffalo, elk, deer, and every variety of wild game with which the forest once abounded; and produced spontaneously the most valuable medicinal plants, furnishing specifics for every disease to which his red children were exposed. The old Indian reminded them of their obligations to the Great Spirit for all these benefits, especially for sending them fruitful showers, and now blessing them with a good crop of corn.

He advised that they ought to evidence their sense of obligation to him by gratefully feasting on his bounties there provided for them and by heartily engaging in the manly sports and exercises of the day. He then spoke of the "pale faces," whom he represented as the first murderers and oppressors. He ascribed their own sad reverses to the anger of the Great Spirit for affording these murderers an asylum on their shores. It was their duty to exterminate, if possible, these intruders on their soil, at least to drive them south of the Ohio. He said that their late victories over the whites, particularly their signal defeat of St. Clair, were evidences of the returning favor of the Great Spirit. He concluded by exhorting them to deeds of valor and to the conquest of their enemies as a certain passport to the boundless hunting grounds in the far, "far west," beyond the vast waters where the Great Spirit would never suffer the "pale faces" to enter.

All listened to this speech with deep attention, the listeners improving each brief pause to utter some monosyllable expressive of the various feelings that by turns inspired them. At the concluding sentence, as if actuated by one sentiment, they simultaneously sprang to their feet and uttered a shrill and prolonged whoop.

With great animation, they commenced their sports. The first of these was running on foot over a straight course of about one hundred yards, in which the principal competitors were Wapawaqua, Catawa-waqua, Wapunnoo, and Captain Walker. They did not allow Moore to join in their sports at the beginning.

For the first time having an opportunity of witnessing the fleetness of the Indians, Ollie noticed that in running, as in walking, they turned their toes in, hindering the full force of the muscles of the leg. Their movements resembled more the bounding of deer than the more rapid steps of whites, whose lower forward efforts bore them only onward. Ollie believed that the Indians may run longer at great speed; yet in a short race, they were generally less fleet than whites. Wapawaqua, whose movements were lower and more rapid, won the race, though Moore swore that he could give him twenty steps and beat him in a hundred yards.

In the wrestling that followed, Wapunnoo, brother of the Loons, and Captain Walker, both tall and powerful men, bore off the palm. In repeated trials with each other with various successes, they acknowledged Walker victor. Walker several times severely threw Wapawaqua, who now insisted that Walker should wrestle with Moore. To this Walker objected, intimating that it would be rather a stoop to wrestle with a prisoner. With Wapawaqua insisting and at the same time leading Moore forward, Walker reluctantly advanced to meet him. Their first assays, as is usual with practiced wrestlers, were but partial trials of each other's strength and skill. At length exerting their powers, the contest was long and apparently doubtful. Each raised the other, by turns, from his feet, and seemed about to be thrown with violence by his antagonist or bent to the ground by his powerful arms.

Then availing himself of an unguarded movement of his adversary, Moore, with a trip of his foot and a sudden twist of his body, threw him to the ground, yet partially with his arms sustained him while falling so that he suffered no injury. Mortified at his failure, and more than half-angry, Walker sprang to his feet. Again closing with Moore and straining every muscle of his body, he put forth all his strength. The struggle was short, for Moore, being now excited, lost sight of his former prudence and by a powerful effort raised his antagonist on his hip, pitched him heels over head, and stretched with violence his whole length upon the ground. This occasioned a loud "*waugh!*" from the other Indians and gave Wapawaqua great gratification. Moore, perceiving that he had roused the resentment of Walker and excited the jealousy of the rest, strove to allay their feelings. By magnifying the strength of his antagonist and ascribing his own success rather to accident than to superior power and skill, he soon succeeded in restoring good humor.

It being now about noon, the Indians suspended their sports to partake of the plentiful feast provided by Coohcoocheeh. There was boiled jerk and fish; stewed squirrels and venison; and green corn boiled, some in the ear, and some cut from the cob and mixed with beans; squashes; and roasted pumpkins. For bread, besides that prepared in the ordinary way from corn meal, they had some made of the green corn. It was cut from the cob and pounded in a mortar until brought to the consistency of thick cream, then salted and poured into a sort of mold of an oblong form made of corn leaves, more than half the length and twice the thickness of a man's hand. Baked in the ashes, it was very palatable.

The guests did ample justice to the entertainment, eating very heartily out of the wooden bowls in which Coohcoocheeh served their dinner. They held the bowls in their laps, using their own knives to cut their meat, which they held in their fingers. They used the horn, wooden, and pewter spoons of their hostess in eating their succotash. As they finished their dinner, putting down their bowl, each man and woman said, "*Ooway nelah, netapee hooloo,*" literally, I have done; my stomach is full. All dined and enjoyed for a few minutes the (with them) great luxury of smoking.

The Indians were extravagantly fond of spirituous liquor, the men and the women, when they could obtain it, drinking to excess. Aware, however, of its mischievous consequences, they always, before deliberately commencing a drunken revel, selected someone to remain sober. To this person they committed their knives, tomahawks, and other dangerous weapons; and it was his or her duty carefully to hide and retain these until after their carousal, when they should become perfectly sober. In consequence, it was very rare at their revels that more serious injuries than bruised eyes or bloody noses occurred. When at their drinking bouts, brawls did take place with blows and wounds; but the injuries they suffered were entirely overlooked when they were afterwards sober, all their acts committed in a state of inebriety being ascribed wholly to the "fire water."

When the Indians finished their meal and their smoke, Coohcoocheeh produced a small keg of rum, to the great gratification of the guests. Both men and women took a hearty draught. Then the men, giving their knives and tomahawks in charge to Coohcoocheeh, arose to renew their sports.

The men now formed a circle. Within it and near the edge, one of the strongest, lying on his back, held a piece of rawhide firmly in his hands between his raised knees. They had softened the rawhide previously by soaking it, and it was so slippery from greasing as to require a powerful grasp and a strong hand to wrest it from his grip. The men followed each other at the distance of about three feet, moving several times around the circle in quick time with elastic step, sinking alternately on each foot, and sang, *"A yaw whano heigh, how-wa-yow-wa,"* in one of their most monotonous tones. Each Indian then in succession gave a loud *"whoop-haw,"* and suddenly stooping and firmly grasping the rawhide, strove to draw it from the hands of its holder. Failing in this, or drawing it suddenly from his hands, some not infrequently were thrown flat on the ground, to the no small amusement of the others. They deemed that wresting it from the hands of the holder or raising him by it from the ground erect upon his feet to be a proof of superior strength.

Dancing began. An old man pounded with one stick upon a small drum and sang at the same time, slowly or more lively according to the kind of dance, regulating the steps of the dancers who kept exact time with the music. The men moved in an outer and the women in an inner circle, stepping lightly and rather gracefully sinking with a rocking motion, first on one foot, then on the other. Changing the form, they faced each other in lines, sometimes springing up briskly, with a sort of galloping motion. Another time, with their bodies bent forward, they slowly raised both feet at once and brought them down heavily, uttering a *"heigh"* at every jump. This latter was the Roasting Ear Dance, or Ne-pa-na-qua-weh.

It was now the middle of the afternoon, and both men and women, with the exception of Coohcoocheeh, were more than half-drunk. Moore had prudently retired with Mr. Ironside across the Maumee. With their advice, Ollie had withdrawn to the cornfields, where looking through a small hole in the back of the viewing shed, he could without danger witness the movements of the Indians. They now drank more frequently, some dancing singly, others in groups, some singing, some whooping, and some quarrelling. At length, "uproar wild and deep confusion reigned." About this time Wapawaqua, smarting probably under the recollection of the severe falls he had received from Walker, laid hold of him and insisted on another trial of his skill in wrestling. Unfortunately, Walker threw Wapawaqua into the fire, which burned him severely. This disaster served as a signal to end the festivities, and in a very short time, all the guests departed for their respective homes, staggering off in different directions.

They went away singing: On their way home from their carousals, they gave notice of their coming—singing, or rather roaring, their drunken song, *"Ha yaw ki-you-wan-nie, Hi haw nit-ta-koo-pee."* They varied their rather plaintive and dirge-like notes more than with their generally monotonous tunes. Sung quicker or slower, louder or less vociferously, the song not only marked the age and temper, but also with great certainty, the degree of intoxication of the individual. Someone very drunk prolonged each note, sometimes sounding as if he had made a sudden lurch to one side, or a stagger on the other. If the Indian was one whom drunkenness rendered more savage and brutal, his wife, or any member of his family with whom he may have been offended when sober, now had a warning, which they seldom neglected, to keep out of his way. Occasionally, they used the cover of inebriety to revenge, with impunity, some injury they received when sober.

CHAPTER THIRTEEN

BECOMING INDIAN

C OLONEL SPENCER WROTE to his brother-in-law, Aaron Ogden. The family was not too worried that the Indians would kill Ollie, because of his nature, but the family was very grieved by it. They hoped that god would save his life.

This was the low point of Colonel Spencer's life. He opined that he had always gotten his living with endless toil. In addition to ordinary toil, there also was a severe drought that summer that was greatly cutting production. People in Kentucky were suffering in particular.

He continued that he was getting up there in years and could no longer endure hard labor. He had a small stipend from his county judgeship, but it wasn't enough. He decided that if a position for judge of the territory opened up, he was as qualified for it as anyone and he might as well have it. After all, he was already present and ready to work. He hinted that something might be done to his advantage with the aid of the president. Colonel Spencer referred to the position left open by the death of the Honorable Samuel H. Parsons, who had been appointed as judge of the territory. While traveling to his post in the west, he drowned when some violent rapids destroyed his canoe.

Colonel Spencer was pessimistic. He did not expect luck in financial matters as he had never had it before, and he knew he had to get on with his work regardless of what positions might or might not become available. He closed by mentioning to Ogden the he was confiding in only him.

Colonel Spencer neglected his duties as head of the county militia, for he wrote in September that he would have complied with an order of Sargent's earlier, but he was "uncommonly busy." He surely was, as he had lost the labor of a son, and he likely spent time writing letters trying to affect his rescue.

Spencer promised Sargent that he would bring the militia into compliance with law, but he believed it best to go "step by step." The men were very reluctant to go to public duty and leave their families unprotected.

OLLIE REACHED THE AGE of eleven on September 14, unremarked.

HENRY KNOX WROTE on September 16 to President Washington concerning the planned visit of the British Ambassador, or Minister Plenipotentiary, George Hammond. "Agreeably to your request, I have sounded Mr. Hammond. [He has] returned from the eastward a few days ago, and will set out on Wednesday the 19th for Mount Vernon."

President Washington would privately request that the ambassador affect Ollie's rescue by writing to Lt. Governor Simcoe of Upper Canada. Surely, Washington was happy to do this for the son of an officer who had served him and the American cause so well.

WAPAWAQUA, FULFILLING a duty to his new brother, educated him in the ways of an Indian man as provider, teaching him to hunt. Ollie accompanied him and William Moore on fishing trips, canoeing the Maumee near Blue Jacket's Town and skillfully shooting the fish in the clear water.

On one such trip Ollie saw from the canoe the body of a youth of fourteen who with his sister, a girl of sixteen, the Indians had taken prisoner from some settlement on the Ohio a short time after Ollie's capture. The youth's drunken master had tomahawked, scalped, and mangled him in the most brutal and barbarous manner and not taking the trouble even to bury him, left him to rot near the edge of the Maumee.

At Coohcoocheeh's, having nothing to do except to bring water and collect wood for cooking, Ollie had some leisure. He occupied himself in hunting with a bow and arrow, the use of which he became quite expert, frequently shooting birds, and at one time killing a fine rabbit. He bore it to the cabin with no small degree of pride and to the great satisfaction of the old woman, to whom it furnished a delicious repast. Her granddaughter So-tone-

Spencer, O.M., Carleton & Lanahan.

goo congratulated him, telling him that he would soon become a man and a hunter.

Sometimes Coohcoocheeh permitted him to visit the Trader's Station on The Point, where Mr. Ironside always welcomed him, and his wife, the daughter of Coohcoocheeh, treated him with great kindness. It was on one of these visits in the woods above the point that he saw William Wells, then a prisoner at large among the Indians, sent by Colonel Hamtramck to look for him. Having learned the boy was there, Wells sought him out.

Wells, a former Indian captive, was a very active man, 5'6" or 8" tall, with auburn hair and freckles. In 1784, at age thirteen or fourteen, he had gone fishing with some other boys at a pond, where Miami Indians kidnapped them. William quickly embraced the life of a warrior, and while a member of the Miami tribe, claiming that he was a lost white man, Wells lured the flatboats of white settlers to shore along the Ohio River so that the Indians could plunder and slaughter them.

Wells had an Indian wife, possibly the sister of the Miami war chief, Little Turtle, and she was among those taken hostage by Scott and Wilkinson in 1791 and imprisoned in the Picket Fort.

Wells had left the Indians due to a dispute with Simon Girty in which they butted heads over a leadership role at the Battle of St. Clair. Wells had nearly received the entire command of three hundred Seneca and Miami warriors who devoted themselves to taking the cannon at the battle, by claiming that Girty was "getting to be old." Instead, Wells and Girty shared the command, but Girty's friends decided to kill Wells afterwards and had a vendetta against him. Wells left the Indians to preserve his life and got a living by serving as an interpreter for Hamtramck, out of Vincennes.

Wells questioned Ollie very particularly about his name, family, and station in his white life, in order to confirm his identity. He did not mention to him any possibility of leaving his captors.

He was quickly on his way, but not before privately making an offer to ransom him, an offer not accepted.

He later communicated the information about Ollie to Hamtramck, the officer commanding at Post Vincennes, who sent it to Colonel Wilkinson at Fort Washington, and he immediately to Colonel Spencer.

While Ollie had abandoned all hope of seeing again his home and his beloved kindred, and he was striving to become reconciled to his fate, his friends were making active preparations for his release. Measures were in operation that in a few months afterward resulted in his deliverance. Through the influence of General Washington, the British minister at Philadelphia wrote letters to Colonel Simcoe, Lieutenant Governor of Upper Canada, and his friends conveyed them by an express dispatched through the state of New York to Niagara, near where Simcoe lived.

AFTER A COUNCIL IN 1791 in which the tribes could not agree on a united course of action, they had decided to call another meeting for the following year. The Grand Council was to meet at Captain Johnny's town, on the east bank of the Auglaize, up river of where Coohcoocheeh lived. Blue Jacket had traveled widely to gather tribes for this meeting.

By this time, Ollie was probably aware that he was in quite a nexus of peoples. The confluence was a place of retreat for a minimum of seven Indian cultures, with villages of Shawnee, Delaware, Nanticoke, Cherokee, Miami, Mingo, and Wyandot in a ten-mile radius. The natives living there and those who were now gathering for the council were three fourths of all the Indians remaining east of the Mississippi, only a few thousand. Ominously, because of the recent wars that had disrupted the growing and hunting seasons, all of these Indians were more and more dependent on the British for supplies.

At the Grand Council that met beginning on September 30, 1792, Simon Girty interpreted, the only white man allowed, as he had gained an Indian military following after co-leading the attack on Dunlap's Station and the burning of Abner Hunt.

In addition to those already named, there were a large number from west of the Mississippi. "Besides these there were so many nations that we can not tell the names of them," said chief Cornplanter, a chief of the Seneca who had avoided getting involved in the American Revolution and after the war secured a tract of land on the Allegheny for his people, bringing in Quaker teachers and beginning an agricultural life for his followers.

Some wanted to mediate a peace based on their recent victories, others pressed for more warfare. They met with the aim of united action in a Confederacy, with four factions of Indians. First, the Six Nations had already lost their land in the New York region to the Americans and did not want more war. Second, those Iroquois who had backed America in the Revolution, led by the Senecas, lived on reservations surrounded by settlers and felt vulnerable to attack. They favored negotiation with the United States. Third, some Indians who had lost their land east of the Muskingum River felt it was impractical to remove the white settlers already there but would fight to retain the rest of Ohio. Joseph Brant supported the Muskingum boundary and got the support of the Lakes tribes, the Wyandot, Ottawa, Ojibwa, and Potawatomi. Last, the Shawnee, Miami, Mingo, and Delaware in the region who were not yet dispossessed felt strongly that the

Ohio River must be the boundary (many Delaware and Shawnee who would not fight at all had already emigrated to Spanish lands around the Mississippi River). The Creek and Cherokee from the south, and the Sauk and Fox from the Mississippi River area participated in the council, as well. As many as 4000 Indians, warriors with family members, were in the region. The British fed them all during the conference.

There was no real resolution at the council. The Six Nations encouraged a peace path through land negotiations, but the rest insisted on the Ohio River boundary even if it meant war, based on the 1768 treaty the Iroquois had made at Fort Stanwix with the British. Ultimately, as expressed by the Mekoche master of ceremonies Red Pole, a peace chief of the Shawnee, the Indian position was, "We do not want compensation. We want [restoration] of our country."

The Seneca, who had come on behalf of the Americans, bought the natives some time by sending a deceptive report to President Washington, keeping from him that they would have the British as mediators and that there would be no compromise on the Ohio River boundary. They scheduled another conference for 1793 to mediate with the Americans, and Henry Knox promised to appoint commissioners to meet with them.

After the conference about the middle of October, a group of fifty Shawnee warriors gathered at Coohcoo-cheeh's cabin, from Snake's and Blue Jacket's villages, including Wapawaqua and Catawa-waqua. They, 150 Miami, and 247 Wyandot and Mingo, led by Simon Girty, with two white prisoners as guides, prepared to join an expedition against the Americans, concerning heavy provisioning of the outposts seen by their spies. They planned to strike at the packhorses at the fallen timber between Forts St. Clair and Hamilton, and missing that, they would go to Columbia. Girty said they "would raise hell to prevent a peace." Ollie was appalled at the thought of them attacking the people in the Miami valley, possibly including those at Columbia and even his own family.

The fifty Shawnee halted near their cabin to consult with Coohcoocheeh on the probability of the success of their expedition. The old woman immediately entered her sanctuary, where she remained nearly an hour. During a part of that time, while sitting under the viewing shed, Ollie could hear noise as of a stick striking the sides of the cabin, the beds, and particularly the kettles within it, and afterward the low humming sound of her voice. He supposed she was uttering her incantations.

Young as he then was, he could not help at times looking on the old woman with a superstitious fear mingled with awe. He did not believe that she was divinely inspired, but thought it more than probable that she interacted with evil spirits.

She came out soon after with a countenance unusually animated and with a look of great wildness. She stretched out both arms. Gracefully bringing the tips of her fingers together as if encircling something, she exclaimed, *"Mechee! mechee! mechee!"* The Indians instantly interpreted this to mean many scalps, many prisoners, and much plunder. Fired with the confident expectation of success, they immediately proceeded to join the main body.

Ollie had never before seen so large a force of Indian warriors. He could not but admire their fine forms and warlike appearance as they marched in single file to the river or stood erect in their canoes with their rifles in their hands, crossing the Maumee. At the same time he shuddered at the thought of the lives that would be taken and the hundreds that through their instrumentality would soon be made widows, orphans, and childless.

The war party joined the larger force under the leadership of Little Turtle and passed Fort Hamilton, where the Indians' spies discovered a party of guarded soldiers chopping firewood east of the fort, going in at noon for their dinner. The Indians set an ambuscade, and as the soldiers returned to their work, the Indians attacked them and captured two men.

Upon interrogating these men, the Indians learned that a regular supply convoy, making its rounds with an escort of one hundred soldiers, would arrive at Fort Hamilton on Monday night. There would be nearly a hundred packhorses, as well as the fine horses of a company of riflemen. The convoy made its rounds daily from Fort Washington to Fort Hamilton to Fort Jefferson to Fort St. Clair, each about 25 miles apart, enabling the convoy to spend each night encamped within the protection of a fort.

The Indians retreated a dozen miles and waited for the convoy's return from the outer posts. On the appointed day, they set their trap and waited for the convoy, to no avail. It turned out that on Saturday night, the convoy commander had allowed his men to remain at Fort Jefferson, to rest on Sunday.

The Indians sent out runners looking for the convoy, finding it Monday night encamped two hundred yards east of Fort St. Clair. Before dawn on Tuesday, November 6, the Indians attacked the camp from three sides, not exposing themselves to fire from the fort. With the crack of their rifles and their well-known yells, they drove the soldiers from their camp and began plundering it and securing the horses.

The army formed into three divisions next to the fort and counterattacked the Indians. The natives' force was at least twice the size of the Americans, enabling them to move off with the horses and other loot. The regulars pursued them on foot.

The Indians continued their retreat and only fired back when closely pressed. After sunrise, the now mounted Indians outdistanced the soldiers, who gave up and turned back.

Only a handful of horses remained, and the Americans set about caring for the wounded and burying their half dozen dead. One man's wound was the loss of his scalp. He received a stunning blow, and three Indians, as he reported, "fell to skinning his head." He survived this and lived for many years.

ABOUT THE MIDDLE of November, Ollie's fear and awe of Coohcoocheeh did not lessen when the Indians under Little Turtle returned victorious. They had taken several scalps, a large number of horses, and a great deal of baggage. Wapawaqua and his brother each possessed a good horse and a number of new blankets, and some of the Indians carried home tents, camp kettles, and many other articles. The Shawnees gave Coohcoocheeh part of their spoils—six blankets, several pounds of tobacco, and a small keg of whiskey—in gratitude for the aid that they did not doubt she had afforded them in achieving their victory. Their late success, if possible, increased their confidence in her supposed supernatural power.

At this time, Ollie's previous fear nearly came true as he had yet another life-threatening narrow escape. When the Indians returned victorious from their raid, they celebrated with liquor, and Catawa-waqua seized him in a drunken rage. He tied him to a stake with the intention of torturing him by burning. According to Spencer family lore, Coohcoocheeh, who was developing quite a fondness for him, saved him from her son with a stratagem, cajoling or tricking him, and aiding Ollie in his escape.

THE LIEUTENANT-GOVERNOR of Upper Canada, John Graves Simcoe, acknowledged a letter from the British ambassador, George Hammond, on November 17: "I have forwarded Your Excellency's letter, relative to young Spencer to Colonel England, who commands at Detroit."

THE WEATHER HAD NOW become cold, and Coohcoocheeh had Ollie throw aside his summer clothes, being not only too thin for the season, but nearly worn out. A white shirt, blanket capot (a hooded coat made from a blanket), blue leggings, and waistcloth supplied their place, so he was dressed in full Indian costume.

Although the labor of gathering their corn was over, he found pretty constant employment. He had now to make fires, carry water both for cooking and drinking, wash the hominy when boiled in ashes, and assist the old woman in getting wood. One afternoon in December, Coohcoocheeh being busy sent him alone to cut and bring home an armful of wood. Taking the axe, the pecawn (a long strap for tying up the wood), and their faithful dog who generally accompanied him, he went about a quarter of a mile up the bottom. He cut some wood, tied it into a bundle, and was just about to place it on his back, when the dog, moving off cautiously a few dozen yards, sat down near a small tree. Growling fiercely and striking the ground with his tail, the animal first looked up toward the top of a sapling, and then at Ollie as if to inform him there was game there and to ask his assistance. Picking up the axe, Ollie walked deliberately to the dog and followed the direction of his eyes. He saw on a limb about sixteen feet from the ground an animal of a dark gray color mixed with red, with a white belly and round head, altogether resembling a cat, but four times larger than the largest domestic cat, and crouched like that animal when ready to spring upon its prey.

Ignorant of its nature and not apprehending any danger, he threw several sticks at it to induce it to come down. At length, he hit it severely on the head, and it sprang to the ground within a few feet of him. The dog instantly seized it, and a fierce contest ensued. The dog, being strong, active, and courageous, several times caught the animal by the throat, but was as often compelled to let go his hold, so fiercely and powerfully did his antagonist draw up his hind feet and apply his sharp claws to his breast and sides. Indeed, Ollie now began to fear that the cat would conquer the dog, whose ardor seemed to have considerably abated and who fought with greater caution.

Approaching with the axe and taking advantage of an opportunity when the dog again attempted to seize the throat of the animal, he was fortunate to hit the cat a severe blow on the head, completely stunning him. He left him to his enraged antagonist, who soon finished the work of death. The dog, though severely wounded, appeared to be delighted, now standing over his fallen enemy as if exulting in his death, and now jumping around him, wagging his tail with pleasure. Ollie turned the animal over several times and marked its length, which from his nose to the end of its tail he judged to be about four feet. Then examining it particularly, for the first time he suspected that it was either a wild cat or a young panther (probably a lynx).

Leaving his wood and shouldering his prize, Ollie marched home, and with no small exultation, threw his load down before Coohcoocheeh. She raised her hands with surprise and exclaimed, "*Waugh haugh—h! Pooshun!*" It proved, indeed, to be a large male wild cat, an animal equally insidious and dangerous, according to its size and strength, as a panther. If it weren't for the presence of the dog and his own ignorance of its nature and of his danger, it might have destroyed him.

This exploit, with which the old woman associated great courage and daring, raised him very much in her estimation. She heard all the particulars of the affair with great satisfaction, and frequently saying, *"Enee, wessah,"* (that is right; that is good) said he would one day become a great hunter. Placing her forefingers together, by which sign the Indians represent marriage, and then pointing to So-tone-goo, she told him that when he became a man, he would have her for a wife.

Ollie had now acquired a sufficient knowledge of the Shawnee tongue to understand all ordinary conversation, and indeed the greater part of all that he heard, accompanied as their conversation and speeches were with the most significant gestures. Often in the long winter evenings, he listened with much pleasure and sometimes with deep interest to Coohcoocheeh. She told of the bloody battles of her nation, particularly with the Americans, and of the great prowess of her ancestors with their chivalrous exploits and "deeds of noble daring." She also related some interesting events of her early life; her courtship and marriage; the great strength, bravery, and activity of her then young husband, Cokundiawthah; and her own youthful charms. Her memory seemed a great storehouse, out of which she brought "things new and old."

In almost all her tales, whether tragic or mirthful, whether of great achievements in the battle and in the chase, or whether relating some diverting incident or humorous story, she mingled many superstitious ideas. She spoke much of supernatural agency and of her own frequent conversations with departed spirits. To the beaver, she gave both the faculty of reason and the power of speech. She taught Ollie a song that a beaver sang to an almost desponding hunter, stranded by high waters and half starved. Encouragingly, the animal told the hunter that the freshet would soon subside and that beyond the stream he should find plenty of game:

Sawwattee sawwatty,
Sawwattee sawwatty,
Sawawkee meechee noo kahoohonny;
Kooquay nippee ta tsa;
Waugh waw waugh whaw,
Waugh waw waugh whaw.

Coohcoocheeh made a great effort to teach Ollie to dance, an accomplishment not so easily acquired as at first one might suppose, from the great simplicity of their steps. Grace with them consisted principally in the motions of the body. The action of their limbs, adapted to facilitate and perfect these motions, were not the chief exhibitors of grace and skill. It required much practice to combine both successfully.

Having seen his elder instruct his younger sister in dancing, Ollie had learned several steps, particularly the balancer, and single and double chassé. Sometimes for the amusement of Coohcoocheeh, he gave her a specimen of the manner of his dancing; with the slower and simpler steps she seemed to be amused, occasionally laughing heartily at what to her appeared so ludicrous. But when he attempted a hornpipe, whirling round frequently, or capered along in a double chassé, so ridiculous did it appear to her, manifesting as she thought such a want of grace and dignity, that usually with some marked expression of contempt she put a stop to his further exhibition.

Coohcoocheeh was remarkably nice in her cookery, scouring her kettles often and washing her bowls and spoons. Nothing offended her more quickly than the appearance of slovenliness. Although Ollie stood pretty high in her favor, he sometimes incurred her displeasure by his neglect, particularly by his want of cleanliness, as she thought, in performing some of his household duties.

IN ORDER TO PROTECT and aid his brother-in-law, Aaron Ogden wrote to Jonathan Dayton, his friend, long- time colleague, and a member of the U.S. House of Representatives, that Colonel Spencer sought a government position in the territories "by reason of his not being able to get on his lands which he designed to cultivate, on account of the savages." Colonel Spencer had mentioned the "mischievous" Indians in his letter, but Ogden primarily blamed his age and the drought for his difficulties. He reminded Dayton of Colonel Spencer's "activity, his sobriety, his honesty and his worth," and went on to say, "you also well know how he deserves from the public on account of services in the war and on account of his patriotism."

Not long after on December 29, Colonel Richard England, who commanded at Detroit, wrote to Simcoe:

Immediately after I was honored with Your Excellency's command relative to Oliver Spencer, a Prisoner boy, taken by the Indians in the neighborhood of Fort Washington, I applied to Colonel McKee to endeavor to obtain his release, and an express was instantly sent by him to his correspondent at the Glaze where the boy is, and have the honor now to enclose you a copy of the answer he received. I regret exceedingly that our endeavors have not yet been as successful as my anxiety for a boy under his description induced me to hope, but we have so far succeeded as to ensure the boy being properly taken care of, and as the Colonel proposed going to the Foot of the Rapids as soon as the ice is sufficiently formed as to admit of his

traveling, there is little doubt but from his influence
he will be able to obtain his release, and bring him
with him on his return here, where every possible
care shall be taken of him by me till the navigation
opens and a proper opportunity offers of sending him
to you in order that he may be restored to his
parents.

I did not receive a letter which Mr. Hammond
in his letter to you mentioned to have addressed to
me, and which I beg you will be pleased to inform
him, lest he should consider me inattentive in not
acknowledging it, as I suppose it related to this
unfortunate boy.

Hammond was the British diplomat who had met
with George Washington. As for his care, Mr. Ironside was
the agent in the matter.

ON A VERY COLD MORNING about the middle of January,
Coohcoocheeh rose before day, and intending to make
some hominy, boiled the corn with some ashes in the
water for some time to remove the hulls. It was Ollie's duty
to cleanse the corn from the hulls, and as it had been long
enough in the ash mixture, she ordered him to get up and
perform that duty.

The old woman's temper was very quick, and when
roused, she was like a fury. By no means particular in
selecting an instrument of punishment, when her poker
was not at hand, she seized a knife, axe, billet of wood,
anything within her reach, and hurled it at the
unfortunate subject of her wrath. Since Ollie did not rise
immediately, she uttered her customary *"Oogh!"* followed
by a stroke of her poker. Not giving him time to put on his

moccasins, she hurried him off with the kettle of boiling corn and a large coarse sieve to the river. The wintry weather had frozen over the Maumee for some time, and through the ice, about six inches thick, they had cut and kept open a hole for the convenience of getting water. Placing the large sieve by the side of the opening and emptying the corn into it, he proceeded to dip up water, pour it on the hominy, and then rub it well to take off the hulls.

He had not finished his work when his bare feet, all this time on the ice, were so pained with cold that he could endure it no longer. He stepped into the hominy and enjoyed the luxury of its warmth until the old woman espied him. Calling him loudly by his Indian name Meecheway, and uttering several *"ooghs,"* she ran down to the river, furious with rage. She hurled her poker and inflicted a severe blow on his back, felling him to the ice. Immediately springing up, he ran on, leaving her to finish the hominy, and did not return to the cabin until her anger had subsided.

Coohcoochcch was not being unusually cruel to him to make him walk barefoot on the ice. The Indians hardened the bodies of their children to the weather by making them bathe in cold water each day. He was lucky that she didn't have him immerse himself in the river.

Also, when deep snow covered the ground in the middle of winter, Ollie was often obliged to spring from his bed at the well-known dreaded sounds *"ki-you-wan-nie,"* the drunken song. He would seize only a blanket and run and hide behind the nearest log or tree, or throw himself down in the snow, where he lay for more than an hour, not daring to move until the drunkard Catawa-waqua had gone off. Once with this, Ollie narrowly escaped death again. Unfortunately, he had again offended the man, who some nights afterward, returning home drunk from the

Miami village a few miles west of them, came so near to their cabin before the boy was aware of his approach that he scarcely had time to escape. Entering the door, the man inquired for him. When Coohcoocheeh told him that Meecheway was absent, he struck his knife several times through the skins on his bunk. He then seized a cat lying near him and threw it on the fire, placing his foot upon it and keeping it there. The poor animal squalled most piteously the while until Coohcoocheeh jerked it out and threw it into the snow.

CHAPTER FOURTEEN

RANSOMED

L IEUTENANT-GOVERNOR John Graves Simcoe of Upper Canada wrote to the British Ambassador George Hammond, "I enclose for Your perusal the copy of a letter and the enclosure that I have lately received from Colonel England by which you will see the Alacrity which that Officer has shown to perform Your Excellency's commands, and the dictates of the humanity of his own mind—and I dare say it will give pleasure to You to be able to convey the substance of the intelligence of the Young Man's safety to his relations—should He be sent here— You may be certain of all attention being shown to him."

In addition, William Wells finally arrived at Vincennes after his tour of the region. Hamtramck was able to inform Sargent on February 6, 1793, "Will you be so good as to give my compliments to Colonel Spencer and tell him that agreeably to your request I have made inquiry of his son and find with very great pleasure that he is alive. He is at La Glaise in a family of the Six Nations who lives with the [Shawnee]. They demand 300 Dollars for him; but if this treaty takes place he will no doubt have him for nothing. The Indians have promised him to take good care of their prisoners."

IT WAS NOW NEAR the close of February, when sharp frosty nights and days of warm sunshine, succeeding the extreme cold of winter, constituted what in early times in the west they called sugar weather. Most families drew their year's supply from the sugar tree (sugar maple), and some made quantities of sugar for sale. Coohcoocheeh and her children took their large brass kettle, several smaller ones, some corn and beans for their sustenance, their bedding, and indeed all their household furniture and utensils, except for the hominy block. Closing their cabin door and placing the customary stick against it, they crossed the Maumee below the mouth of the Auglaize. Then packing their baggage on a horse, they proceeded four or five miles down the river to a beautiful open woods, principally of sugar trees intermixed with blue ash, elm, and poplar. Here Coohcoocheeh had made her sugar for many years, and here they found a comfortable bark shelter. There was every convenience for sugar making, save kettles, which they now supplied. The old woman tapped the trees, and she gave Ollie employment as well—dusting out and setting the trough, carrying the sap, cutting wood, making fires, and occasionally attending to boiling the water at night.

They had a remarkably fine season and had been for several days employed, during which time they collected sap sufficient to make probably a hundred weight of sugar. Then one evening near sunset, as they sat quietly around the fire, a messenger came and spoke privately with Coohcoocheeh. He informed her that the British Indian agent from Detroit had arrived at The Point and had purchased Ollie through Mr. Ironside. Wapawaqua was absent on a hunting expedition, and he had authorized Mr. Ironside to dispose of him. Mr. Ironside had sent the messenger to conduct him to The Point.

Whether she thought the sudden joy that the news of his release from captivity would inspire might prove injurious to him, or whether she herself, now rather attached to him, was unwilling to part with him, the old woman received the intelligence with great seriousness, answering only with a simple *"Hu! enee."* She did not communicate the news to him until the next morning.

That evening she seemed more than usually disposed to converse with him. She repeated her inquiries about his parents, their rank in society, how long they had lived on the Ohio, and many such questions. She asked him particularly of the place of their former residence, and he told her that they once lived not far from the seashore and near New York, that their forefathers were English who came from the island on the eastern side of the great salt lake, south [sic] and east of them.

Her brow for a moment seemed deeply clouded, and the mournful tone of her voice betrayed her mingled feeling of melancholy and regret. She spoke of the first landing of the "pale faces" from their monstrous canoes, with their great white wings, as seen by her ancestors. She continued with their early settlements, their rapid growth, their widely spreading population, their increasing strength and power, their insatiable avarice, and their continued encroachments. The red men were no longer powerful. Diseases had reduced them, civil wars had thinned them, and long and various struggles, first with the British (*Met-a-coo-se-a-qua*), then with the Americans or Long-Knives (*Se-mon-the*), had diminished them. The invaders would not be satisfied until they had crowded the Indians to the extreme north, to perish on the great Ice Lake, or to the far west. Pushing those who should escape from their rifles into the great waters, at length, they would exterminate all.

She spoke of the anger of the Great Spirit against the red men, especially those of her own nation, nearly all of whom had perished. She and her children, the remnant of her race, would soon sleep in the ground. There would be none to gather them at the feast of the dead or to celebrate their obsequies.

Soon her countenance kindled with animation and her eyes sparkled with pleasure; when changing the mournful theme, she ended with a most glowing description of the beautiful hunting grounds, the ever-enduring abode of the brave and good red men. These she described as lying far, far beyond the vast western ocean and as being ten-fold larger than the great continent of America. There, she said, the changing seasons brought no extremes of heat or cold, wet or drought. None was sick; none became old or infirm. She pointed to the large poplars near them, some of which were five or six feet in diameter and rose eighty feet without a limb, and spoke of the largest trees of that country as being twenty times larger and spreading their broad tops among the stars. Corn, beans, pumpkins, and melons, she said, grew there spontaneously. The richest fruits loaded the trees; perpetual verdure covered the ground; the flowers on the prairies were forever blooming and fragrant. The springs were abundant, clear, and cool; the rivers large, deep, and transparent, abounding with fish of endless varieties. Innumerable herds of buffalo, deer, elk, moose, and every species of game stocked the fine open woods. In short, there was a paradise containing all that could delight the mind or gratify the senses, and to crown all, it was the exclusive home of the Indian.

The little Canadian Frenchman, for such was the messenger, listened with that attention which among the Indians is inseparable from good manners. He frequently expressed his admiration and even his wonder, though once or twice he turned Ollie, smiled incredulously, and said, "Ma foi! dat is grand contry."

It was very pleasant when they arose early the next morning, the last day of February 1793, and the Frenchman expressed his intention to set out immediately for The Point. Coohcoocheeh now for the first time communicated to Ollie the information the man had given her on the preceding night. In addition, she told him that he should go down to Detroit, cross the great lake in a big canoe, and performing a large circuit, arrive at his home on the Ohio. She spoke of the happiness of his family, especially the joy of his mother, at his safe return. She expressed her own regret in parting with him, having, as she said, begun to regard him as her child. She concluded by saying that if he should grow up to be a man, he must come and see her. Affected even to tears, while taking his hands in both of hers and cordially pressing them, she said farewell. Poor So-tone-goo sobbed loudly as Ollie took her hand, for the moment deeply affected himself, as he said goodbye. Leaving the cabin, he now followed the Frenchman at a brisk pace. Frequently, he looked back at its inmates who were still standing near it, until the intervening trees hid them forever from his sight.

The sun just rising seemed to shine with unusual splendor. Never before, as Ollie thought, had it appeared so bright and beautiful. He was at first "as one that dreamed," scarcely crediting the fact that he was no longer a prisoner. Gradually, however, as he left his late dwelling farther and farther behind him, becoming assured and conscious of the truth that he was indeed free, he was like a bird loosed from its cage, or a young colt from its stall. To suppress his feelings or restrain his joy would have been impossible. He laughed; he wept; he whistled; he shouted; and sung by turns. Never had he moved with step so elastic, now skipping over logs, jumping, dancing, and running alternately, while the Frenchman, whose name he found on inquiry to be Joseph Blanche, sometimes stopped and looked at him intently as if suspecting that he was more than half insane. By degrees, however, this extreme of joy subsiding, he became more temperate, confining the expression of his happiness to singing and whistling, which he kept up almost without intermission until they reached the Auglaize.

Stepping into a canoe and crossing that river, in a few minutes, they entered the hospitable dwelling of Mr.

Ironside. This gentleman received him with more than his usual kindness, and congratulating him heartily on his release from Indian captivity, introduced him to Colonel Matthew Elliott, the British Indian agent, and to a Mr. Sharp, a merchant of Detroit who had accompanied him to the Auglaize. The latter was a teacher by profession and had gone to Detroit for a job, but the position had no longer been available. He remained and became a successful trader in the Northwest region after the Revolution, eventually becoming an agent for the Miami Company in the Maumee-Wabash region.

Matthew Elliott was a Scots-Irishman who arrived in America in 1761. He volunteered with Bouquet's expedition, in which the British commander put down a native rebellion which was prompted by their desire to purge their lives of white influence and return to native ways. Afterward, Elliott remained on the frontier and began a long career as an Indian trader, traveling in the Shawnee country, building an extensive trade with them, and marrying a Shawnee woman.

Elliott had acted as a spy for the Patriots as the revolution neared, reporting on British and Indian activities, until the Americans wanted the supplies that he intended to trade with the Indians to use in their war effort against the British. Much to the American's resentment, he continued his trade with the Indians, who would use those supplies to raid along the frontier. No feeling for the American cause was evident in Elliott, and he believed that anyone who had the opportunity to get the high prices he was getting in wartime would do as he was.

He mounted his usual trading expedition in 1777, but Indians soon attacked him and seized all his goods, horses, and employees. Some Christian Moravian Indians who had followed behind him saved his life. When he tried to return to the Americans, they treated him with suspicion, so Elliott turned to the British side, which he probably felt was going to be the winning side anyway.

In 1781, the British sent Elliott to remove the Moravian Indians from the Tuscarawas River. These Christian Indians had built an extensive settlement with large fields and cattle and pigs, but the British did not want them close to the Americans because they believed that their leaders, David Zeisberger and Johann Heckewelder, were American sympathizers. Elliott was without gratitude to the Moravians for saving his life, and he made them leave their crops in the field. In addition, Michael Herbert, Elliott's servant, said that while they were packing horses, his master said, "that with these goods he expected to make the greatest speck he ever had made; that the Moravian Indians had at each of their towns great stocks of horned cattle, which when once distressed by the warriors, he could purchase of them for a song; (a few dollars per head,) while he would get forty dollars a head at Detroit."

Elliott received Ollie with considerable hauteur and with a look that spoke that his noticing him was condescension. Governor Simcoe had sent him with the express order to affect his ransom and convey him to Detroit. Yet, as if such a service was degrading, he pretended that being at Auglaize on public business, he had accidentally heard of him, and actuated wholly by motives of humanity, procured his release by paying a ransom of one hundred and twenty dollars. Ollie, having understood from Coohcoocheeh that he was to be sent home to his parents, was not a little disappointed in finding, as he supposed, that he was the property of an individual and subject to be disposed of at his pleasure. However, he soon comforted himself with the thought that the same humanity that had moved Elliott to affect his ransom would influence him to perfect the generous act by restoring him to his friends. At the worst, living with Elliott would greatly improve his condition. Elliott had conveyed to Mr. Ironside the same false impression, that his ransom was altogether his own private affair. Had Mr. Ironside known the truth, that gentleman would have immediately undeceived him, equally scorning such pitiful deceit to magnify generosity and incapable of trifling with the feelings of one in his hapless situation.

Ironside's wife now kindly invited him to breakfast, but Elliott objected to the trouble that it would give her. He ordered Joseph to take him over to James Girty's, where he said they would provide their breakfast. Girty's wife soon furnished them with some coffee, wheat bread, and stewed pork and venison, of which he ate with great gout, it being so much better than the food to which he had been lately accustomed.

He had not more than half breakfasted when Girty came in, and seating himself opposite to him, said, "So, my young Yankee, you're about to start for home."

Ollie answered, "Yes, sir, I hope so."

That, Girty said, would depend on his master, in whose kitchen he no doubt should first serve a few years' apprenticeship as a scullion. Then taking his knife, while sharpening it on a whetstone, he said, "I see your ears are whole yet, but I'm [damnably] mistaken if you leave this without the Indian ear mark, [so] that we may know you when we catch you again."

Ollie did not wait to find whether he was in jest or in downright earnest, but leaving his breakfast half finished, he instantly sprang from the table, leaped out of the door, and in a few seconds took refuge in Mr. Ironside's house. On learning the cause of his flight, Elliott uttered a sardonic laugh, deriding his unfounded childish fears, as he was pleased to term them. But Mr. Ironside looked serious, shaking his head as if he had no doubt that if Ollie had remained, Girty would have executed his threat.

Everything being now ready for their departure, they took their leave of Mr. Ironside and his wife, Ollie with feelings of gratitude for their kindness, which he never forgot. Several of the inhabitants on The Point wished them a good voyage and him a safe return home. They seated themselves in a small open bateau, steered by Joseph and rowed by a stout Canadian whom he called Baptiste. They soon cleared The Point and began to descend the Maumee.

As they passed Coohcoocheeh's cabin on the northern bank, Ollie took a last look at the spot where he had spent more than seven months of hopeless captivity and very many hours of painful anxiety and fearful apprehension. Nearly eight months before, he had arrived there, weary, exhausted, half-famished, sick, desponding, and a prisoner, truly an object of pity. Now he was ragged, dirty, bareheaded, and very much tanned; his looks were by no means inviting. Still, he enjoyed good health, and what with him seemed then to comprise almost every blessing, he was free from savage captivity. Turning his back forever upon his late residence, with tears of gratitude he devoutly thanked God for his deliverance. As he thought about the ever-rolling current, aided by every stroke of the oar, wafting him nearer and nearer home, he felt a pleasure impossible to describe.

Of Elliott and Sharp, he had but an indistinct recollection: they were both men of only ordinary size, having nothing remarkable in their appearance. Elliott's hair was black, his complexion dark, his features small. His nose was short, turning up at the end. His look was haughty and his countenance repulsive. Sharp, on the contrary, had light hair and a fair complexion, with a smirking look, and a countenance indicative of shallowness.

After half an hour spent in light and unimportant conversation, Sharp, merely to pass away the time, requested Ollie to relate the particulars of his captivity. However, he appeared but little interested, often interrupting him to make some observations on persons or things as they passed down the river. He then made several inquiries about his family, the Miami settlement, and Fort Washington. This led to a more general conversation and drew from Elliott many ungentlemanly remarks and disparaging observations about the Americans.

Sharp then observed that being so full of notions of liberty and equality, they would make rather stubborn servants and that he thought the boy would be no great bargain. "However," he continued, looking at him, "I suppose you will not have much employment for him?"

"Not much," replied Elliott, "besides cleaning knives and forks, blacking shoes, running of errands, and waiting upon table."

With an expression of disgust and indignation, Ollie turned his back upon him. The truth was, he more than half doubted his having anything to do with him except to convey him to Detroit. He asked no more questions of either of them, and when questioned, answered as briefly as possible.

He amused himself with looking at the numerous fish swimming in the clear stream, or at the lofty trees on the banks, and seeing here and there an Indian hut or village. Now he listened to the cheerful song of the boatmen as the one plied his oar and the other his paddle, timing their strokes as exactly with their music as a soldier would the tread of his left foot with the beat of the drum.

On the first night after leaving the Auglaize, they slept at a Wyandot village. The next morning they reached the rapids.

Alexander McKee and his deputy Elliott kept a storehouse at the Rapids of the Maumee, from which they led and encouraged the Indians battling against the Americans. During the battle years, the British completely supplied the dependent Indians by sending food, weapons, and cloth from Detroit across Lake Erie and up the Maumee River to the foot of the rapids, from where the Indians took their share of the goods.

Alexander McKee's father had been a licensed Indian trader, and the son grew up immersed in that world. He spoke several Indian languages and variously a translator and diplomat on behalf of the British army. The British had rewarded McKee with land and political positions for his service, in which he had been able to keep an uneasy peace with Indians who were disaffected with the growing settlement of their land and the problems that came with it. During the Revolution, he chose the British side, and it was with this man and Elliott that Simon Girty had fled to the British.

The British had made McKee a Captain of the Indian Department after he fled to Detroit, where he related useful military information about Fort Pitt. McKee had had British instructions to restrain the cruelty of the Indians and to ransom captives throughout the Revolution. Sometimes he succeeded in doing so. He also participated in ambushing the American force at Blue Licks. After 1790, McKee at first urged restraint to the warriors when he thought there was a chance of a negotiated settlement. In the Battles of Harmar and St. Clair, McKee provided guns, intelligence, and food to the natives, signaling the support of his government.

McKee's compound was a small fort built by the British at the end of the Revolution with eleven storehouses for weapons, ammunition, and food. Ollie later wrote that they stopped there only for the night. This may have been the case, but he may have been playing the peacemaker. Another captive believed he met Ollie there. John Brickell said, "I think I saw Spencer once. I saw a large lad, who, if I recollect right, said his name was Spencer: he was with M'Kee and Elliott as a waiter, or kind of servant, and if I remember right, he was at the rapids."

The Delaware had taken John Brickell from near Pittsburgh, and he wrote of the gauntlet, "for they fell to beating me so that I was knocked down, and every thing that could get at me beat me, until I was bruised from head to foot. At this juncture a very big Indian came up, and threw the company off me, and took me by the arm, and led me along through the lines with such rapidity that I scarcely touched the ground, and was not once struck after he took me till I got to the river. Then the very ones who beat me the worst were now the most kind and officious in washing me off, feeding me, etc., and did their utmost to cure me. I was nearly killed, and did not get over it for two months."

Whingwy Pooshies, or Big Cat, a chief of the Delaware, took him and treated him as one of his family. He mainly hunted with the men and traveled all around on the Scioto, Hockhocking, and Licking Rivers, and Jonathan's Creek. He later said that the "Delawares are the best people to train up children I ever was with." They never hit and scarcely scolded him, but pointed out people as good or bad examples.

John later earned money by supplying game to settlers using the hunting skills he learned from the

Indians. He would become the first white settler at the confluence of the Scioto and Olentangy Rivers where Columbus, Ohio now stands.

In the morning, Elliott took Ollie on horseback to a Wyandot village situated on the Maumee just above the entrance to Lake Erie. The two boatmen with their bateau left them and proceeded to their home at Frenchtown. Here Elliott placed him in charge of some Wyandots with whom he had contracted, probably for a gallon of rum, to convey him to Detroit. He mounted his horse in company with Sharp and rode off, leaving him again to the mercy of the savages. The Indians, eight or ten in number, commenced drinking pretty freely directly after Elliott left them. Soon becoming half-drunk, they began to sing, dance, shout, and wrestle, as usual. Among them was a youth of about fourteen who, while Ollie was sitting quietly as a spectator on one side of the tent, came over, pulled him up, and insisted that he should wrestle with him. This he refused, objecting to the great inequality of their years, size, and strength. Being urged, Ollie at length consented, and as he was very strong for one of his years, and withal quite active, in a very few seconds he laid the Wyandot youth sprawling on the ground. In a second effort, the youth was more successful, throwing Ollie down, but the moment he struck the ground, Ollie gave a sudden spring and threw himself over the youth. As he struggled by force to get up, Ollie held him down until he asked him to let him rise.

Mortified and angry, the youth got up, blackguarding him in broken Shawnee, and seizing him by the hair and passing his finger around his head, said he would scalp him. That moment Ollie gave him a severe blow in the pit of the stomach, which made him lose his hold on his hair and nearly knocked him down. Ollie now stood in an attitude of defense, determined to resist any further insult or violence.

The youth did not now approach him.

Supposing his anger had cooled, Ollie turned round and walked a few steps with the intention of sitting down.

With this opportunity, the youth drew his knife, and stealing behind Ollie, stabbed him in the back. He no doubt intended to inflict a mortal wound, but the knife, fortunately striking the lower part of his shoulder blade, glanced down across the ribs without entering the body.

An old Indian now interfered, and discovering from the flowing blood that the youth had badly wounded him, he stripped off his capot and pressed the wound firmly. He then applied a large quid of tobacco to its orifice and covered it with a compress secured by a bandage over his shoulder and round his chest, effectually staunching the blood.

Early next morning, so great had been Elliott's care for him, two old Indian women took charge of him and placed him in the middle of their canoe. They set out for Detroit, about forty-five miles distant; and paddling along the edge of the lake and up the strait, they arrived at that place on the evening of March 3.

Detroit's population at that time was around 2500, including 2000 French Canadians, 250 slaves, both Native-American and African-American, and 250 British, the latter building Fort Lernoult at Detroit in 1779 in anticipation of an American attack.

The two old women delivered him to Colonel Richard England, the officer commanding that garrison.

CHAPTER FIFTEEN

A JONAH

GOVERNOR SIMCOE HAD informed Colonel England about Ollie's family and particularly about his relatives. Simcoe instructed England to receive him, to provide clothing and everything necessary for his comfort, and to send him on to Fort Niagara as soon as the navigation of Lake Erie should open. Colonel England found that he was personally acquainted with some connections of Ollie's mother. His sense of duty, as well as from a disposition to oblige his friends, would have assured Ollie of a favorable reception, but independently of these considerations, being both a gentleman and a man of great humanity, he received him with much kindness. Regarding his wretched appearance, with sympathy for his condition, he followed only the generous impulse of his nature in ministering to his relief and comfort. After asking him some brief questions and kindly assuring him of his future welfare, he addressed himself to Lieutenant Andre, an officer of the same regiment. Mr. Andre was expecting him and on hearing of his arrival had repaired to the colonel's quarters. Colonel England committed him to his charge, observing that Mr. Andre would of course take pleasure in making the necessary provision for him.

Mr. Andre immediately took him by the hand and led him to his quarters in the same barracks only a few doors distant. Requesting him to sit down, he retired from the apartment. In a few minutes, a servant entered and set before him some tea, bread, and butter. He supped, arose, and was retiring from the table when two women, whom, as he supposed, mere curiosity had kept standing at one end of the room looking at him intently while he was eating, now advanced. Each unceremoniously took him by the hand, led him out of the apartment, and conducted him to a chamber.

Here they stripped off all but his shirt and carefully threw his clothes out at a back window beyond the palisades of the town. Before he had time to tell them of his wound, they seated him in a large washtub half filled with water and suddenly tore off his shirt, which had adhered fast to the bandage round his shoulder. This inflicted for a moment acute pain and extorted from him a loud scream. Their surprise at this soon ceased when he told them that an Indian had stabbed him in the shoulder. When they saw the blood from the open wound running down his back, alarmed, one of them ran to inform Mr. Andre. The other with a rag immediately staunched the blood and deliberately proceeded to scour his person with soap and water, and by the time the surgeon arrived, had affected a complete ablution.

On probing the wound, which the surgeon found to be about an inch wide and three inches deep, he pronounced it not dangerous. Fortunately, he said, the knife in entering had struck the lower posterior point of the right shoulder blade and taken a direction downward. Had it entered an inch lower, or nearer the spine, it probably would have caused death.

From the lack of clothes, it was late the next morning before Ollie could get up. Receiving at length a temporary supply of a roundabout (a waist length jacket) and pantaloons from the wardrobe of Ensign O'Brian, brother of Mrs. England, and a pair of stockings and slippers from one of the women, he made his appearance in the breakfast room. He met Mrs. Andre, wife of the lieutenant. She very kindly took his hand and congratulated him on his deliverance from the Indians, though she could not help smiling at his singular appearance, dressed as he was in clothes which, although they fit the smallest officer in the garrison, hung like bags on him.

Mrs. Andre made very particular inquiries about his mother, whose maiden name was Ogden, and his relatives on her side. Telling him that she had been a Miss Ogden, she made their relationship to be that of third cousins. This unexpected information gave him great pleasure. To find among strangers and in highly-polished society one who was not ashamed to acknowledge as a relative a destitute boy far from friends and home, could not but be truly gratifying. But Mrs. Andre possessed none of the false pride of those who, governed wholly by artificial circumstances, while they "have respect to the man in gay clothing," feeling as if degraded by condescension to the unfortunate, "say to the poor, Stand thou there." She was kind and amiable, as she was handsome and accomplished. Although quite young, apparently not more than twenty, she supplied to him the place of a mother.

Her husband, one of the handsomest men Ollie ever saw, very affable in his manners and frank in his disposition, treated him with great kindness. After seeing that he was comfortably and indeed genteelly dressed, he introduced him to the families of Mr. Erskine and Commodore Grant. There he found boys and girls of nearly his own age who cheerfully associated with him and took pleasure in showing him the town, the shipping, the fort, and whatever else Mr. Andre thought would afford him gratification.

Here, too, he frequently saw William Moore who, through the influence of Colonel McKee, a countryman and an old friend of his father, had obtained his liberty

and given him employment in the agency. He seemed quite
contented and even happy, amusing himself in his leisure
hours in shooting at a mark, or in running, wrestling,
jumping, or other athletic exercises. Perhaps Moore was
paying his way home with a few wagers.

The situation of Detroit, on the western bank of the
strait, connecting Lake Huron with Lake Erie, and about
ten miles south of Lake St. Clair, is familiar to many. In
the 1790's it was a small town containing only wooden
buildings, few of which were well finished. Surrounded by
high pickets enclosing an area of probably half a mile
square, of which houses covered only about one-third
part, lying along the bank of the river, as they called the
strait. There were three narrow streets running parallel
with the river and intersected by four or five more at right
angles.

At the ends of the second street on the south end of
town were the entrances into the city, secured by heavy
wooden gates. Also there adjoining on the west was a
space about two hundred feet square, enclosed on a part
of two sides with low palisades. Within, occupying the
south side was a row of handsome three story barracks for
the accommodation of the officers. Buildings of the same
height for the soldiers' quarters stood on the west and a
part of the north side. The army used the open space as a
parade ground, where every day the adjutant exercised the
troops.

In the northwest corner of the large area, enclosed
with pickets on ground a little elevated, stood the fort. An
esplanade separated it from the houses. Surrounding it
first was an abatis of treetops, having the butts of the
limbs sharpened and projecting outward about four feet
high. Next, there was a deep ditch in the center of which
were high pickets, finishing with a row of light palisades,
seven or eight feet long, projecting horizontally from the

glacis (ground sloping away from the fortress). Covering not more than half an acre of ground, the fort was square, having a bastion at each angle, with parapets and ramparts high enough to shelter the quarters within, which were bomb proof entirely from the shot of an enemy. Its entrance, over a drawbridge and through a covered way, was on the east side facing the river. On each side were long iron cannon carrying twenty-four pound shot and which the officers called the "British lions." On each of the other sides were planted two, and on each bastion four cannon of various caliber—six, nine, and twelve pounders.

A company of artillery under the command of Captain Spear garrisoned the fort, while two companies of infantry and one of grenadiers of the 24th (Colonel England's regiment) had their quarters in the barracks. The balance of the regiment was at Michilimackinac and other northern posts. By the side of the gate near the end of the officers' barracks was another twenty-four pounder, and for the protection of the east side of the town, there were two small batteries of cannon on the bank of the river.

In the spring of 1793, anchored in the river in front of the town were three brigs of about two hundred tons each. The *Chippewa* and the *Ottawa* were new vessels carrying each, eight guns, and the *Dunmore* was an old vessel of six guns. There was also a sloop, the *Felicity*, of about one hundred tons, armed only with two swivels, and not in the best condition. Built in 1774, the *Felicity* could carry forty men and fifty barrels, with a burthen of fifty-five tons, and it took six men to sail her. All belonged to His Majesty, George III, and Commodore Grant commanded them. There were besides several merchant-men, sloops, and schooners, the property of individuals.

Meanwhile, Colonel England wrote of Ollie's arrival to Lt.-Governor Simcoe on March 17, 1793:

*It gives me much pleasure to acquaint you
that after many difficulties I have at length
succeeded in getting the release of the prisoner boy,
Oliver Spencer. The repeated application made by
his father and friends through a variety of channels,
made this a matter of much more difficulty and
greater expense than it otherwise would have been,
and indeed if it was not for the influence of colonel
McKee I much doubt if I should have been able to
prevail on the family the boy was with, to have given
him up. Money to a very considerable amount was
offered to them through other channels and this
naturally made them more anxious about him than
they otherwise would have been, and increased their
demands for him. His ransom and other expenses
cannot I am confident be considered very
extravagant when compared to the very desirable
object of restoring him to his family. It all comes
under sixty pounds New York Currency, which sum I
will pay as I wish to keep my word strictly with
those I rescued him from and beg to be informed how
or to whom I am to apply for this money. The Indians
state that five times that sum was offered to them for
him and they had increased his purchase to Five
Hundred Pounds, which by much difficulty the
correspondents of Colonel McKee and influence
removed. The boy on his way from the Glaze met
with a very unlucky accident, but as it is not now
likely to be attended with any bad consequence will
not trouble you with a detail of it. He is at present
under the surgeon's hands and daily recovering with*

*the assistance of some warm baths, a plentiful
application of soap, a supply of linen, and all kinds
of clothing and necessaries, he is restored to a
Christian form. He is as tenderly attended to as
possible by Mrs. Andre (a lady of the Regiment) with
whom he is connected, and who received from her
friends letters relative to him. I propose to forward
him to Niagara as soon as the communication opens
by water, in the mean time it would be kind to inform
his family with his situation provided any
opportunity offered.*

IN THE SPRING of 1793, while the British rescued Ollie from
his captivity, Wapawaqua and his friends continued their
raids on the settlers along the Ohio.

John Van Bibber was recuperating from smallpox
at his maple sugaring camp on the north shore of the
Ohio, opposite Point Pleasant. With him was his slave
David, a man of prodigious strength, able to lift a barrel of
whiskey by the rim and drink from the bung while
standing.

John's sixteen-year-old daughter Rhoda and her
older cousin Joseph Van Bibber had recovered from the
pox, and canoed over from Point Pleasant to assist John.

David was in a distant clearing; John read in the
cabin yard; while Joseph and Rhoda prepared a dinner.

David ran toward them shouting, "Indians!"

John ordered the teens into the cabin, but they ran
for their canoe. A party of twelve to twenty Indians that
included Wapawaqua divided and half ran after the canoe.

They shot Rhoda through the chest when she was a
few yards offshore, and she died instantly. With the
Indians' threats, Joseph returned to shore and they took
him prisoner.

The people of Point Pleasant heard the shots and lined the shore, soon launching a canoe. Included in the party were Nathan Boone and perhaps Colonel Daniel Boone. While crossing the river, they fired more than 100 shots.

Back at the cabin, an Indian fired his musket through a gap in the logs and grazed David's head. In response, John fired back through a gap with a long fowling piece loaded with sixteen rifle balls, hitting a group of Indians. He killed one warrior and wounded three others, breaking Wapawaqua's arm.

John, not knowing his daughter was dead, begged the men from Point Pleasant not to follow the fleeing Indians. This spared Joseph, who managed to escape the following year at Detroit.

For giving the warning, John rewarded David with the dead Indian's gun and silver trinkets from his body. More importantly, John gave David his freedom. He lived to old age in the Teay's Valley south of Point Pleasant.

OLLIE HAD SPENT almost four weeks very agreeably at Detroit, becoming much attached to Colonel England and particularly so to Mr. and Mrs. Andre, who treated him with great kindness, and to the family of Mr. Erskine, also very friendly and polite to him. Near the close of March, the lake being entirely clear of ice, though there was still some danger from easterly storms, they thought that the navigation to Fort Erie would be tolerably safe. Colonel England issued orders for the sailing of the *Felicity*. Ollie felt a momentary regret that he must so soon separate from these kind friends and acquaintances.

Everything being in readiness, and the sloop preparing to weigh anchor, he took leave of Mr. and Mrs. Andre, thanking them with tears for their parental kindness. So affected was he that he could scarcely pronounce the word farewell. He also took a very affecting leave from Colonel England, acknowledging with gratitude his obligations to him. The Colonel wished him a prosperous voyage and safe return to his friends. With a small bundle containing a few shirts and stockings, accompanying the sailor who was waiting to conduct him, Ollie proceeded to the sloop's boat, and in a few minutes more, was safely on board the *Felicity*.

With a light breeze they proceeded down the strait, but the wind being from the southwest, they went but little faster than the current, as they were obliged to tack very frequently from side to side of the river. Anchoring at its mouth, they lay there during the night. The next morning, the wind freshening a little from the same direction enabled them to spread their lower sails, topsail, and topgallant sail. About the middle of the afternoon, they anchored in Put-in-Bay, a fine harbor in the western part of Lake Erie, formed by North, Middle, and South Bass, the Strentian (Green Island), and some smaller islands.

The wind being light and variable, and there being some appearance of a change of weather, Captain Fleming thought it most prudent to remain here until morning. Taking Ollie into the ship's dinghy, with two oarsmen and a couple of hooks and lines, they rowed round the bay, trailing the lines from the stern. Passing along the north side of a little island at the mouth of the bay, Gibraltar Island, which is convex, steep and rocky, they caught several fine bass, one of which Ollie had the pleasure of drawing into the boat, on which they made a delicious meal.

On a high rocky point of this island stood a very large tall tree, towering above the adjacent woods, on the top of which was an eyrie. Here Ollie first saw the noble American eagle (Bald Eagle) and amused himself for some time watching several of them. Without the least apparent exertion, they gracefully, yet with amazing velocity, made a circuit of the bay; gradually rising and contracting their sphere with each circuit, until suddenly rising, they seemed a mere speck in the blue sky. Then as suddenly descending, almost with the rapidity of thought, to mid-air, they began to wheel around, doubling their sphere with each circuit as they descended, some settling on the trees, others darting on their prey. One of them perched on the high tree near the nest where his mate could be seen, probably hatching her eggs, and whose place he took soon after as she left her nest for food or recreation.

Early next morning, the first day of April, they weighed anchor, having a light breeze from the south. Sailing eastwardly, in a few hours they passed between Point Pelee and Middle Islands. At four o'clock in the afternoon, their sloop being a pretty good sailer, they had made about fifty miles, when the wind suddenly coming round began to blow fresh from the east. They continued onward, however, regularly tacking from southeast to northeast as near to the wind as the vessel would progress, until after sunset, with the wind still increasing.

They were now out of sight of land. The water all around them seeming to touch the horizon, the curling waves cresting with foam and appearing to mingle with the clouds, presented to Ollie a novel, sublime, and yet fearful spectacle. He retired to his berth on the larboard (port) side of the cabin about ten o'clock, and notwithstanding the noise of the waves and the pitching of the vessel, fell into a sound sleep. The wind increased to a tempest, and to proceed became impossible. For some time, they lay to under a close-reefed jib and main sail, when the captain, seeing no prospect of the storm abating, and fearing that the rolling of the sloop would unship her mast, gave orders to put her about. In coming round to starboard, they were nearly upset.

The tilting of the boat threw Ollie from his berth against the opposite side of the cabin, waking him. The next moment, a heavy sea struck the stern and forced in the cabin windows, pouring in several hogsheads of water, in which he was tossed about from side to side. It was nearly a minute before he could gain his feet and ascend to the deck. The crew soon closed the dead lights and cleared the vessel of water. The captain advised Ollie to return to his berth in the cabin, but he preferred to remain on deck, thinking that if the sloop were wrecked, he would have a much better chance of escape.

Although scudding almost under bare poles, merely carrying enough sail to steer the vessel, they were going at the rate of twelve knots an hour, pitching and rolling with the heavy swells. They sometimes feared that they might lose their mast; or that the seams of the rather old and unseaworthy vessel would open, making her founder; or in the shallow lake, she would be dashed to pieces against the bottom. Providence, however, kindly preserved them, and just after daylight, passing the fearful breakers on the north side of Point Pelee, they soon anchored safely in Put-in-Bay.

Tom, the cook, who was held as an oracle on board the sloop, openly declared that their being driven back by the storm was in consequence of their sailing from the bay on Friday, being besides the first day of April, to which all the crew assented, adding that they were lucky in getting safely back.

They spent a part of Saturday afternoon on an excursion through the Middle Bass Island, on which they killed several large rattlesnakes. Ollie narrowly escaped one at least three feet long, over which he stepped as it crossed the path. The captain, who had gone to a small pond a few hundred yards ahead of them to shoot ducks, returned in a short time running and out of breath. He declared that when he had fired at some ducks, a monstrous snake, more than sixteen feet in length, issuing

issuing from the long grass by the edge of the water, made directly toward him and pursued him for more than a hundred yards. On their return to the sloop, they caught some fine bass, which more than compensated them for the loss of the captain's ducks.

The next morning being Sunday, with the wind fresh from the south, and the weather being favorable, they again weighed anchor and stood out of the bay. Tom prognosticated that they should have a prosperous voyage. His predictions seemed likely to be true, as they sailed finely this day. Tom entertained them with several marvelous stories and extraordinary adventures, of which he had a store; and many would have compared with those of "Sinbad the Sailor." Besides these, he had a great variety of nautical songs, some of which, such as "Sweet Poll of Plymouth," and "All in the Downs," he sang with considerable pathos. Others of bloody battles and brilliant victories he sang with great spirit, but none of Ollie's entreaties could prevail with him to sing "Cease, rude Boreas," which he said was to be sung only on shore over a good can of grog, in company with wives and sweethearts.

The wind, favorable all Sunday, veered round before Monday morning, blowing very fresh directly ahead. Soon after daylight, when in sight of Long or Puttshawk's Point and not much more than a hundred miles from Fort Erie, to their great disappointment, a storm even more furious than the first compelled them to put about and drove them quite back to Put-in-Bay, which they reached on Monday evening. On Wednesday morning, they again sailed; and on the following day, a furious storm, carrying away their topgallant mast, again drove them back. On returning this time, Ollie was extremely sick from the pitching and rolling of the sloop and began to be discouraged, fearing they should never get across the lake.

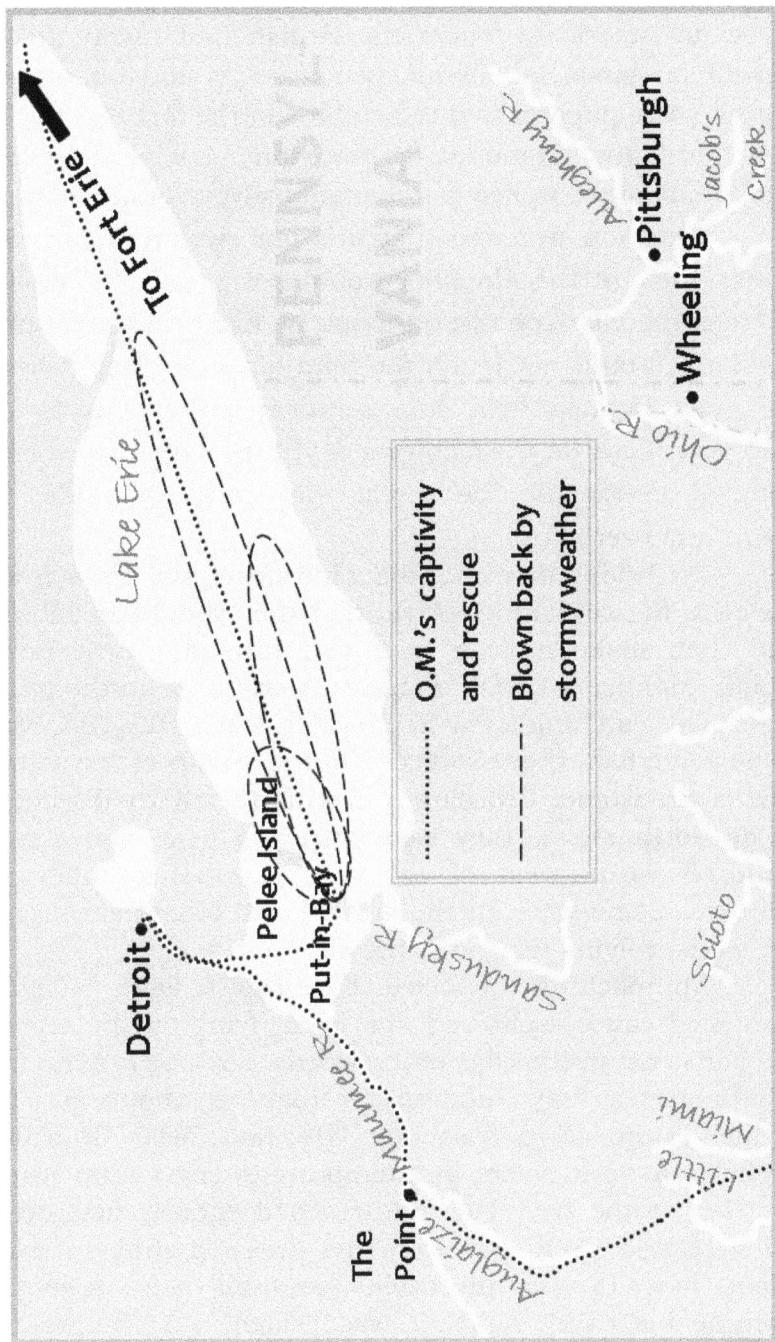

They had in the hold of the sloop an ill-looking man, said to be an American, whom the British had taken up at Detroit on suspicion of his being a spy and on whose person some papers, said to be plans of the fort and town, they had found. Pronouncing him guilty, Colonel England had him chained in heavy irons and conveyed to Niagara.

Tom now declared that this man was a Jonah, on whose account the Almighty would not permit the vessel to cross the lake—one who though he had escaped justice on shore, would not reach the land alive. So deeply were the crew imbued with this sentiment, that but for a discovery made on the following day, they might have been tempted to execute the threat they privately made, to throw him overboard.

On Friday morning, the wind being still fresh from the east, the captain proposed that they should go fishing and then make a little excursion through North Bass Island. Making a circuit round westerly and northerly in their boat, catching a few fine bass, a small sturgeon, and some white fish, they proceeded to the middle of the south side of the island. Crossing it in a northeasterly direction to its north shore, they were attracted to a spot a few hundred yards west of them by a great number of vultures. Some were on the ground and others sitting on the trees or flying around in the air.

Approaching the place, they saw a light, bateau-fashioned canoe, split and shattered, lying on the top of the bank just in the edge of the woods. Looking around for a few minutes, they found not far from the canoe a man in a high state of putrefaction. He had been drowned probably a week before in attempting to cross from Point Au Plait to the bay. The vultures had entirely destroyed his face and neck; but from his dress, a drab colored capot, overalls, and moccasins, and his skin, seen by opening his calico shirt, it was evident that he was a Canadian Frenchman.

Tom immediately explained the cause of their detention and the storms repeatedly driving them back. He declared that the Almighty would not suffer them to cross the lake while this man lay unburied, and instantly seized the poor Frenchman's paddle, which lay near him. With the aid of another sailor, working sometimes with his hands and sometimes with a stick, in about an hour they succeeded in digging a grave about two feet deep in the soft sandy ground on the top of the bank. Into this, they placed the corpse, dragging it up by the shoulders. Tom drew from his pocket a prayer book, and opening it at the burial service, he handed it to the captain, who read it with great solemnity. They now filled up the grave and planted at its head the paddle with its blade upward, and threw brush and logs over it for its protection.

When satisfied that they had done a good work, they returned to their boat and rowed backed to the sloop. In about an hour, Tom prepared for them an excellent dinner of fish and potatoes. Ollie had become hardened to the sight of gore, and they ate with gusto, their appetites from the exercise of the morning being very keen.

On Wednesday, April 13, the wind changed to the southeast and the lake became calm, allowing them to again set sail. On Friday evening, they safely anchored opposite Fort Erie.

On the following morning, taking leave of the sloop's crew, Ollie went on shore with the captain. He introduced him to the officer commanding the fort, at the same time delivering to him a letter written by Colonel England. They detained him here only a few hours and then put him on board a small barge in the charge of a corporal and four soldiers. In a few hours, they conveyed him to Fort Chippewa. This was a blockhouse garrisoned by a lieutenant and thirty men on the north side of Chippewa creek, some dozen yards from its mouth and about two miles above the falls of Niagara. The boy passed the night there.

On the following morning, a man whom the lieutenant provided to conduct Ollie escorted him down to the falls. He would never forget the sensations with which he first heard it, sensations growing more and more intense as he approached nearer and nearer to it—the feeling of apprehension with which, while passing down the rapid current of the river, he bent his body instinctively to the shore as if to make the boat cling to it. They landed, and Ollie observed the first small break of the water was close to the British shore, just above the head of the long narrow island, extending almost from the mouth of Chippewa to the falls, and at the foot of which, there was a small mill in the direction of Goat Island. A glance from there to the middle of the river struck him with dread as he marked the second break (as it was called), where a part of the mighty river, sweeping down a steep ledge of rock, rose and rolled in fearful swells that threatened instant destruction.

But no language could describe his feelings when he stood just in front of *the awful precipice and first saw the vast volume of water rushing over far beyond the angular summit rock of its upper bed*, extending from its western bank to Goat Island and plunging down down into the deep abyss. Then he measured with his eye the giddy height of the foot of that island, presenting a face of solid rock rising perpendicular from the depths below. A beautiful unbroken sheet of water fell between it and the eastern bank, facing the west, and in front of which in clear warm sunshine was a brilliant rainbow with its ample arch spanning the width. Troubled water, rising and bounding from its fearful plunge back to the foot of the tremendous cataract, there forced again into the dread abyss, again emerging, rolled tumultuously down, a mighty torrent.

In 1739, two Seneca warriors who lived north of Lake Erie were returning home from a visit to Fort Niagara. They were paddling a birch bark canoe and heading up the river above the falls, drinking some brandy they had acquired at the fort. They planned to hunt deer later in the day on an island some distance above the falls, but the liquor caused them to fall into a slumber. The boat slipped back down the stream, and one of the men woke up to hear the roar of the falls. They were in the rapids just above the island in the middle of the river, just above the falls. The gravity of his situation sobered him immediately, and he shouted at the top of voice to wake his companion. They paddled for their lives toward the island and joyfully landed there, but after their relief subsided and they thought about what was next, it came to them that their situation was grim. A method of escape did not readily present itself, and they would starve on the tiny island.

They eventually formulated a plan. Linden trees grew in abundance there, so they decided to peel off the bark and make rope from the inner fibers. They soon made a rope ladder as long as the depth of the falls, which they fastened to a large tree growing at the edge of the cataract, from which they dropped the length of the rope down the falls. They were able to climb down the rope to the rocks at the bottom and throw themselves into the roiling water at the base of the falls. The men tried again and again to swim, but the turbulent waves tossed them back onto the rocks, flaying the skin from their bodies. Realizing the task was impossible, they climbed back up the ladder to the island.

After some time, passing Indians heard them call, and those men rushed to Fort Niagara to ask for the advice and help of the commandant there. The British leader consulted with his officers, his men, and the Indians, who were well acquainted with the current on both sides of the island. The natives remembered that the water at the upper end of the island was not very deep, nor the current there as strong, having watched Indian boys wade far out into the water there.

They adopted the following plan: the commander had the fort blacksmith attach sharp spikes to some poles, and he gave two young Indians four of the iron-shod poles each and a bag of food for the men stranded on the island. The officers went along to witness the plan and to offer aid. The nimble warriors went to the east side of the river above the island; and driving the poles into the bottom to support themselves against the strong current, the water sometimes above their knees, they waded diagonally to the flow and safely reached the island. After feeding the two wretches there, they gave them each a pair of poles, and brought them back across the current without further injury.

After spending about two hours in viewing the stupendous cataract, Ollie and his guide descended on a path around them and proceeded to Queenstown, where finding a wood boat going down to Fort Niagara, the boy immediately got onboard. Arriving there an hour after, he delivered a letter to the commanding officer. Richard England had determined that Ollie should not stay with Lt.-Governor Simcoe, writing, "You may privately mention to the Governor, that as I don't consider him by any means an amiable boy to keep in his family, the sooner he gets rid of him the better."

On the surface, this is mystifying, as Ollie always endeavored to be amiable. He had numerous of issues that could have made him irritable: missing his family; the stress of frequent threats to his life from Catawa-waqua; the threats from Elliott to make him a servant, along with the keg of whiskey left with those who were to transport him to Detroit, with the resulting stabbing; the uncertainty of his present situation; and even possibly missing Coohcoocheeh and So-tone-goo and some aspects of his life with them. In addition to these events, he *was* "full of notions of liberty and equality," which he would have been youthfully unaware was painful to the Loyalists. A damning epithet by Simcoe was "the fellow has been infected by republicanism."

The commander conducted him to the quarters of Lieutenant Hill, whose wife received him with great kindness.

CHAPTER SIXTEEN

HOME AGAIN

IN THE 1790'S, the southwestern part of the state of New York was almost an unbroken wilderness. Except for a log ferry house on the top of the high bank opposite Queenstown, near the present site of Lewistown, there was but one house on the road. The road was really a footpath between Niagara and Canandaigua, a distance of a hundred miles. The sole house was a tavern near the western bank of the Genesee, probably ten miles south of the spot where Rochester now stands. The best mode of traveling then was on horseback, but as little communication existed between the western part of New York and Niagara, opportunities suitable for Ollie's return to his friends seldom occurred. He had therefore to wait patiently until such opportunity should offer, or until Governor Simcoe should provide some mode of conveyance.

Ollie was very comfortable in the family of Mr. Hill and spent his time quite pleasantly for about a week at the fort. Lieutenant Hill was adjutant of the 50th regiment of infantry, a part of which, with a company of artillery, garrisoned Fort Niagara, and a part was stationed at York, Upper Canada, on the west side of the lake nearly opposite. Frequently, by his invitation, Ollie accompanied him when he marched the troops not on duty out of the garrison, which he did on every fair day in order to exercise them. It was astonishing to see with what precision the British regulars went through the manual exercise, marching and performing the different military evolutions, and how quickly the officer, noticing the slightest error or fault, not infrequently punished the delinquent by a stroke with his rattan over the knuckles or on the shins. The troops here, though almost perfectly disciplined, were in Ollie's opinion inferior to the 24th, who besides made a much more showy and, as he conceived, a more martial appearance. The uniform of the 24th was a white vest and pantaloons with black half gaiters, a long scarlet coat faced with deep green and laced with silver at the buttonholes, skirts and wrists. That of the 50th was drab under clothes, and long scarlet coats faced with light green, without any ornament. The former wore their long hair powdered, clubbed at the neck, and spreading like a fan between their shoulders; the latter had their hair queued.

With Lt. Hill, Ollie was much pleased. He appeared to be what is generally termed a clever man, plain yet urbane in his manners—not brilliant. His principal recommendation was his natural kindness and frankness, his sociability as a companion, and his punctual observance of his duty as an officer. Being at least fifteen years younger than his wife, whom he treated rather with deference than with affection, it was probable that fortune, rank, or some consideration other than love influenced his union with her. His wife was at least forty, tall and lean, with large and homely features, in her attire very neat and simple, polished though rather precise in her manners, quite intelligent and fluent, and possessing a very amiable disposition. During his stay with her, she treated him with the kindness of a mother, carefully repairing his shirts and clothes. When Ollie left her, she presented him with a calico needle and thread case that he might learn to mend his own clothes when occasion should require. This he carefully preserved for many years, often finding it useful.

From the habit formed when young, he ever after carried a needle and thread in his pocket book, and often thus remembered that benevolent lady gratefully.

Fort Niagara had a very commanding situation, built on the high bank at the mouth of the strait connecting lakes Erie and Ontario. The scenery around it was at once romantic, grand, and sublime. Above were the high precipitous banks, or rather mountains, covered to the water's edge with trees and huge masses of rock, between which the broad and mighty water contracted below the deafening cataract into a comparatively narrow stream, boiling and foaming and whirling along the mighty chasm, rushing for several miles with resistless impetuosity.

A few miles below on the Canadian side, seemingly hanging on the face of the mountainous bank, stood the large white mess house and quarters of the Queen's Rangers, constituting the principal buildings of Queenstown. On a small plain between the end of this hill and the lakeshore was the small but neat village of Newark, then the residence of Governor Simcoe.

On the west, north, and east, the dark deep waters of Ontario presented a vast expanse, bounded only by the horizon, inspiring the beholder with mingled wonder, delight, and awe. Here, especially in the "still night," you might hear the deep, heavy roar of the mighty cataract as the coming of the desolating tornado. Indeed, it may be heard distinctly "as the sound of many waters" on Lake Erie more than twenty miles distant.

Ollie had been at Fort Niagara about a week when one afternoon Mr. Hill informed him that there was an opportunity for him to return to his friends, and Governor Simcoe had directed him to send him over to Newark immediately. Tying up his small wardrobe in his handkerchief, in a few minutes, he was ready to comply with this brief notice. Taking a hasty leave of Mr. and Mrs. Hill, they soon conveyed him across the Niagara and conducted him to Navy Hall, a "miserably little wooden house," roughly built, at the mouth of the Niagara River, the home of Governor Simcoe.

Simcoe had been a young British officer in the Grenadiers, fighting in the battles of Brandywine, Germantown, and Monmouth. At Brandywine, he captained the British Grenadiers in the charge on Osborne Hill and was directly engaged in fighting Colonel Spencer's regiment. The British got the upper hand.

Simcoe soon commanded the Queen's Rangers, roaming the countryside and performing impromptu raids. Once when pretending to be rebel rangers, they burned some flatboats, a Dutch meetinghouse, and a forage depot, before moving on and seeing at the Somerset Court House a prisoner chained to the floor and starving. Angered by this, Simcoe released the prisoner and allowed his men to burn the courthouse.

The fires gave away their position and the Jersey militia set an ambuscade. As Simcoe passed through a break in a fence, too late, he saw some men hiding behind some bushes and logs right next to the fence opening. The last words he heard were "now, now" before five shots felled his horse, and he was stunned senseless by the violence of his fall.

The Jerseyans took Simcoe to Borden Town and gave him a parole to walk about the town. Of course, the townspeople were unfriendly, and Simcoe said to his sergeant that if they attacked him, he would attempt to escape. Someone who overheard him misquoted the conversation as, if he were insulted, he would attempt to escape.

Following this, Simcoe wrote that he was surrounded by a "quicksand of deceit and calumny" when he was taken to Burlington and locked in the jail. This was uncommon treatment of officers, men of honor normally remaining under voluntary captivity in rented rooms in people's homes.

After writing his complaints to his commanding general, his treatment became worse. Simcoe wrote, "a few evenings ago I was taken from my bed, and moved into rooms which had been occupied by felons for months, and placed among their filth, and closely locked up; this was by order of Mr. Read, Secretary to the Council, and at a time when the Governor held out to me a prospect of exchange, which, till that moment, I did not suspect to be delusory." After this, Simcoe became determined to escape.

Simcoe's sergeant and a servant had gone voluntarily with him into his captivity. Allowed to move about freely, they learned that there were a number of British prisoners of war put to work in the neighborhood and also that the carbines and ammunition of Colonel Lee's dragoons were locked in a room at the jail. Simcoe had the idea to get eight or ten of the British to assemble, steal the guns, and all would escape together by taking some of Colonel Lee's horses by stealth.

Simcoe's sergeant got an impression of the key to the armory in the jail, and with the aid of another prisoner, an armorer from one of His Majesty's ships, made a key of pewter. Then one day the jailer entrusted the sergeant to let Simcoe out of his room while he was away, and the two men opened the armory with the false key. They saw that the guns were in good condition, but when they tried to lock the door again, the soft pewter key broke in the lock. Simcoe said this was the most anxious moment of his life, for they expected a party from Colonel Lee at any moment, and if it discovered them, the sergeant and the armorer faced execution.

They got the armorer, who ingeniously cut the key, dropping it into the lock. Lee's men arrived soon after and opened the room without difficulty. The sergeant made another key, and they were ready to put the plan into action.

In the meantime, a much-chagrined Simcoe had written to General Washington: "Gov. Livingston told me I was a prisoner of the State, a distinction I never till then was acquainted with." Simcoe reasoned that he was actually under the authority of Washington himself, and soon after obtained his release on Dec 26, 1779.

Simcoe returned to England after the war, where he was instrumental in designing a new government for Canada. Britain installed him as Lt. Governor of Upper Canada in June of 1792. Though he had a vision for Canada and was enthusiastic for the position, still he considered the undertaking a "species of banishment," a kind of punishment for his role in Britain's loss of her American colonies.

The governor received Ollie with great courtesy and introduced him to Thomas Morris, Esq., of Canandaigua, who had arrived at Newark only the day before. The governor remarked that he had acquainted that gentleman with the request that had been made to him by the British minister, at the instance of Ollie's friends, to ascertain where he was and to release him from captivity, and of the fortunate result of his efforts. He concluded by saying that Mr. Morris, at his request, had kindly consented to take him as far as Canandaigua.

Mr. Morris made some inquiries about Ollie's family and relatives, said he was well acquainted with his uncle, Colonel Ogden of Elizabethtown, New Jersey, and that he would with pleasure convey him to Canandaigua. He had no doubt Ollie would have an opportunity of returning to his friends from there.

In answering the inquiries made of him by Governor Simcoe, Ollie spoke of the conduct of Colonel Elliott, particularly of his leaving him in charge of the Indians at the mouth of the Maumee, of the injury he had suffered, and of the danger he had in consequence incurred. On hearing this, Simcoe appeared to be quite indignant. He spoke of his instructions to Elliott to convey him to Detroit; and remarked to Mr. Morris that such conduct in a British officer would have subjected him to trial before a court martial, but he was obliged to overlook many improprieties in the agents who had such influence with the Indians and were so necessary to His Majesty in his associations with them.

Elliott surely acted alone in his mistreatment, for Simcoe's sense of propriety and honor would have overridden any personal preference. He also had had his own experience as a prisoner, with little control over his own fate, increasing the chance for true empathy with Ollie. Even so, he later allowed Elliott the plum position of Superintendent of Indian Affairs at Amherstburg, and thus the British held him in esteem until 1797, when they removed him from office for questionable practices.

Mr. Morris now remarked that he proposed to set off from the ferry house early the next morning and that he would wait for Ollie until evening at Queenstown. He arose and took his leave.

Of Governor Simcoe's person, his figure was commanding; his features were manly; his countenance was open; his manners, though dignified, were affable; and in his conversation, he had all the frankness of the soldier. Ollie had the honor of taking tea that afternoon with his lady, Elizabeth Posthuma Gwillim Simcoe, a very handsome and intelligent woman. Her father, Thomas Gwillim, was a major in Wolfe's army at the Battle of the Plains of Abraham and a Colonel at Gibraltar. He had died in 1766, and her mother had died at her birth. Mrs. Simcoe had helped her husband recuperate after his captivity and six years of war service.

Unfortunately, she was afflicted with so great an impediment in her speech that to Ollie, it was painful to converse with her.

After tea, Ollie took leave of Governor and Mrs. Simcoe, and a servant appeared at the gate with two fine bay horses. He mounted one, and when the servant received his orders, "Spin him along," they set off at a rapid canter. Traveling at half speed uphill and down, in less than an hour, they arrived at Queenstown.

Thomas Morris was the son of Robert Morris, of Philadelphia, the great financier of the Revolution. Thomas had returned from Europe in 1788, where he had spent five years being educated at Geneva, and then two years at university in Leipzig. His father's goal was to educate his sons "to participate in the honor of serving a free people in the administration of their government." Recently, his father had sent him to administer the selling of the entire Genesee country in western New York, over a million acres purchased from the state of Massachusetts, and the young man would successfully negotiate a treaty with the Six Nations. Thomas Morris had attended a 1790 council at Tioga Point, and at that time, the Seneca adopted him into their tribe. Red Jacket gave him his own former name, Otetiani, meaning Always Ready.

Crossing the Niagara about dusk and ascending the high bank, Mr. Morris and Ollie entered the ferry house where they found Mr. Nathaniel Gorham, one of the proprietors of Canandaigua, and a "colored" servant who had traveled with him to the frontier. Here they spent the night.

On the next morning after a very early breakfast, Mr. Morris again provided a separate horse for Ollie, and they set out on horseback for Canandaigua. Traveling rapidly and stopping only an hour at noon to rest and feed their horses and to take a luncheon of biscuit and cheese, they rested at night at an Indian village. On the next day, they dined at about twelve o'clock at a tavern near the west bank of the Genesee and arrived at Canandaigua a little after dark. They thus performed a journey of nearly a hundred miles through the wilderness along a footpath in two days. Here Ollie was placed in the family of Mr. Sandford, a tavern keeper with whom Mr. Morris boarded, Mr. Morris being then single and not quite having finished his large and elegant house at the west end of the town.

Canandaigua was in 1793 a neat village, containing about forty houses scattered along the principal street, leading westward for more than a mile from the long narrow lake of the same name. The native town of the same name that the Americans burned on September 10, 1779, in the expedition against the Iroquois, had been a large town with thirty neat houses, many with the fireplace in the center, in Indian style. There also had been two posts with war mallets, for the torturing of prisoners.

Mr. Sandford's house, a large two-story wooden building painted white, and making a very respectable appearance, stood at the head of the main street, facing the lake. Near this house on the north was the village schoolhouse where Mr. Upham taught about forty girls and boys. Below it was the residence of Mr. Chapin, agent for the Seneca, the eldest of whose sons traded with the Indians, exchanging his goods for furs and skins, while a younger one acted as an interpreter.

While waiting for an opportunity to go to New York, Ollie spent his time very pleasantly at Canandaigua, where he employed a part of his time at school with Mr. Upham and occasionally amused himself in fishing at the outlet of the lake. Mr. and Mrs. Sandford treated him with

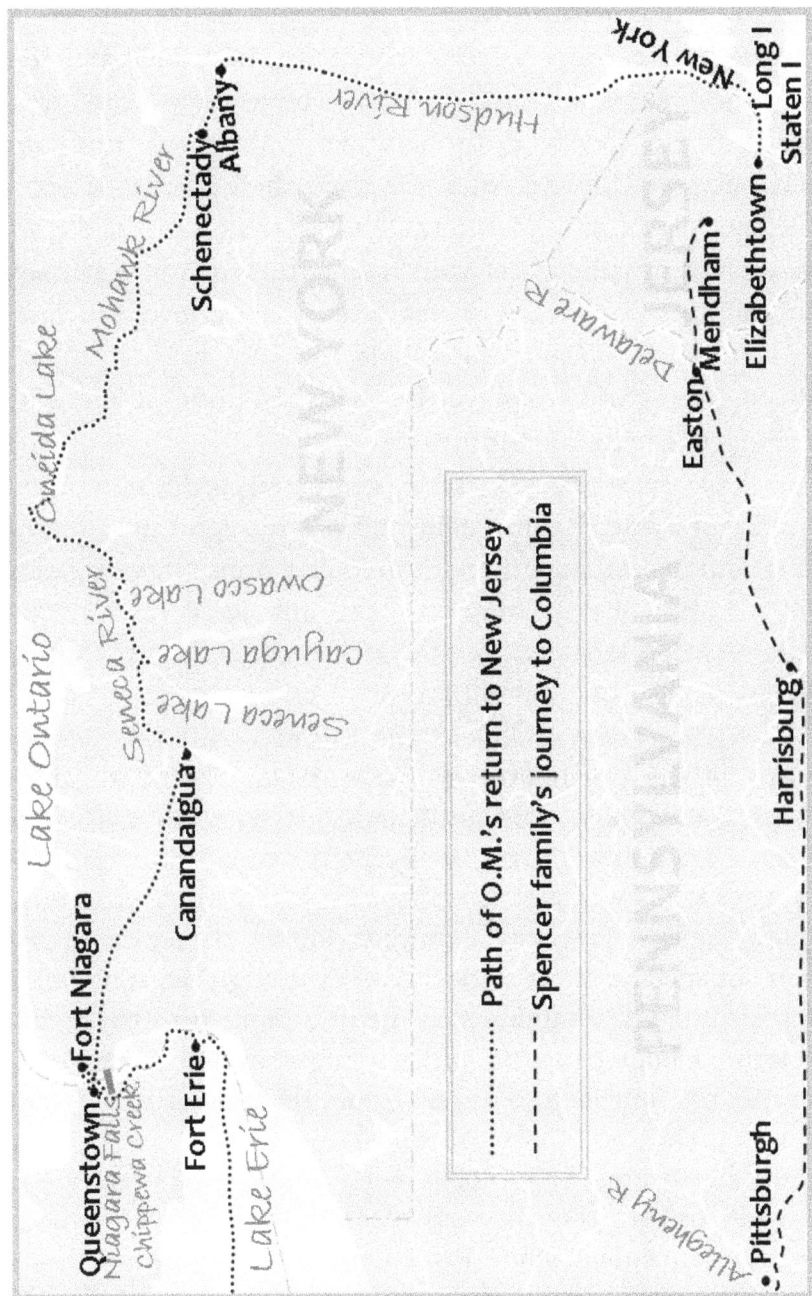

parental kindness, but never from a stranger did Ollie
receive such benevolent and generous treatment as he
received from Mr. Morris. The man had incurred the
expense of purchasing a horse to convey him from
Niagara. He defrayed the charge of his boarding and
schooling at Canandaigua. He furnished him with some
summer clothing, and when Ollie was ready to set out for
New York, supplied him with money to bear his expenses.
For all this, he would never afterward receive the least
remuneration. When Ollie took leave of him, it deeply
affected him, and whenever he thought of him, it was with
feelings of the liveliest gratitude.

At Canandaigua, Ollie remained until about the
middle of June. Having collected a large quantity of furs,
bear and deerskins sufficient to load a pretty large bateau,
Mr. Chapin, being ready to set out for New York to
replenish his stock of goods, at the request of Mr. Morris
consented to take him with him.

Their bateau lay in the outlet about three miles
north of the north end of Canandaigua Lake, to which
point there was water sufficient for bateau navigation.
From this point, having loaded the bateau with peltries
conveyed in wagons from the village, they proceeded
slowly down the narrow winding outlet. Sometimes they
were obliged to stop and cut away trees that had fallen
across it, and sometimes to get out and drag their flat-
bottomed boat over the riffles. They traveled in this way
for nearly four days, passing the several outlets of the
Seneca, Cayuga, Owasco, and other lakes, the stream
gradually becoming larger and its obstructions fewer. On
the fourth day they arrived at the mouth of the Oneida
outlet, here called Three River Points, distant from Canandaigua by land about sixty miles, but at least one hundred
by water. Ascending the outlet, they crossed the Oneida

Lake, about thirty miles in length, to the mouth of Wood Creek. They with much difficulty forced their bateau up this small, crooked stream to within a mile of the Mohawk. Portaging across the ground where Rome now stands, but where then on the Mohawk stood a solitary house, they proceeded down that river to Schenectady. From this place, Mr. Chapin conveyed his peltries in wagons, and they drove to Albany, where they stayed a day or two. Finally, they embarked on board a Dutch sloop for New York, where they arrived on the second day of July.

Here Ollie took leave of Mr. Chapin, and on the next day took a passage across the bay in an open ferryboat (the only ferryboats in use at that time). They narrowly avoided an upset by a sudden gust of wind.

OLLIE ARRIVED SAFELY at Elizabethtown, New Jersey on July 3, very nearly one year since his capture, and sought out one of his sisters. She and his relations were delighted to see him; but the happiness he experienced in returning to the home of his childhood, after an absence of nearly three years, in which he had endured so many privations and hardships and encountered so many dangers, must have been far superior to theirs. When he retired to rest on the evening of that day, gratefully reflecting on the past goodness and mercy of God to him, he on his knees devoutly thanked him for the exercise of his gracious providence toward him, preserving, sustaining, and protecting him, and restoring him in safety to his friends.

The next day, being the Fourth of July, there was a very splendid celebration at Elizabethtown, which Ollie enjoyed very much. He also had the pleasure of seeing his distant relative, the late Governor Bloomfield, who was highly gratified with the narrative of his captivity and his account of Indian manners and customs. The governor found interesting the custom of Indians and had written much about the Iroquois in his journal while an officer with one of the New Jersey regiments in the Revolution. He took great pleasure in hearing his Indian songs and seeing him dance after the Indian mode. He subsequently placed an announcement of his return in Kollock's *New Jersey Journal*:

New Jersey Journal, Elizabeth-Town, July 17, 1793
On the 10th [*sic*] instant, arrived here in good health, by the way of Detroit, Niagara and Genesee river, Oliver Spencer, Jun. a youth of twelve [*sic*] years of age, only son of Col. Oliver Spencer, of Columbia, in the western territory, from whence he was taken last July, by two Shawanese Indians, and carried into their nation, where he was detained a prisoner, until redeemed a few months past, at the price of sixty pounds, through the kind interposition of Col. Richard England, on the application of the lad's numerous connections and friends.

This notice brought people from far and near to see him, some no doubt merely from the regard they bore to an old and esteemed friend or acquaintance, whose son he was, but the greater part came from mere curiosity as they would flock to an exhibition of wild beasts, expecting to see something at least half savage. At first, Ollie took pleasure in giving an account of his captivity, in answering the numerous inquiries that were made of him, in singing and dancing in the style of the Indian, and uttering the various Indian yells. They supposed that he performed so naturally and exhibited, as they fancied, such a wildness in his looks and manners that some frequently remarked in an under tone, "How much he looks like an Indian!"

Indeed, he had so endeavored to accept his fate while among the Indians that he was well on his way to "becoming Indian," though Catawa-waqua's frequent attacks prevented him from liking Indian life as well as he might have. Most children who were with the Indians for two or three years refused to ever return to white life when given the opportunity. This phenomenon was probably due to the Indians' humanity among themselves, coupled with the pleasure of living a wilderness life. Considering the fate of the Indians, it was fortunate for Ollie that his rescue came when it did.

Being obliged to repeat the same story and answer the same questions frequently twenty times a day to different companies and individuals, he became so heartily tired of it that at last he gave only brief answers, often uttering a simple yes or no to the inquiries that were made of him. Indeed, from the circumstance of his then repeating so often the story of his captivity and for weeks answering so many inquiries, he became averse to saying anything about it. He acquired a habit of replying so tersely to questions asked of him that later in life, he felt mortified when by his brief answers to questions on this subject, he seemed to have checked further inquiry and to give room to suspect him of a want of politeness, or even of civility.

His parents desired for him to remain safely in New Jersey. He soon settled into life at Elizabethtown with his sister and brother-in-law, Mr. Halstead, occupying a regular portion of his time with school.

CHAPTER SEVENTEEN

DEFEAT OF THE SHAWNEE

A RUDE LOG HOUSE was the first humble sanctuary of the first settlers of Columbia, standing amidst the tall forest trees on a beautiful knoll. On the holy Sabbath they assembled to hear the word of life; but they met with their muskets and rifles, prepared for action, and ready to repel any attack of the enemy. While the watchman on the walls of Zion was uttering his faithful and pathetic warning, the sentinels without, at a few dozen yards distance with measured step, were now pacing their walks and now standing with strained eyes endeavoring to pierce through the distance, carefully scanning every object that seemed to have life or motion.

At the end of each service, Colonel Spencer reminded them to carefully guard the settlement. Once, two members brought a freshly taken Indian scalp into the church during the service.

At the Maumee Rapids, in July of 1793, the Indians met in another great pan-Indian conference close to Alexander McKee's storehouse, home, and trading post. Simon Girty again was interpreter. The British wanted peace and an Indian boundary state. The Shawnee and their allies wanted the Ohio River as boundary, abandoning Brant's Muskingum line, and Simcoe supported them in order to maintain unity. Simcoe told his agent "to exert your ascendancy over the Indians." This McKee did and reassured them the British backed them on their stand of the Ohio River as their boundary line.

For their part, the Americans wanted a large portion of Ohio and their negotiations were mostly for show. The army under General Anthony Wayne was making lengthy and thorough preparations, slowly advancing, building small forts as supply depots along the way. The commissioners whom the Americans sent to negotiate on July 7, 1793 allowed that the king had ceded only *his* right to the Indians lands in the Treaty of Paris in 1783. This was an empty admission, as the commissioners still demanded a good bit of Ohio.

The Indians wanted their land back, and because of their wins, they felt they must fight because it was God's will. The Indians debated and then made an ultimatum. They said, "It appears strange that you should expect any [concessions] from them, who have only been defending their just right against your invasion. We want peace. Restore to them our country and we shall be enemies no longer."

The now inevitable events played out. By May, at the Rapids of the Maumee, McKee issued provisions from the British. Northern Indians mobilized by Blue Jacket, following a battle plan to cut the Americans off from their rations, successfully attacked a supply convoy intended for Fort Hamilton. They chose to attack convoys because there would be no surprising Anthony Wayne as had happened to St. Clair's army. Each day Wayne sent the quartermaster, a surveyor, and front guard to set up new camps, each with sites marked out in hundreds of yards square, trees cut and laid in breastwork two to four layers high, a bastion at each corner, a gateway, all tents inside, and fortified outposts set up at a distance for the guards.

In June, the Americans deflected a native attack on Fort Recovery, and the northern allies abandoned the cause.

As the American army continued its cautious advance, Colonel Spencer made a special request of Winthrop Sargent, Lt.-Governor of the Northwest Territory, asking for a day to be set aside to "implore divine aid" for the Army against the Indians. In response, Sargent declared a day of "Fasting, Humiliation, and Prayer" for August 14 to "supplicate the Sovereign God of Heaven and Earth" to "bless the Armies of the United States" in order to "end the savage war within our country."

The Americans were ready for the conflict. In addition to the chain of well-supplied forts that Wayne had created, the general had the resources to answer Colonel Spencer's request for cannon. Wayne ordered the commander at Fort Washington to send a three pounder and a cask of powder to Columbia.

The Indians prepared for battle, as well. Blue Jacket kept much of his force together but had trouble keeping them in battle readiness, as the Indians fasted before battle with the hope of surviving a wound to the gut.

They finally met in battle on August 20, 1794. Wayne's army had advanced along the Maumee and made a temporary post for keeping their stores and baggage. Their spies reconnoitered the position of the enemy, who were encamped behind a thick brushy wood and the British fort (near present Toledo).

At 8 o'clock in the morning the army again advanced in columns, according to the standing order of march, the legion on the right, its right flank covered by the Miami Indians, one brigade of mounted volunteers on the left, and another in the rear. A select battalion of mounted volunteers moved in front of the legion sufficiently advanced so as to give timely notice for the troops to form in case of action. There was still the possibility in the minds of the Americans that the Indians would cede to their demands.

After advancing about five miles, one corps received so severe a fire from the enemy, secreted in the woods and high grass, that they were compelled to retreat. The legion immediately formed in two lines, principally in a close thick wood which extended for miles on the left and for a very considerable distance in front, the ground covered with old fallen timber, probably caused by a tornado. This made it impracticable for the cavalry to act with effect and afforded the enemy the most favorable covert for their mode of warfare. The savages formed in three lines within supporting distance of each other and extending for near two miles at right angles with the river. They were in full force in front, in possession of their favorite ground, and endeavoring to turn the American's left flank.

With orders to gain and turn the right flank of the Indians, the second American line advanced to support the first with the whole of the mounted volunteers, by a circuitous route. At the same time the front line advanced and performed a bayonet charge, rousing the Indians from their coverts. When the natives were up, the line delivered a close and well directed fire on their backs, followed by a brisk charge, so as not to give them time to load again.

The legionary cavalry turned the left flank of the enemy next to the river with such an impetuous charge by the first line of infantry that the Indians, Canadian militia, and volunteers were driven back in a short time. Although every possible exertion was used by the officers of the second line of the Legion and mounted volunteers to gain their proper positions, only part of each could participate in the action, the enemy being driven in the course of one hour more than two miles through the thick woods by less than one half their numbers.

Wayne concluded, "This horde of savages, with their allies, abandoned themselves to flight, and dispersed with terror and dismay, leaving our victorious army in full and quiet possession of the field of battle, which terminated under the influence of the guns of the British garrison,..."

After the battle, Wayne's army destroyed all of the crops and villages along the Maumee and Auglaize Rivers.

IN THE MONTHS following this battle, many of the chiefs were still not ready to meet with the Americans, and the Indians still created mischief.

Ollie's townsman William Moore had purchased his way out of captivity, and back in the Miami valley region, was again on a hunting excursion. He was about a mile and a half east of one of the stations on the Little Miami River where he killed a deer, skinned it, prepped the hide for packing, and washed his hands in a brook, all the while singing an Indian song he had learned when with the Shawnee. Suddenly, someone joined in singing in Shawnee. Moore sprang up and raced for some thick woods to the west, chased closely by several Indians. They probably knew him and wanted to capture him again, since they did not fire their guns.

The lead Indian was very short, but very fast, faster than Moore. As he gained on him, they came to a large fallen tree, which Moore vaulted over in one bound. The Indian could not do this and had to go around the tree, allowing Moore the lead he needed to escape to the safety of the nearby fortified station.

WITH THE BRITISH no longer supporting them, the Shawnee finally made peace in the Treaty of Greenville of 1795, ending the Shawnee dream to reclaim Ohio. The land sessions of the treaty represented the reality of where the Indians were living then anyway, to where the Americans had already forced them to withdraw. The peace chiefs rallied and founded Wapakoneta just north of the treaty line, the Shawnee capital for the next forty years. In August and September of 1796, the Americans distributed the first of perpetual peace annuities at Fort Defiance, built at The Point, across the river from Ollie's former home with Coohcoocheeh.

When the war ended, Ollie's parents sent for him. On September 14, 1795, being then fourteen years old, he set out on horseback on his return home in company with a Mr. Crane and General Schenck, then on his first visit to the west. They performed the journey to Pittsburgh in ten days. From there, they and their horses descended the Ohio on a flatboat, arriving at Columbia about the middle of October.

The joy of his parents on seeing Ollie is more easily imagined than described. With tears and embraces, they welcomed his return. They spent the day in affectionate inquiries about the past. Around their family altar that evening, devoutly and gratefully, his pious father led them in thanksgiving and praise to the Father of mercies for all his past-unmerited goodness, particularly for Ollie's preservation and safe restoration to his home.

COLONEL SPENCER'S SERVICE in the Revolution helped end his son's captivity. Usually, prisoners returned from Indian captivity by treaty, by purchasing their own freedom, or by family members traveling into Indian country and striking a deal or spiriting the prisoner away, but Ollie was rescued by direct diplomatic means, perhaps the only person to be so treated. This was due to Colonel Spencer's connections created by his dedicated and successful service in the Revolution.

CHAPTER EIGHTEEN

STRUGGLING TO THRIVE

A S AN ADULT OLLIE distinguished himself from the other
"Olivers" in the family by styling himself as O.M. His
broad life experience made him, as written by an
associate, "characterized by a peculiar urbanity and
suavity of manner, which, while it forbade not the
approach of the humblest individual, never failed to
command the respect and esteem of every one." Aided by
education and the social position and relative wealth of his
family, in 1798 at the age of seventeen, he entered public
service, and the people of Hamilton County elected him as
Deputy Recorder. He soon found business opportunities in
the south, and announced in the newspaper *Liberty Hall*
in March of 1800 that he was leaving for Natchez.

While trading in the south, he accepted a request
from the governor of the Mississippi territory to join his
militia staff in the capacity of Quartermaster, or supply
officer.

Doctor Oliver H. Spencer, his nephew whom he had
grown up with as a brother, was now living in New
Orleans. After an apprenticeship with Dr. Richard Allison,
the Army surgeon, O.H. studied medicine at the University
of Pennsylvania and graduated in 1803. As soon as he
finished his examinations, O.H. booked passage for New
Orleans, where he began practicing medicine and kept a
pharmaceutical shop. He soon became an army surgeon.

On December 20, 1803, Doctor Spencer wrote to an
uncle, "The troops take possession of the Province of
L[ouisiana] at 11 O Clock while I am writing to you, our
friends are on their way to meet them coming in. Every

class of people from different motives have been expecting the change with anxiety for some time . . . Oliver has not altered much since I saw him last, I feel peculiarly happy that his conduct has secured the esteem of many good men and gained him that of Govr Claiborne."

These were gratifying words from a "brother." As an officer in the militia, O.M. had a role in the military ceremony transferring New Orleans from France to the United States. Napoleon's representative received the American dignitaries at City Hall. The prefect read the official papers ceding Louisiana, exchanging ratifications, and delineating the powers of the new possessors, while the Americans stood on either side of him. When they finished the legal proceedings, the Army and militia began the flag exchange. O.M. commanded this detachment.

They lowered the French flag and raised the American flag simultaneously. At midway, they paused the flags a moment, and began the celebration with cannons firing, trumpets playing, the Stars and Stripes now rising, amid joyous shouting.

One of O.M.'s letters recounts the event: "[I] mounted the first Guard (with regular & my own corps) in the principal Fort of this place planted the first American flag, & fired at least three hours without intermission from forty 24s. I commanded a Garrison four days (until I got sick) of forty men & five subalterns, so you see I've done something."

After his discharge from the militia, he also participated in the social life of the area. Remember that Doctor Spencer is *his* nephew, though by one year the elder. O.M. wrote to an uncle, "I have not yet seen the Ladies, but shall next Sunday at the Ball. They are all enquiring for Doct Spencer's nephew. You see he has told a fine story, & I'll profit by it handsomely.

"I intend making my bows to them in perfect French style _a la militaire_, assuming the most egregious consequential airs (the only thing that carries in this place) and cutting the most astonishing first chop scrapes.

". . . I have the greatest attention paid me by Doct. Spencer & the family. Every evening I am charmed with the Piano of Miss Celest. She is indeed a fine girl, & I have some mind to court her—20,000$ is nae deaf nits."

He was enjoying a little joke. "Nae deaf nits" literally means "not empty nuts," a quote from a 1718 poem by Scotsman Allan Ramsay, "Lucky Spence's Last advice." Its subject is the dying advice of a brothel keeper to her prostitutes on how to take their clients for all they are worth.

He did think of himself as a lucky "Spence," but he likely did not really have it in him to attempt to take Miss Celest for all she was worth.

Being plagued by bouts of malaria in the south, for his health's sake he returned to Ohio, resumed his life as a merchant, and married Miss Electra Oliver on January 13, 1805. She was the daughter of Colonel Alexander Oliver of Marietta, a Revolutionary War officer from Massachusetts who arrived in the region before the Spencer family in the spring of 1790, their family at that time suffering with hunger. So great in that summer was the scarcity of breadstuffs that her mother was obliged to send her children from the house while she prepared bread for her boarders, who by some fortunate circumstance had obtained a bushel of corn meal.

After his marriage, O.M. began as a clerk at the Miami Exporting Company, a trading company that outfitted boats with goods to trade in New Orleans, incorporated on April 15, 1803 at the very first session of the Ohio General Assembly, beginning business in Cincinnati in 1804. It had a banking feature in its charter, and it became the first bank in Ohio after failing as a trading company. It issued notes payable to the bearer and assignable by delivery only, and it issued bills that were redeemable in the notes of other banks, but not in specie, which is money in coin. On March 1, 1807, it opened its first office in Cincinnati, relinquishing all other commercial projects. The subscriber made the first payment or two in cash, and then paid off the rest with dividend reinvestment.

He became cashier within eighteen months of his first employment with the company. The following spring he re-entered public service as County Recorder.

Colonel Spencer began to lose his health. Joseph Bloomfield wrote to Jonathan Dayton in 1799, referring to nine years previously, "In April 1790, Col. Spencer engaged to pay attention to my land in the North Western territory, & received the Original land Warrant and [some money] . . . I have not had a line of information respecting the land from Col. Spencer, . . . and I wish not to trouble him."

In addition, Governor St. Clair wrote of Colonel Spencer in March of 1800, "In the county of Hamilton, Oliver Spencer commands. He is an old officer, but has been altogether inattentive to the militia, and is either too old or too indolent to give much attention to it in future." Of course, Colonel Spencer was not indolent; he was becoming infirm. He hung on for at least a decade, dying after a short illness in 1811, and John Cleves Symmes began his obituary, "Few mortals in this age of depravity, have maintained a more undeviating line of integrity, benevolence, and religion, than the late Col. Spencer of Columbia." He filled it with many interesting biographical details, including Colonel Spencer's favorite battle, that first small battle at Springfield. He ended it with, "Thus prepared for, and resigned to the will of heaven, he patiently waited under all dispensations of providence 'until his change come' 'gathered like a shock of corn fully ripe' on the 22nd day of January, 1811, his lamp of life expired in the seventy-fifth year of his age." Touchingly, it was also the date of his fifty-third wedding anniversary.

In the same year as Colonel Spencer's death, O.M. remembered his "solemn vow that if he was saved and restored to [his] dear family he would dedicate [his] life to God." He was ordained as a Methodist minister in 1815, a position achieved after a four-year trial. He had no formal training. His brother O.H. wrote to their uncle in October 1813, "Entre nous, I am sorry Oliver is so much disposed to preach; like a slow and undermining disease I am afraid it will continue to increase until his business and health the future welfare of his family will be injured by [illeg.] her influence. I [told] him that I am Christian, but I wish to see the divine tenets of my faith in the hands of men regularly taught, and whose business it is to inculcate the doctrines of our [faith]. "

Despite O.H.s discouragement, preaching was important to O.M. and he continued it on a part time basis.

In the meantime, in 1810, people had poured into Ohio and with them came rising prices, stimulating speculation. Men loaded themselves with land, expecting to sell at a profit. Ohio chartered twenty new banks that issued cheap notes with little security, based on confidence. This inevitably led to trouble, as easy money soon sparked speculation, land fever, and inflation, which was quite a challenge for O.M. since he was now bank president. He coped by going into the mercantile business in addition to his banking position, postponing a hoped for early retirement, and buying huge tracts of land himself.

WHILE O.M. WAS ESTABLISHING himself and raising a family, Wapawaqua and his family remained with Blue Jacket awhile. They eventually followed the chief, Quitawepea, or Captain Lewis, as the Americans called him.

Blue Jacket and the Shawnee Tecumseh worked together with similar ideals, working to create a confederacy of tribes, which was Brant's idea begun at the Sandusky council of 1783. Tecumseh had inherited what was by then a longstanding tradition. They insisted that only through the confederacy could the Indians sell their lands, and not in a piecemeal fashion through individual tribal treaties. They also continued to work through the British to recover their lands. They held the view that with the Treaty of Greenville, the United States had acknowledged that the tribes owned their lands jointly. They also advocated greater Indian identity and self-sufficiency. In varying degrees, they still wanted to return to the life the Indians had before the arrival of the settlers, making what they used instead of buying it, wearing skins and in particular, abandoning liquor.

Opposing this in 1802, a number of Shawnee chiefs, Black Hoof, Big Snake, Lewis, and Paumthe visited President Jefferson. Captain Lewis, born on the Pickaway Plains and participating as a boy in the Battle of Point Pleasant in 1773 on the Kanawha River, now headed a town on Stony Creek in Logan County. He was a handsome well-formed man who took great care in his appearance, having a graceful demeanor and dressing with elegance. Even his horse and equipage evoked wealth and elegance. He was a superior hunter, but not known as a warrior or orator.

Lewis's power and position came by accident. When on his 1802 presidential visit, he first visited Secretary of War Henry Dearborn in Washington, D.C. with the Shawnee delegation, looking for cattle and tools to build frame houses. They were ready to make agricultural improvements and to keep animal stock. They also requested a new trading post for Fort Hamilton. General Dearborn believed that Captain Lewis's appearance and manners meant he was the most important person in the party. He was mistaken. Black Hoof was now head civil chief of the Shawnee, but Dearborn gave Captain Lewis a medal, and the Indian proudly showed the medal to his fellows on his return. The awarding of the medal was taken as the wish of the Americans that Captain Lewis *be* a chief among them, and he was now an honored authority.

Then in the winter and spring of 1804-5, there was an epidemic of either smallpox or influenza. The Indians believed such things happened because of the sin of witchcraft, using supernatural power for harm, which angered the Great Spirit, who showed his displeasure by visiting them with illness. Many Shawnee felt they must find the cause of the displeasure and reform.

By 1806, Tecumseh's brother Lalawethika declared himself a Prophet to whom the Great Spirit was speaking directly, revealing the means for saving themselves. The Prophet said the Great Spirit was not the same god that made white people and the Indians' recent misfortune came from abandoning the mode of life that their god had given them. The Prophet was against racially mixed marriages, fraternization with whites, and the use of white manufactures and provisions.

This was a couple of hundred years late in realization, pure nostalgia. They had loved and heavily traded and used the white man's goods for centuries. They had inter-married for their own benefit to create powerful family ties with traders. They had married the captives they had taken in order to replenish their reduced numbers. Their numbers were falling because of continual warfare and slow family growth, due to the hunting and trading lifestyle that they were now struggling so dearly to maintain, and to their love of and susceptibility to alcohol.

Captain Lewis offered the Prophet and Tecumseh hospitality while they prepared a new town at Greenville, situated well within the land that the Shawnee had ceded to the Americans at the Treaty of Greenville. Lewis's village, established in 1806, was just above the mouth of Stony Creek, standing on a ridge above the west bank near present DeGraff, also a few miles inside the cession.

Most of the Ohio Shawnees, living in the neighborhood of Wapakoneta, stuck with Black Hoof and their other chiefs. Black Hoof and the Prophet were at odds, the Wapakonetans wanting aid to farm as whites did. Many Indians resisted farming because working in the fields would metaphorically turn the warriors into women.

The Prophet was apparently a powerful preacher, for Indians from many tribes came to hear him speak or to even catch a glimpse of him. Members of the Shaker religion who visited said that his town at Greenville was "powerfully charged with religious fervor."

Such a gathering of Indians made the whites nervous, and there was talk among them to mount a militia expedition to scare off the Indians. There was also continual threat of another war between the U.S. and Britain.

Soon after, Blue Jacket went to Stony Creek with the news from Governor William Hull of the Michigan Territory that hostile Indians of the west, the Sac and Potawatomi, were forming a confederacy against the United States. Weary of war, and seeing the natives' situation played out again and again with new tribes, Wapawaqua moved his family to Stony Creek. He had remained unchangeable in his opposition to the "pale faces," bravely resisting their continued aggressions so long as there appeared to be the slightest hope of preventing their further encroachment. He then yielded to the power of circumstances, submitting calmly to his fate.

Most of the Shawnee were not to be drawn into the confederacy against the United States, but Blue Jacket was concerned that Tecumseh's band would be branded with similar ill intentions. This could threaten the new town of sixty houses they were building at Greenville.

Tecumseh, Lewis, and Blue Jacket visited the Ohio governor at Chillicothe, insisting they were not preparing for war, but only reforming the Indians. After speaking privately with the governor, they went with him to the state courthouse in Chillicothe, sat with him in the jury box, and spoke about their peaceful intentions in front of a packed audience. This calmed the whites and they abandoned the expedition against the Indians, but the native presence at Greenville still alarmed the whites, since the settlement was inside of the treaty line. In 1807, William Wells, now the American Indian Agent at Fort Wayne, ordered them to move.

There were other rumblings, too. On April 25, 1807, Wells wrote to Secretary of War Henry Dearborn and declared, "It appears very clear to me that the object of this Shawnese Prophets is to dislodge the chiefs of his nation and become the first chief himself."

The Prophet and Tecumseh removed to the Wabash near the mouth of the Tippecanoe in 1808. This land belonged to the Miami, who were opposed to the Prophet but couldn't get him to move because of his large number of supporters.

Blue Jacket's influence ended with his life in 1808, when he died in his village on the Detroit River.

The year after, Tecumseh traveled to the Wyandot and Seneca living on a reserve on the Sandusky River. White settlement around them hemmed them in, and Tecumseh tried to lure them to a life on the Wabash, for more warriors for the Prophet.

While Tecumseh was away, the Delaware, Miami and Potawatomi signed the Treaty of Fort Wayne, ceding lands on the Wabash. When Tecumseh returned, he threatened to kill the chiefs who had signed and stated that he would not allow whites to survey or settle the lands. He afterward worked for a number of years to create a military confederacy, traveling widely recruiting tribes west of the Mississippi and throughout the Great Lakes region. All the while, the British had been supplying encouragement with clothing, arms and ammunition in order to have allies if America attacked Canada, but when it became clear that Tecumseh was planning to lead with an attack on America, the British ordered their Indian agents to use their influence to restrain the natives.

To a large number of the citizens of Miami County, assembled at Piqua Town, on August 24, 1811 Captain Lewis made a speech to declare good wishes, and "to ratify all the treaties that have been made between us." This was a definite break between Captain Lewis and his followers at Stony Creek on one side, and Tecumseh and the Prophet on the other.

While Tecumseh was away, the Prophet was unable to restrain the masses of Indians Tecumseh had gathered, who began murderous attacks. The people on the frontiers requested relief from the President, and he sent them the 4th U.S. Regiment under the command of Governor William Henry Harrison, with volunteers from Kentucky flocking to his standard.

At the end of September 1811, Harrison began a march up the Wabash with a force of around 900 men, including the 4th Regiment, militia, and 130 dragoons. They halted within the boundaries of the United States and sent Delaware and Miami Indians as messengers to The Prophet, who received them insolently. The reply to a demand to deliver up the murderers and some stolen horses came in the form of a small war party that wounded one of Harrison's sentinels. The Delaware chiefs with Harrison assured him that their only satisfaction would come from force.

Harrison set out to face the Prophet, whose strength was increasing daily with Indians from beyond the Illinois River. He managed to get a force of 800 men within a mile and a half of the Prophet's town, and the Prophet agreed to meet with him the following day. Instead, the Indians attacked before dawn with a force about equal in size to Harrison's. The Americans held their ground and drove the Indians back in the Battle of Tippecanoe.

The Prophet had told his followers that the Great Spirit would protect them; the American's bullets would not hurt them; and they would have light while their enemies would be in thick darkness. During the battle, the Prophet kept himself safe on a nearby hill as he sang a war song.

The natives fought harder and more openly than usual, believing in the claimed supernatural protection. Their fatalities were similar to the Americans, around fifty for each side, a difficult blow for the Indians, whose mode of life made growing their numbers a great task. On Tecumseh's return, he and the Prophet remained undeterred and continued their preparations against the Americans. Attacks continued along the frontier in 1812, but the government held back from any more expeditions.

Then President Madison, along with a pro-war congress, declared war against Great Britain on June 18, 1812 due to British maritime impressments, or drafts, of Americans for their ships in their war against France; to continued fear of the Indians; and to coveting of British soil. A Representative from Virginia declared, "Agrarian cupidity, not maritime right, wages this war . . . we have heard but one word—like the whippoorwill, but one eternal, monotonous tone—Canada, Canada, Canada."

CHAPTER NINETEEN

WAPAWAQUA AND THE AMERICAN CAUSE

THAT SUMMER there was a lot of fear of all natives among the settlers in Ohio. To investigate and calm matters, the governor called for a treaty at Piqua, Ohio, where Indian Agent Johnston kept his home. Johnston reiterated, "There is not any danger to be apprehended from the Shawanese at Wapakoneta or Stony Creek." At the same time, he began arrangements for a council with the Indians. It resulted that the locals went so far as to gather the friendly natives into a few villages, for the protection of the settlers, but also to protect the Indians from the hostile native holdouts.

The Americans mounted a military expedition into Canada that summer under General William Hull. When Hull arrived at Brownstown below Detroit on the American side, he supervised an intertribal council. Black Hoof from Wapakoneta attended, as well as Lewis of Stony Creek, Tarhe (the Crane) from Sandusky, and Walk-in-the-Water. These Indians were unimpressed by the latest British efforts to attract them and chose to go along with the Americans. Canadian tribes, the Ojibwa of Lake St. Clair and the Iroquois on the Grand River, sent representatives offering neutrality in exchange for protection. Tecumseh stayed at British Fort Malden with 300-400 Indians.

On July 12, 1812, Hull invaded Canada, but the old Revolutionary War soldier was not up to the task. He soon retreated to Detroit and surrendered when Indians flanked the fort.

Before Hull's surrender at Detroit, when the Ohio governor learned of the situation facing Hull's army, he raised 1200 troops, headed by Brigadier General William Henry Harrison, and marched them to Urbana. At that time, Kentucky also gathered 5500 troops, and they rendezvoused in mid-August. When the men learned of Hull's surrender, they became preoccupied with the idea of wiping away the disgrace. They also were concerned that Indians who had been waiting to see where the chips fell would now side with the British and create havoc on the frontier.

On September 3, Harrison and his troops arrived at Piqua, and the Logan County Shawnee acted as spies, or rangers, for them. On Oct 23, 1812, John Johnston wrote to Harrison from his agency at Piqua, "You may depend upon my furnishing the Shawanoese. They will I suppose meet you at Upper Sandusky. [Chief] Logan will be here this night or in the morning and [I] shall make him Chief of the party."

Wapawaqua and Catawa-waqua were two of those spies, though perhaps not in the Logan party. Catawa-waqua, fighting in the American cause, was killed near Manary's blockhouse a few miles from Bellefontaine by one of the American rangers, supposing him to be a spy of the enemy. The confusion arose because, as John Johnston wrote, "The [hostile] Indians are hovering about and only want an opportunity to strike. Their signs continue to be seen in this neighbourhood."

General Harrison moved his depot to Fort Meigs, where he resisted a siege by the British in May of 1813, and he was convinced that the British would not initiate another attack on American soil. "[A]s long as they have Malden to defend or my army to destroy, every Indian that they can obtain will be brought down to that place."

IN JUNE OF 1813, O.M. gave a "Masonic Sermon" with the
theme "But covet earnestly the best gifts; and yet show I
unto you a more excellent way." The best gifts were
"eloquence, knowledge, faith and good works." He
expressed, "To recommend the pursuit of knowledge, we
need only to contrast the 'dark periods of antiquity,' and
the barbarous manners of our ancestors, with the present
state of the civilized world, or compare the uncultivated
and ferocious savage, with those whom knowledge has
enlightened and refined." He was indeed grateful to be
rescued from captivity.

That same summer he wrote to his sister Sarah,
sharing some of his preaching at her request, "I rejoice to
hear that you are still endeavouring to deny yourself, to
take up your cross daily and follow Christ, and though
this course of conduct will unavoidably expose you to
[illeg.]tion, this must not deter you from steadily evincing
your attachment to your Lord by your daily acts of
obedience & holiness." In the ensuing year, he became a
deacon, then later an elder, and also spread the Christian
word literally as president of the Miami Bible Society.

ON JUNE 21, 1813, there was an Indian Council at
Franklinton, Ohio, with Harrison and fifty chiefs of the
Delaware, Wyandot, Shawnee and Seneca tribes attending. Harrison wanted the Indians to either join the
Americans in the war or show loyalty by moving into
designated villages, the President wanting no false friends
ready to turn with the tide of the war.

The chiefs and warriors unanimously responded,
"They had long been anxious for an invitation to fight for
the Americans."

The General then made clear to them that they
must conform to the modes of European warfare. They
must not kill or injure defenseless prisoners, old men,

women, or children. Harrison was especially eager for them to do so because if they could do it, this would prove what the Americans suspected—that the British had made no effort to prevent the Indians fighting for them from being brutal in their mode of warfare.

Harrison caused a lot of amusement by promising them British General Proctor as a prisoner, with one condition. He began by telling them that he had learned through spies that Proctor had promised to deliver Harrison "into the hands of Tecumseh if he succeeded in capturing Fort Meigs, to be treated as that warrior might desire." Harrison's counter promise was that Proctor would be their prisoner, "if they could take him, provided they would only put petticoats on him and treat him as a squaw."

The Delaware and Shawnee turned out about two hundred warriors to march to General Harrison's relief. In addition, "The Wyandots within our lines, the Senecas and Mingoes have also turned out their disposable force, about two hundred more. The whole intend to continue with the army during the campaign," John Johnston informed the secretary of war. In addition, The Crane, Capt. Anderson, Black Hoof and the Snake pledged two hundred and fifty-nine of their warriors to fight in defense of the United States. About twenty of them rounded up cattle foraging in the woods and drove them to Fort Meigs. The army issued them blankets as part of their pay.

On Sept 4, 1813, Harrison expressed in glowing terms the friendly relations between the local Indians and the Americans:

> *The conduct of the Shawanese upon a late*
> *and Similar Occasion ought to satisfy every one that*
> *they are disposed to listen to and redress every*

complaint when properly made & supported—when one of their young men in July last Shot one of our citizens he was immediately apprehended by the Chiefs and Surrendered to Genl [John] Wingate at St Marys [Ohio]; two of these very Delaware Indians, who have been most Strongly suspected, have lately proven their fidelity in a Very exemplary manner, by the rescue of one of our Officers from a party of hostile Indians—I request your Excellency to take immediate Steps to afford Security to these people. They have thrown themselves upon us for protection—The faith of the Country has been Solemnly pledged that this protection Shall be afforded them. Many of their Warriors are now here rendering important services to the army—If any man has just Cause of complaint against them, let him come forward, he Shall be heard and redressed. —were I not perfectly convinced that the suspicions against these people are groundless, I should be one of the last men in the country to lend them countenance and Support—But a long acquaintance with them gives me some right to judge, and their recent conduct, present situation and future hopes Convince me that their fidelity to the United States is unquestionable—

THE AMERICAN CAUSE took a decided turn for the better on Sept 10, when naval officer Oliver H. Perry won the Battle of Lake Erie and the lake came under American control. With this victory, the Americans hastened their troops forward to the mouth of the Portage River.

On September 20, they began transporting the army of nearly 5000 men across the water, including the friendly Indians. They left all their horses and sailed in armed vessels, encamping on six-acre Middle Sister Island on the 25th.

Two days later, they landed three miles below Amherstburg, Canada, where they found that the British had fled, taking every single horse with them. They left a regiment to guard the town, and soon the Indians who had sided with the British came in, for they were discouraged by British losses and hadn't followed Proctor's retreat. The Ottawas, Chippewas, Potawatomis, Miamis, and Kickapoos agreed to bring in women and children as hostages and "to take hold of the same tomahawk with us, and to strike all who are or may be enemies of the United States, whether British or Indians." The Wyandot came in soon after, but didn't join the fray.

Harrison pursued Proctor with 3500 of the men—a simple task, since Proctor hadn't destroyed any bridges. Captain Perry went with his force went up the River Thames, using his cannon to drive the Indians and others away from partially destroyed bridges.

They met the British in battle on October 5, in the Battle of the Thames, where the friendly Indians helped as flanking scouts for the American regular army in their effort to seize the artillery. The British were in an impromptu defensive position—they had about-faced on the road to Moravian town, and the American cavalry broke the British lines immediately with an impetuous charge, with most of the British force surrendering. The British Indians, better situated in some woods, fought hard, but after the Americans killed Tecumseh, his followers fled. Proctor rushed into the forest on foot and escaped, sparing himself petticoats.

By December 1, 1813, the Americans discharged the friendly Indians to reoccupy their hunting grounds for the winter. John Johnston wrote to the Secretary of War, "I have this day drawn on you in favor of Oliver M. Spencer, cashier of the Miami Exporting Company for six thousand dollars, which will nearly close my expenditures—the pay of the Indians under my care who served with the N.W. Army until the close of the campaign on the River—amounted to $5000."

The following summer, Brigadier General Lewis Cass went to Detroit, again with a band of select warriors, joining with the American Army to attack Canada again. The Indians were quite willing to go against the British army and Canadian settlers, but did not want to fight the other tribes. When Cass reached Detroit on Aug 13, 1814, he sent the Indians he had brought with him from Greenville up the River French, with orders to penetrate, if possible, to the location of American General Ethan Brown and his men. Cass believed the Indians would provide important services to the advance force, if they could reach it. If they could not, they would so alarm the country that they would make it necessary for the British County Officers to detach a considerable force to protect the area. The Indians went up the Thames River and across to Fort Talbott, taking prisoners and plundering, but killing no one, as instructed.

The Americans were so well pleased with this chosen force of Indians that they requested more of them. In response, seventy-four Shawnee, Delaware, and Wyandot were equipped under chiefs Lewis, Wolf, and Civil John.

On October 9, General Duncan McArthur, an Ohio Senator and Brigadier General in the U.S. Army, started northward from Detroit with his Indian force and 750 men from Ohio and Kentucky, with five small field cannon.

Ethan Brown had been under siege at Fort Erie, and McArthur marched towards Burlington Heights to aid him by destroying the flouring mills in the region of the Grand River, which the British were using to grind their grain.

To prevent the British of learning of the plan, the Americans sent a false report, labeled as secret, that they were mounting an expedition against a village over 100 miles above Detroit. They counted on spies intercepting it.

To continue the deception they made a feint to the north, circling Lake St. Clair and crossing the St. Clair River on the twenty-sixth, and headed southeast to the Thames River. Above the Moravian town of Delaware, the forward guard captured a "British sergeant who was proceeding with intelligence of the expedition directly to Burlington Heights."

On November 4, a detachment surprised the inhabitants of Oxford, who believed an army of 2000 must be on their doorstep, or else the move would be too bold. General McArthur promised them protection and disarmed the militia, giving them parole; but he threatened to destroy the property of anyone who sent intelligence of his advance, and ended up burning the houses of two men who went anyway.

Militia, Indians, and dragoons gathered to oppose him at Malcolm's Mill, but McArthur used the stratagem of placing 100 men to make camp with as much noise and action as possible, while the majority of troops snuck off. Some of the men in the camping ruse fired at the enemy Indians and some made camp. The main body of McArthur's force, about 550 strong, headed to Malcolm's Mill and crossed the millstream, using a pile of driftwood that lay across it as a bridge, coming upon the lightly fortified rear of the enemy's camp. An officer wrote, "Our Indians had crossed with the general and as soon as they came in sight of the enemy they raised their usual hideous yell which produced such a panic in the Canadians that the whole of them fled in confusion at the first fire." When the Kentuckians heard the rear flank of their own troops approach, they charged across the bridge to attack the enemy's front, gaining the breastwork without a shot as the Canadians fled. General McArthur gave chase and captured many, but nightfall ended the attempt. The British had eighteen killed, nine wounded and over a hundred and thirty taken prisoner. McArthur had one killed and six wounded.

The next day, they burned Malcolm's Mill and soon continued on to Sovereign's Mill, where sixty-five of the militia who had fled in the attack on Malcolm's Mill had gathered. Seeing such a large force, they surrendered themselves, and McArthur gave them parole. After burning the mill, that evening they encamped near Dover, having captured thirty more militia.

On the return journey, at an old Indian village called Muncie Town, on the Thames, they constructed rafts for the sick and wounded, whom they placed in the care of the Indians. After this successful expedition, the Indians returned safely to their hunting grounds in Ohio, and the Treaty of Ghent ended further hostilities on Dec. 24, 1814.

After the war, Captain Lewis relocated his village a few miles north to within Indian Territory, to Lewistown in present Bloomfield Township, and the Indians continued to adjust to their new condition after the war. Minister James Hughs informed Governor Worthington in May, "I visited these Indians last week and preached to them a great number attended and behaved very decently. Capt Lewis and his wife have lodged with me in this place two nights this week they appear to be anxiously seeking after knowledge and improvement. They wish you to visit them to give them advice."

The Americans set a plan in motion. Agent John Johnston wrote, "My object . . . is to collect the Indians at one point, to build them a mill, and place one or two laboring men with them assist them in farming, they would then have no objections to parting with the surplus of their lands in an amicable way." He continued, "It ought not be forgotten that the 7/8 of the Indians living on this tract of country were the firm friends of the United States during the late war."

DURING THESE YEARS, Wapawaqua commenced an annual visit to O.M.'s home in Cincinnati. The brothers reminisced, O.M. in broken Shawnee, as his sons listened with fascination. He learned that Coohcoocheeh had passed, but did not chance disturbing her resting place by revealing its location. Once he rode out with Wapawaqua, and they retraced the steps of their escape with Wapawaqua refreshing his memory with the names of the streams partway up the Miami valley.

O.M. acquired thousands of acres in central Logan County, including land that natives lived on below the boundary line on Rum Creek. The land was not far from Lewistown. Perhaps a home for O.M.'s native brother?

In the spring of 1816, the President of the United States appointed O.M. Spencer as a commissioner to superintend subscriptions for the newly chartered Second Bank of the U.S. The people disliked this bank, for it paid in specie, which meant that the local banks had to reduce their practices of easy loans and easy money, causing depreciation. It also shipped specie out of the area to the east to pay government loans for imported goods, making it unavailable locally. This was particularly bad at a time when notes were depreciated—a double setback—and the speculation bubble burst.

Greatly overvalued real estate secured the loans to farmers, and money was in permanent improvements. The price of farm goods fell so low as to hardly pay transport to market and land became nearly unsellable.

By autumn of 1820, the notes of the Miami Exporting Company were at a 31% discount and in May of 1821, an angry mob forced the closing of the M.E.C., the last bank in Cincinnati. Banking did not return to the city until 1825. The devaluation of bank notes financially ruined nearly everyone in the area, including O.M.—just as devalued currency had financially ruined his father.

During this time, O.M. was a member of the Select Council, which was Cincinnati's town council, director of the Apprentices' Library, and a trustee of the new Cincinnati Asylum. He served on the Board of the Cincinnati and Dayton Turnpike Road Company.

His mercantile company did not survive; and in April of 1826, he wrote to a friend in Congress, requesting assistance in finding employment. He told him that he'd written to William Henry Harrison informing him "that being out of business, I found it extremely difficult to support my family comfortably, and requesting him, should any office affording a small income be created this session . . . that he would use his influence and solicit yours, to obtain it for me." O.M.'s name was associated with the banking disaster, and no office became available for him.

In this same year, using his ample spare time, he became a member of the board of directors of the Cincinnati Equitable Insurance Company (an insurance company still in existence). He was also on the board of directors of the Board of School Trustees and Visitors, which helped to form the public school system.

By 1829, land was increasing in value in the state, and comparatively, there was no scarcity of money. Increased income from land sales was helpful to him. His sister Dorothy shared in a letter to their sister Sarah in Mississippi on March 29, 1832, "Brother and the family are well. I think he looks better than he has for a great while."

CHAPTER TWENTY

THE SHAWNEE JOURNEY WEST

THE INDIANS GAVE in to the now inevitable. By the 1817 Treaty of Fort Meigs, made at the foot of the Maumee Rapids, the Indians ceded more land and moved to small Ohio reservations. One of the signers again was "Quitawepea," AKA Captain Lewis, and he and his followers, the Lewistown Shawnee as they became known, were left with a tract of forty-eight square miles. The Treaty of St. Mary's in 1818 granted them an additional 8,960 acres with their partners, the Lewistown Seneca. They began collecting the annuities promised them at treaties, and turned to learning the new style of husbandry. The Society of Friends, or Quakers, placed a mission at Lewistown beginning in 1819, with the goal to educate and civilize the Indians with an "emphasis on elevating the character and sphere of women."

As O.M. wrote, the Indians in general are not kind and affectionate to their women, whom they treat rather as slaves than as companions. They compel them not only to perform the drudgery of the household, but even to work in the field, it being thought disgraceful for an Indian to labor. He had often seen families traveling. While the poor woman bent under the weight of a heavy load and the girls carried packs or the smaller children on their shoulders, the "lazy" Indian in front carried nothing but his rifle and blanket, and the boys only a bow and arrows, or a reed blowgun.

It took several years to sort things out, but eventually the U.S. Government paid the warriors who had accompanied Lewis Cass from Greenville to Detroit for their service. They also compensated them for losses during the war. The Indians of "Lewis and Scoutash's Town received $1227.50," the Shawnee at "Wapakonetta $420.00," and the "Senecas at Lewis Town, $219.00." The Indians were also compensated $5821.11 for land improvements that they were forced to abandon in the 1817 Treaty of Fort Meigs.

There were complications and difficulties immediately. The American Indian Agent John Johnston lived at Piqua, below the treaty line. White settlements surrounded his agency, and in order to get their annuities, or even to get advice, the Indians were forced to travel through white settlements. As the Governor of the Michigan Territory pointed out, "Under any circumstances to pay the Indians twenty miles within a white settlement is impolitick because it brings them into contact with our people at time when they have means of purchasing any quantity of whisky."

The American plan was to suffer the presence of the Ohio Indians until they got the idea themselves to move west. Lewis Cass sympathized, "I do hope they will be allowed to enjoy their property in peace, until they express a wish to abandon it."

In 1823, Captain Lewis attempted to move his people west of the Mississippi. He visited General William Clark at St. Louis and explained, "We are surrounded in Ohio, Indiana and New York by a dense white population. We have few lands left to hunt on. There is too much whiskey. We want our own laws, and to receive teachers of husbandry among us, so that we may enjoy the blessings of agriculture and industry." Since this was in agreement with American policy, he received support, but few followed him. The Shawnee and Delaware already at Cape Girardeau, Missouri joined his confederacy. They received a tract of land west of the Mississippi that displaced "wild" Osage Indians.

Those Indians remaining at Lewistown had a great deal of respect for John Johnston. During a period when the Indian agent was under attack by the U.S. Government for taking a cut, or "premium" from the Indian annuities, the Shawnee and Seneca of Lewistown wrote and signed a petition in his favor. They said of Johnston, "by your good advice through him, we have been brought safe through all our difficulties and we cannot help respecting him as long as life remains." Among the signers was "Wa pa moek or White Loon." This was Wapawaqua. Johnston defended taking a part of the annuities, with "now that there is no publick provisions issued to them near the frontiers, I am often obliged to feed large numbers of them [along] with their horses."

In May of 1825, Lewis and members of his confederacy met in council with eastern Indians at Wapakoneta, but the eastern Indians refused to be drawn in. Johnston explained why: "The Indian Lewis who has continued this visit and the plan of removal, is very unpopular with our Indians. He was dismissed from office some years ago by his people for fraud and falsehood and moved westward in disgust, is now endeavoring to raise a party of his own on the Arkansa and draw subjects from here. He is not confided in in this country, nor will the Indians in Ohio listen to him. This information would have been given long since to Gov. Clark if he had thought proper to have corresponded with the Agent; ...Lewis has undoubtedly deceived him and I am induced to look upon the whole visit as not calculated to benefit the Government or the Indians. There was not a person in the deputation [to the President] who had the shadow of authority to act for the Indians in Ohio."

Not that Johnston was opposed to moving the Indians west. He considered it part of his duties as Indian agent and imparted to the Secretary of War, "Since the year 1818 I have moved from Indiana and Ohio over the Mississippi very near three thousand souls, and am still every year moving some." However, he felt, "The earlier a permanent provision is made for them the better. It is due to the character of this Government and Nation to provide such a retreat for the primitive inhabitants of the country. Whatever may be alleged to the contrary they never can be saved on what is called Reservations. They must have a country and an independent character, under certain modifications assigned to them, [or] their race will perish."

The Indians continued farming and making improvements on their Reservations, but they did not thrive, living as they were, surrounded by whites. A census taken in 1829 showed that there were 132 Shawnee and 198 Seneca served by Johnston's Piqua Agency, but the totals showed 98 deaths and only 70 births. Indian Agent John McElvain wrote, "their thirst for strong drink is beyond conception, and are great cause of the disease, . . . great pains hav[e] been taken for some time past, by all employed in this agency to convince the Indians that the course they were pursuing would eventually ruin them, which has had a good effect."

The government exerted further pressure upon the Indians by dividing their annuity between them and the Indians who had already gone west. The Indians protested in an 1830 letter to "Our Great Father the President of the U.S. Father this all that we can see, and why should the money be sent to Mississippi when all the chiefs are all here that were present at the Treaty."

Why indeed? As Johnston wrote, "This division of their Annuity will at once decide the Shawanoese on emigrating West of the Mississippi, and if the Government will continue myself in charge of them and the Shawanoese and Senecas of Lewis Town, I hereby engage to effect the removal of the whole."

In addition to any impulse to save the Indians, the Indian agent's true purpose was no mystery, as Johnston continued to explain, "The lands owned and occupied by the Indians in Ohio is now become very valuable and must under proper management soon fall into our hands. There [are] some situations that would command $100 an acre. Their occupancy is greatly desired for the purpose of enabling the state to complete those [illeg.] plans of internal improvement, which she has commenced."

Under this continual pressure and not thriving in their situation, the Shawnee finally decided to go west. The Lewistown Shawnee and Seneca traded their lands for a 60,000-acre tract west of the Mississippi in the treaty of July 20, 1831. Initially, traders offered the chiefs bribes for their lands and then "told the Indians that they must sell their lands to get the money to pay" claims that they had against them. The Lewistown Indians didn't fall for any schemes, though. O.M. sent two of his adult sons, Henry and Alexander, to watch out for his friends' interests. They attended this treaty and no other, and signed as witnesses.

After the treaty, the Shawnee sent an entourage to Washington for financial aid for their journey west, but President Jackson was entirely unsympathetic. But, as John Johnston wrote, the Shawnee in his agency had garnered some respect from the Americans by "their uniform attachment to the United States since the peace with General Wayne in 1795. They consider themselves entitled to much consideration. They being a leading Tribe were without doubt the salvation of these frontiers during the late war."

Secretary of War Lewis Cass agreed with the Shawnee and went to Congress on their behalf, obtaining funds for the removal.

In early June of 1832, James B. Gardiner, Special Agent and Superintendent of Indian Removal, worked tirelessly to prepare the Ohio Indians for their move to the Kansas region. He promised Cass, "I shall use my best exertions to comply with your instructions, and to conduct the emigration in such manner as shall consummate the benevolent intentions of the Government towards the tribes under my charge."

Gardiner spent a week speaking with the principal men of Wapakoneta, Hog Creek, and the Lewistown Shawnee and Seneca. This larger group received a grant for 100,000 acres of land set apart for them in a Missouri treaty of 1825. They were to have the land near their friends or anywhere else in the region that they liked.

The principal Shawnee chief, John Perry, said in good English "that they had [not] bought land at all, by ceding their reservation in Ohio. He considered that the Government had made them a present of the tract of land west of the Mississippi, and that they were receiving a fair equivalent for their reservation in Ohio, by getting the principal part of the avails of it when sold, and being removed and subsisted one year at the expense of the United States."

They camped at the farm of John Johnston while preparing for the move. The agent's diary listed for Sept 28, 1832, "Shawanoese, Senecas, and Ottawas removing west of Miss. in Provisions, Pasture, Horse feed apples, etc $35.00. Destruction of Timber in camping on my Farm when moving westward of Miss. $29.00."

The Indians had debts of about $1000, and they would receive a total of $16,000 in the summer. $13,000 was for improvements made on their lands, and $3000 was the first installment of a perpetual annuity. They also had chattels to sell.

Gardiner attempted to persuade the Indians to travel west by water due to its ease; but the Indians were unanimously averse to it. "They know nothing about steamboats. They do not wish to 'move by fire,' nor to be scalded 'like the white man cleans his hog,' . . . Some of their little children might be drowned. Their native modesty revolts at the use of the only convenience on board a boat to obey the calls of nature."

If they traveled by steamboat, the government would have to pay to transport the natives' many good horses, probably the most important consideration, so Gardiner yielded to their wish to travel by land.

There were many arrangements for wagons, wagon-masters, pioneers to cut the way, and an interpreter. America delivered blankets and Russia sheeting to Bellefontaine, the sheeting for the Indian women to use to make tents. As for food, Gardiner estimated that the rations allowed were too little. Gardiner suggested to Cass, "You would be as unwilling as he, or any other man, to have them complaining for want of food while under your charge. I would not presume to dictate, but I am strongly persuaded that the present ration will prove too little. But if there would be an impropriety in changing it now, so far as applies to the Ohio Indians, I see no other way we can do to prevent complaints, except to enlarge the muster-roll."

The Indians earnestly requested vaccination against smallpox before beginning the journey. Gardiner believed Cass would comply with their wishes, "although the expense would fall upon the Government, as nothing would be left undone which could promote their comfort and safety." Gardiner pleaded, "In the approaching journey, we shall be as defenseless against sickness and casualties as the public soldiers if deprived of their surgeon."

The Indians were impatient to move on, and some planted no crops and sold off so many of their hogs and cattle that they were in danger of not being able to feed their families if there were any delays. They also were a prey to those around them who knew of their coming wealth, intended for improvements in their new homes. Gardiner cautioned them against contracting any new debts, but merchants tried to get the men drunk to "filch [illeg.] from them the last dollar for which they have sold their heritage amongst us, and the 'graves of their fathers.'"

An account of the emigration follows from the Journal of occurrences kept by the conductors of the "LEWISTOWN DETACHMENT" of emigrating Ohio Indians, Seneca and Shawnee; commencing on August 20, 1832, and ending on the 13th of December, 1832:

August 20, 1832: Agreeably to previous notice given them, the Senecas and Shawnee Indians this day assembled at Lewistown, Logan County, Ohio, to receive rations. At their request, provisions for four days were issued to them. The proper officers of this detachment were present, and inspected the provisions and the issues, both of which were satisfactory. The utmost harmony prevailed throughout the day; and in the evening, the Indians returned to their homes, well satisfied with the manner of drawing, and with the quantity and quality of their food. Each family drew separately.

Since there was no definite time set for the commencement of their journey, and their houses thought the most proper places for them to remain, while rendered unwell from the effects of vaccination, it was considered most expedient for them to continue their former manner of living, until they should recover their health after being vaccinated, and a time fixed for their departure.

August 21: Tuesday, Civil John, the head chief of the tribe, and some of the principal men were called together, by the request of Lieutenant Lane, to ascertain whether there was a possibility of prevailing on them to go by water. Agent James McPherson was the interpreter.

(Author's note: McPherson was serving with a Pennsylvanian regiment in 1781, when he was taken prisoner at Lochry's defeat at the mouth of the Great Miami. Lochry's expedition was a part of George Rogers Clark's bid for Detroit. For several years while in captivity, McPherson worked for the British Indian Department under McKee and Elliott. He was on good terms with the Indians, among whom he was known as Squalakake, or the Red Faced Man. He was not released until the Treaty of Greenville in 1795.)

They say what they have said before, that 'they depended on Colonel Gardiner to carry their understanding of the treaty into effect. They are ready, willing, and anxious to go, and always have been; but it is useless to try to persuade them to go by steamboats." They say, that some of their old and infirm women say, "we will not go in steamboats, nor will we go in wagons; but we will go on horseback; it is the most agreeable manner for us; and if we are not allowed to go so, we can, and will, remain here and die, and be buried with our relatives; it will be but a short time before we leave this world, at any rate, and let us avert from our heads as much unnecessary pain and sorrow as possible.'

In the evening they departed, expressing a desire to hear the final conclusion of their great father, the President, and the Secretary of War, with respect to the route which it is wished they should pursue. They ardently hope that they will be permitted to go by land, on horseback.

August, 22: The Indians remained at home today, and in the evening sent word to their conductor, James McPherson, that they would meet at his house tomorrow, for some purpose which they did not explain.

August 23: The Indians met this morning, agreeably to their appointment of yesterday, and made known the business for which they assembled. It was this, namely: a young man, (one of their friends, and a member of their band,) had just arrived from the Big Spring reservation, to inform them, that the Indians of the Grand reservation were drawing up writings in a secret manner, to establish a claim to a part of the avails arising from the Big Spring reservation, which were affirmed to be unjust by the Indians of the Big Spring reservation, and by the Lewistown Indians, their friends and relatives.

They (the Lewistown Indians) wished the interference of their friends, J. McPherson, and Major Pool, the assistant agent, in their favor, and their co-operation with Colonel Gardiner to protect their rights. They requested that Mr. Gardiner should be informed immediately of their claim, and exert himself to avert its deleterious effects to them and their property.

They were assured that they might rely upon the interposition of these officers in their favor, to protect their rights. They then departed for their homes in peace and confidence.

August 24: The Indians this day collected at a grove, near the house of James McPherson, and received rations for four days. Civil John said that the tribe should be assembled at his house, on Monday next, to be vaccinated.

August 25-26: The Indians all remained at home.

August 27: This day Dr. Lord, with an assistant, proceeded to Lewistown, and vaccinated about one hundred and twenty of them; they were well pleased with the operation.

August 28: Dr. Lord vaccinated the remaining part of the Indians today. Provisions were issued for three days.

August 29-30: The Indians remained at their homes.

August 31: Several of them took their horses to be shod today, to have them in readiness to start. Colonel Gardiner directed this to be done.

September 1, 1832: Several more of the Indians took their horses to be shod.

September 2, Sunday: The Indians remained at home today. At night they made a feast, which is termed by them the "death feast," or feast of death. They celebrate, in feasts of this kind, the good and worthy qualities and actions of some deceased person of the tribe, and mutually and undisguisedly lament their death by tears and lamentation. They adopt some person in his place, for the purpose of perpetuating his name, and the memory of his actions.

September 3: The Indians assembled today, by order of Colonel Gardiner, to receive their blankets, tenting, and rifles, which were given to them. They appeared well pleased with them.

They were told by Mr. Gardiner to make every possible endeavor to be prepared to start in ten days. They said they would do so. They expressed great pleasure at hearing they were permitted to go by land, and that no delay in preparing was allowed. They said that it was their desire to get to their destination as soon as possible. They fear that cannot be done before winter sets in; but they will endeavor to get there this season.

September 4: The Indians remained at their homes.

September 5: Several of them took their horses to get shod today.

September 6-7: They continued making preparations to start.

September 8:   The Indians commenced delivering their chattel property to General J. McLane, the appraiser, for sale.

September 9, Sunday: They remained at home.

September 10:   They continued delivering their property.

September 11:   They commence assembling at Lewistown, in conformity with directions to that effect from James McPherson.

September 12:   They continued assembling at Lewistown. Some of them were engaged in taking more property to sell.

September 14:   They were reminded of the necessity of being prepared by the appointed day to set off. Monday was appointed as that day.

September 15:   The Indians assembled today, and received the amount of money due them for their improvements, from Colonel John McElvain.

September 16:   They remained principally at Lewistown.

September 17:   They received the proceeds of the sale of their property.

September 18:   A part of them attended the funeral of Mrs. McPherson, who deceased yesterday, and whom the Indians had esteemed as a relative more than as a friend.

They say they will start tomorrow; they were reminded of the necessity of being ready, and promised to finish their arrangements today.

They have settled nearly all they owe in the neighborhood. Sixteen horses were distributed among them today.

September 19, Wednesday: Nearly all of them left Lewistown today and encamped at the distance of ten miles.

September 20: Those Indians who started yesterday proceeded to Hardin, a village nineteen miles from where they were encamped. The remainder traveled ten miles.

September 21: Today those who arrived here first remained, and the balance of the tribe came up at night.

September 22: By order of Colonel Gardiner, the Indians remained at their encampment today—order reigned.

September 23: The detachment was ordered to march this morning. We encamped late in the evening at the distance of eighteen miles from Hardin.

September 24: We struck our tents at 8 o'clock, and marched to Greenville, fourteen miles; we could have gone farther, but a severe storm arose to prevent us.

September 25: Upon a solicitation of the principal chief and others, the Indians were permitted to remain in the camp long enough to dry their tents and blankets, which were wet in the rain yesterday.

At 11 o'clock we marched on, and at sunset, encamped at the distance of thirteen miles from Greenville, on the road towards Richmond, Indiana.

September 26: We struck our tents at 10 o'clock, and marched ten miles, being within four miles of Richmond, near which place we were ordered to remain by the superintendent until further orders should arrive from him.

September 27: The Indians remained at camp today.

September 28: Nearly all of the Indians went into town today; some to see the place, some to trade, and some to get intoxicated.

September 29: A severe rain prevented them from leaving their encampment today.

September 30: We were ordered at 12 o'clock by the superintendent to march on immediately. By night, we succeeded in passing through Richmond and two miles farther, making six miles.

Monday, October 1, 1832: Today some difficulty arose among the teamsters, which detained us until 11 o'clock, at which time we left the camp and proceeded through Centerville. Our start was so late and the road being so muddy that we traveled only seven miles.

October 2: Struck our tents at 9 o'clock, and marched thirteen miles and a half, where we halted for the night.

October 3: At 10 o'clock we commenced traveling, and at five gained the distance of fifteen miles.

October 4: We commenced marching at 9 o'clock, and at 5, encamped at the distance of sixteen miles from our last encampment.

October 5: We started at 9 and passed Indianapolis two miles, making today eighteen miles.

October 6: We remained in camp today. Our orders from the superintendent were to remain near this place until he should direct us to proceed. In the evening, the superintendent arrived at Indianapolis.

October 7: We received orders this morning to march a few miles. The Ottawa detachment is but a few miles in our rear. At two o'clock, we left the encampment and marched eight miles.

October 8: We struck our tents at 9, and at 5, encamped at the distance of nineteen miles.

October 9: We traveled thirteen miles today over a very bad road.

October 10: The Indians expressed an anxious solicitude to remain today to rest themselves and their horses, and to dry their tents and blankets, which were wet in a storm last night, etc. Their wishes appeared so reasonable that they were granted the privilege of remaining.

October 11: The detachment marched sixteen miles—no impediment.

October 12: We marched nineteen miles to the Wabash River.

October 13: We were detained late in crossing the river. For the sake of economy, the horses were made to ford the river, while the most of the women and children were taken across in boats. The river was not low enough for it to be considered safe fording for any but men, or those who were good riders.

The detachment marched seven miles from the ferry, (Clinton).

October 14: We marched into Illinois today, to the distance of eleven miles from our last encampment.

October 15: We started this morning about 7 o'clock and marched until dark at a pretty rapid gait, which took us at the distance of twenty-seven miles. There was no water to be had between these two encampments, and the Indians were apprized the previous evening of this fact and ordered to be prepared to start very early, that we might reach the Ambroise River.

October 16:   At the request of the chiefs, and by permission of Col. Gardiner, the superintendent, the detachment remained on the encampment today for the purpose of refreshing themselves.

October 17: We started about 11 o'clock and marched 7 miles to where we encamped. There is no water for twelve miles farther.

October 18: One of the chiefs lost some of his horses, which detained us until 11 o'clock, when we left the encampment. In the evening, we encamped at the distance of twelve miles.

October 19:   We marched twenty-one miles, having traveled late.

October 20: This day early it commenced raining and continued until noon, at which time all the tents were wet and the horses were in the woods. We remained at the camp.

October 21: We struck our tents at 11 and marched fourteen miles.

October 22: We started at 9 o'clock and traveled late; we made the distance of twenty miles.

October 23: We traveled seventeen miles today; the roads were good, and the day fair. We encamped six miles west of Vandalia, Illinois.

October 24:   We traveled nineteen miles; we had an excellent road.

October 25:   By order of the superintendent, the detachment remained stationary. An express was sent by him to St. Louis for information respecting the prevalence of the cholera and the best place and manner of crossing the Mississippi river. He addressed these inquiries to Governor Clark.

October 26: Removed from the road that travelers from St. Louis might not come among the Indians, for it is now understood that the cholera is prevailing there to a considerable extent.

October 27: The detachment remained in camp.

October 28: The Indians remained in camp; quietness was exhibited from every tent; good feeling abundantly prevailed throughout the day. The Indians have not for several days had an opportunity of procuring liquor; they consequently remain sober.

October 29: We this day received orders to march by Col. Abert, who assumed the future direction of the emigration on the 27th.

We started about 10 o'clock, and marched to the distance of fifteen miles on the road to Kaskaskia, where General Clark advised the superintendent to have this detachment of Indians taken across.

October 30: In consequence of some of the principal men of the tribe being behind, the Indians refused to go until they should come up. It was not till past noon that they arrived; and it was then too late to get to the next stream of water; so we were compelled to remain.

October 31: We marched fourteen miles.

Thursday, November 1, 1832: A chief and his son were left behind yesterday to hunt for their horses, and have not yet come up. The chiefs here refuse to leave him any farther behind. They say that they are afraid that they are lost. We were constantly compelled to remain for those behind.

November 2: We struck our tents at 9 o'clock and encamped at 5, having traveled seventeen miles.

November 3: We marched fourteen miles.

November 4: We traveled twenty miles, which brought us within four miles of the ferry at the Mississippi, where we were to cross.

      The conductor rode to Kaskaskia to see Colonel P. Menard, to whom he was directed by Colonel Abert for information respecting the route and assistance in crossing the river. In the evening, the conductor returned to camp.

November 6: This morning the Indians proceeded to the ferry: the wind blew so severely that the ferrymen refused to cross. It continued so all day.

November 7: Today about two-thirds of them were taken over, which occupied their time until dark.

November 8: The remaining part of the Indians was taken over today.

November 9: The Indians remained at the camp for the purpose of getting their horses shod.

November 10: The Indians had considerable difficulty in finding their horses. We started late and only traveled eight miles.

November 11: We traveled eighteen miles.

November 12: We traveled seventeen miles.

November 13: We traveled four miles, one west of the *mine of Burton,* where we encamped for the purpose of having the remaining part of the horses shod.

November 14: We remained today for the purpose of getting horses shod and giving the squaws an opportunity of washing their clothes and blankets.

November 15: It was late this morning before the Indians could collect all their horses; we traveled only eight miles.

November 16: We traveled sixteen miles to the Meramec River.

November 17: A family was left behind a day or two ago, which the Indians say they intend waiting for at this place.

November 18: It rained all day, so much that the Indians would not start.

November 19: It was so cold that the Indians refused to travel. It snowed and blowed terribly.

November 20: A child died this morning (the only death which has occurred in this tribe), which detained us until late. Some horses strayed away, which added to the delay. We traveled seven miles.

November 21: We traveled eighteen miles.

November 22: It rained and snowed so much that the Indians could not travel.

November 23: We marched fifteen miles.

November 24: We struck our tents at 8 o'clock and marched until about 5. We made the distance of sixteen miles. The horses of two of the teamsters ran away, and their wagons were consequently left behind.

November 25: A part of the detachment traveled ten miles, and the remainder continued stationary. The wagons which were left behind yesterday arrived in the evening.

November 26: The Indians who remained behind yesterday, waiting for the teams, joined those in front.

November 27: We marched ten miles.

November 28: We struck our tents at 8 o'clock and continued traveling until late in the evening, by which means we made the distance of eighteen miles.

November 29: We traveled thirteen miles to the Gasconade.

November 30: The Indians remained today for the purpose of waiting for some of their brethren who are behind.

Saturday, December 1, 1832: It commenced raining in the night and continued all day, so that the detachment could not travel.

December 2: We were compelled to cross a stream several times today which nearly swam the horses; so that we were detained along the road so much that we traveled but eight miles.

December 3: We traveled fourteen miles. One keg of powder and one hundred pounds of lead were given to the Indians today by Lieutenant Lane, upon the condition that they should pay for it in game, which should be divided among all as other supplies of provisions.

December 4: We traveled twenty miles today. We started early, had a good road, and traveled late.

December 5: We traveled thirteen miles today, which brought us to White River.

December 6: We remained at the encampment for the purpose of refreshing the detachment.

December 7: About 11 o'clock we left the encampment and crossed White River, and marched nine miles beyond it, making ten miles today.

December 8: We traveled twelve miles, to Gibson's fork of the Neosho.

December 9: We traveled fifteen miles.

December 10: We traveled seven miles to day. We could have gone farther, but it was necessary to halt to get corn and meat.

December 11: We traveled thirteen miles.

December 12: We traveled eighteen miles.

Thursday, December 13, 1832: We traveled twelve miles to the Seneca agency.

I delivered the Indians into the care of Major Kennerly, the agent for the Senecas, agreeably to instruction. They will remain upon the land of their brethren, the Senecas, until an exchange of their tract of land is made, at which time they will remove to the piece given them.

I and my assistant, with the chiefs and others of our detachment, went to examine their tract situated west of the Neosho, and does not extend within less than five or six miles of it; but, in consequence of its being too high to ford, we were compelled to remain on the east side. There was no boat in which we could cross.

The resident Senecas say it cannot be cultivated: that there is scarcely any timber upon it, and but little good soil, and withal, entirely un-adapted to their purposes.

Upon this representation, they refused going to see it, but they have since been over to make an examination of its advantages and disadvantages, but what their conclusion is I have not yet learned.

DANIEL M. WORKMAN,

Conductor of Lewistown Emigrating Indians,

By DANIEL R. DUNIHUE.

Mr. D. M. Workman instructed me to make out this copy and forward it on to the War Department, which I now have the honor of doing. It should have been sent on some time ago, but my recent arrival at home, and unavoidable business, has prevented me until the present time.

Very respectfully,

DANIEL R. DUNIHUE. February 10, 1833.

Finally, the following summer, a second slightly smaller wave of Shawnee left for the west from John Johnston's farm. His diary lists for June 23, 1833, "Last of Shawanese left their camp on his Farm for the west, 100 in all +100 horses, 5 days here."

NOT ALL OF THE NATIVES LEFT, some evidently living independently and quietly, perhaps tolerated because of their mixed blood status. When a Mr. Henry Hone moved his household goods by wagon to his property in Bloomfield Township in Logan County in 1836, he found the Miami River very high, with only the trunk of a fallen tree to help his crossing. While Hone stood on the shore scratching his head, "a number of half-breed Indians" came out from their bark cabins on the bank to watch him. He asked for their help but they were not interested until they learned he had "a small quantity of spirits in the wagon." In exchange for a few drinks of the "whisk," they helped with the crossing, unloading the goods and carrying them across, the horses swimming, and the wagon pulled across by a bed-cord to the end of the wagon-tongue, the goods reloaded, and the journey resumed.

CHAPTER TWENTY ONE

OMEGA

W APAWAQUA'S VISITS inspired O.M. to think of his captivity in active terms again, and in 1834, he had published in the *Western Christian Advocate* in serial form *Indian Captivity: A True Narrative of the Capture of the Rev. O.M. Spencer by the Indians, In the Neighbourhood of Cincinnati*, Written by Himself. Other Christian papers in the country copied it, and the Sunday School Union of the Methodist Episcopal Church published it as a book. It pleased him to do this for charity.

The same year that O.M. had his Indian captivity story published, he renewed his banking duties with the Miami Exporting Company, paying stock, liquidating debt and redeeming notes. In addition, he went into the wholesale dry goods business with the firm Spencer, Strong and Blachly, on Pearl Street in 1834.

After an illness, his health began to fail. His sister Dorothy wrote to their sister Sarah, "Brother has been quite sick. They supposed it [a bout] of <u>Cholera</u>, but [illeg.] he was getting better. There have been some cases in Town, but we have not heard of any proving [fatal] . . ."

Then the government precipitated another financial crash, when President Jackson put out the "Specie Circular" in 1836, in which he advocated paying for government lands only with specie, due to high inflation. The ensuing panic caused creditors to call in loans, and the payment of specie was suspended. Intensifying the depression were crop failures in 1837.

O.M. now eked out a living only as a wholesale dry goods merchant. At his home on Sixth Street (between

Sycamore and Broadway), four of his adult sons boarded with him, Henry, O.M. Junior, and the twins Samuel and Francis.

In addition to aiding in their support, his sister Dorothy and her children asked for occasional financial assistance. He was kind to her with loans and gifts as she needed them, but he was so burthened with his own business, besetments, and difficulties that he felt full of too many cares. When she under necessity asked for assistance again, he resolved to pursue his father's war pension. Colonel Spencer had refused this money, instead taking a commendation. O.M. requested that his sister Sarah write to their uncle, Aaron Ogden, who had in 1812 served a term as governor of New Jersey, to see if something could be done about it. He and all of his siblings signed the letter. She wrote:

> *My Dear Uncle, I am induced to address you at this time on a subject in which I feel assured you will take a warm interest as well as pleasure in tendering your advice to the parties concerned as your relatives & the children & heirs of a Brother Officer in the American Revolution Col Oliver Spencer. It has been lately intimated to me by a relative acquainted with the measure that through the influence of Col Johnson a delegate to congress from the State of Kentucky a law has been passed by that body & a provision made for the officer of different Ranks & grades of the Revolution securing to them & to their Heirs a compensation for their services during the War. I have been requested to unite with the other members of my family in a Petition to Congress during its present session to*

*obtain the half pay due to our Father a full Col brevet
at the period of his quitting service which [was] not
until the close of the American contest with Great
Britain. My Brother Mr. Spencer of Cincinnati has my
Fathers commission the only document in possession
at this period to present (should it actually prove to
be the fact that the provision made by congress
embraces the Heirs of deceased Officers) as well as
the few surviving [illeg.] of the Revolution in the case
it strikes one forcefully that from your personal
knowledge of my Fathers Patriotism and valour
displayed in the service of his country the many
sacrifices he made both in personal property &
money to further her interest & raise the credit of her
paper currency would suppose your representation
of these facts have a strong influence in the
admission of the claims brought forward by his Heirs
his half pay & would your engagements in business
permit we should feel strongly indebted to you my
dear Uncle to second our Petition by drawing up a
brief sketch of our Fathers biography & the
engagements in which he signalized himself during
the Revolutionary struggle to be presented at the
same period to Congress. My Fathers modesty on
this subject was great the only thing I recollect to
have heard him report was that he had been
Honored with the thanks of the Commander in Chief
in General orders, twice when the sacrifices he had
made during the American Contest. The loss of
Property compelled him to remove with the younger
& helpless members of his family to the Western*

*Frontiers exposed to the Horrors of an Indian War &
to many privations & hardships, & to fill up the cup
of Bitterness, the capture of his only son by the
Savages. So far from complaining of regretting the
cause which had reduced himself & family to their
present condition he would console himself with this
remark "I have served my country faithfully." My
dear Mother fret & suffered keenly when she
recalled to remembrance what she believed to have
been my Fathers misplaced confidence in the justice
of government, in his having as I have heard her
mention exchanged three thousand pounds in specie
for Continental money which at length depreciated
until it became as it were a mere blank, & which she
afterwards thru into the fire as waste paper. Had
this Paper had been preserved no doubt but on
producing properly testimony of the manner it came
into possession Congress would have redeemed it.
He had also at the commencement of the Revolution
armed & equipped several of the soldiers under his
command at his own private expense & without ever
making any charge against Government at the close
of the War he attempted to reinstate himself into his
former business. But the depreciation of the
Continental currency & the fear that his certificates if
returned would share the same fate induced him to
part with the greater part of them when they would
only command four & six pence on the pound.
Reserving only a small part with which he
afterwards purchased lands in the Western Country
& his efforts to reinstate himself into business*

proving unsuccessful he was compelled at the age of 50 with his helpless family to remove to the Western Country in the year ninety one. Here after a few brief years of disappointment & patient industry & endurance he closed his mortal cover. He lived, & died a devout Christian. Respect for his memory & a desire to assist the more unfortunate members of his family has led me my dear uncle thus to give [illeg.] from you this testimony to his virtues. I would also ask you candidly to state whether under any circumstance you think the object I have mentioned attainable in the way I have mentioned & to point out a letter made for our ad affair [illeg.], if more certain of success. & if after all no remuneration should be given or granted by Congress yet still I shall love the consolation of owning to do my duty & leaving the event to Providence."

This bid for Colonel Spencer's revolutionary war pension failed. On the contrary, O.M. had to divest himself of his best properties; he lost everything. In early May of 1838, he had to place an ad to sell his lots on Sixth Street as well as his residence there, a "large and commodious house."

Despite his troubles, O.M. kept his faith. He wrote, even if we are troubled on every side, we are not distressed as if there were no way for our escape. Though often perplexed and in doubt about what step we are next to take, yet never should we despair of God's mercy. Though persecuted, we are not forsaken. God does not give us up for a prey to our enemies. Even as we may be cast down and desponding, God does not suffer us to be destroyed. So that while we continue faithful, and trust in his grace, we may constantly say 'the Lord is my helper, & I will not fear what man shall do unto me.'"

WHEN DEVALUED CURRENCY ruined Colonel Spencer, he took advantage of an opportunity to start over. O.M. could not. Weakened by his bout with cholera and with his financial troubles, Oliver Marlborough Spencer died on May 30, 1838, of nervous apoplexy—a stroke.

> *Cincinnati Daily Gazette*, June 6, 1838
> Few are the dispensations of Divine Providence, that happen to our community, more afflicting than the death of Mr. Oliver M. Spencer, who departed this life on the 30th ultimo aged 57 years. His was a life marked with many peculiar events. Some of which he has himself narrated in his "Indian Captivity," which forms a number of the Sunday School Library . . . The sufferings of the orphan, the distresses of the widow and the necessities of the poor and destitute of every description, never failed of finding relief either in the distribution of his bounty, or in the dispensations of his friendly and consolatory admonitions.

His wife Electra and at least eight living children survived O.M. Despite his financial difficulties and the ensuing stress, on reflection, he was grateful for his life and lot. A few years before his death he wrote, "I do not wish to leave large possession to my children not only because it would argue [against] trust in the providence of God, but would most probably lead them to pride, extravagance, dissipation, & perhaps destruction of soul & body. If I can give them a liberal education & a few thousand Dollars each to commence with I think I shall have done my duty & have manifested a sufficient concern for their temporal welfare." He was able to do well enough for his children, for they did well in life.

His oldest son Henry E. Spencer was president of the Firemen's Insurance Company. Politically he was a Whig and was mayor of Cincinnati for four terms, described as "a man of great integrity, fine abilities and very spirited." O.M.'s namesake, Oliver M. became a judge of the Hamilton county courts. Robert became a Methodist minister. Samuel was a farmer. John Collins Spencer and possibly Francis W. Spencer, were "at sea."

Alexander Oliver Spencer went to live in Logan County in the 1830s. He married Kitty McWorkman, the granddaughter of James McPherson, the local Indian Agent. They built a house at Silver Lake, then known as Spencer Lake and planted many catalpa trees there and throughout Bellefontaine, the old trees still surviving in the author's childhood. He died in 1844 of a fever that "carried off" many citizens at that time.

O.M.'s and Electra's only daughter, Anne Elizabeth, is perhaps the most interesting of the children, due to her marriage. She was educated by Mrs. Tevis of Shelbyville, Ky. and at the boarding school of Mesdames Segoyne and Saracene in Philadelphia. Born in 1819, she became a Catholic when she married a naval officer from Maryland who had set up a law practice in Cincinnati, one Raphael Semmes. They eventually moved to Alabama. As the Civil War approached, Anne did not want her husband to resign his U.S. Naval commission to join the Confederate States Navy, terming it "false movements." She and O.M.s sons were Unionists, and at her husband's urging in 1861, she went to visit her relatives in Cincinnati, for "a month or two." A month or two became a year or two, until Semmes became famous for his destruction of Northern merchant ships, forcing her to return to Alabama. Later she referred to her brother Henry as now being "too Yankee & bitter to do any thing to oblige me." She herself had become bitter, for when writing about a southern woman marrying a Yankee officer after the war, she wrote, "What contemptible women they are to unite their destinies with such vandals."

IN ALL, O.M. SPENCER honored his place as the descendent of Puritan forefathers who had "left England on account of the persecutions for religious opinions." He struggled financially in later life, but he never lost sight of his humanity and humility. While raising a family and conducting business, he followed his conscience as a Methodist minister. He was grateful for his rescue from life with the Indians, yet he did what he could for them in his own way with visits with Wapawaqua and having his sons monitor their final Ohio treaty. Most importantly, he wrote about them without malice, remembering his Indian mother Coohcoocheeh and her grief for her people and her sadness at their parting. Perhaps he was allowed a glimpse of her beautiful and abundant hunting grounds.

The Lewistown Shawnee may have had the most orderly transfer of any of the tribes going west, America rewarding them for their actions and loyalty during the War of 1812. They separated from their Seneca partners in 1867 and are now known as the Eastern Shawnee, eventually moving to Oklahoma. Only in recent years have Native Americans been able to openly conduct ceremonies and worship as they please.

In the eighteen years in which I researched and wrote this book, innumerable people expressed interest and support for the project, and I am grateful. Wondrously, those who were the primary receivers of my enthusiasm are still speaking to me, John C. Rupert, Ann Newsom, and Diane Sainato. Thank you for the hours of listening to the latest in research and allowing me to bounce ideas off of you. Special thanks to Ann for traveling with me and helping with the initial research. Many other friends and relatives have read some version of the manuscript and helped with their comments: Jan Savage, Gerald Newsom, Mike Bergman, Ben Rupert, Earl Nelson, Rick Wohleber, Annette Bartz, Anne Filbert, and Bob France. Thanks to Sarah Giesman for graphic art advice for my website.

Numerous reference librarians and archivists have also been of invaluable aid in the researching of this book. Clara Ireland, the former archivist of the Rare Books Collection at the State Library of Ohio, brought an enthusiasm to her job that helped to build mine. John Sugden provided exceptional aid with factual editing and encouragement. I still may not have gotten it all right and any errors are mine. Ellen McCallister Clark of The Society of the Cincinnati was tireless in delving for useful information. Larry L. Nelson of Fort Meigs State Memorial, Ohio Historical Society provided encouragement and perspective early on. Joseph R. Fischer, author of *A Well-Executed Failure* gave me insight into Sullivan's campaign and the Iroquois. It also was my privilege to interview the author Ray Crain before his passing.

Many thanks to the archivists and historians who searched their collections for information on Oliver Spencer-- Laura E. Beardsley, The Historical Society of Pennsylvania; Stewart Butler, National Archives; John Diehl, The Literary Club of Cincinnati; Bette Epstein, New Jersey State Archives; Maureen D. Heher, Beinecke Rare Book and Manuscript Library, Yale University; Christy L. Kaciuba, Burlington County Library; Alfred Kleine-Kreutzmann, Public Library of Cincinnati & Hamilton County; Joan Lanphear, Burlington County Historical Society; Marie Lore, South Street Seaport Museum; Barbara McMillan, Mount Vernon Ladies' Association of the Union Library; Kelly Nolin, Connecticut Historical Society; Eric P. Olsen, Park Ranger and Historian, United States Dept. of the

Interior, National Park Service, Morristown National Historical Park; Carolyn M. Picciano, Connecticut State Library; Margaret M. Sherry, Princeton University; Ann K. Sindelar, Western Reserve Historical Society; Edward Skipworth, State University of New Jersey, Rutgers; Karl P. Stofko, DDS, Municipal Historian of East Haddam, CT; Garry Wheeler Stone, Monmouth Battlefield State Park, New Jersey Park Service; Jean Zajac, New Jersey Historical Society; and the staff of the New York Historical Society.

Marc Arguin, April Miller, and Dan Somers of the National Archives of Canada each provided information that helped me to choose and acquire microfilm that I needed. Christine Colburn, The Newberry Library provided John Graves Simcoe information. George Ironside was sorted by Myrtle Anderson-Smith, Aberdeen University Library; Bob Garcia, Fort Malden National Historic Park, Amhertsburg, Ontario, Canada; John Gibson, Burton Historical Collection, Detroit Public Library; Madeline Malott; and B. Carpenter, Devon Record Office, Exeter, England.

Benjamin Helle, Ohio Historical Society; Fred Sisser III; and Dr. David Riley, University of Medicine and Dentistry of New Jersey helped with enquiries into the Hunt family. Thanks to Norwood A. Kerr, State of Alabama, Dept. of Archives and History; and Kevin Grace, Archives and Rare Books, University of Cincinnati in relation to the Semmes family. Additional information on the *Felicity* was gleaned from the staff of the Milwaukee Public Library. Janice Beattie, NOAA Central Library, helped with a library tour and information on a hurricane. Tony McPherson of the Logan County Historical Society helped with the mystery of Manary's Blockhouse. Boyd Ann McElroy, Georgetown, Brown County looked into William Moore. Many thanks to Daisy Hagan-Bolen, Interlibrary Loan, Columbus Metropolitan Library, for filling numerous requests. Last but not least, thanks to the staffs at the State Library of Ohio and the reading room of the Ohio Historical Society.

ABBREVIATIONS USED

ASPIA	*American State Papers, Class II, Indian Affairs.*
ASPMA	*American State Papers, Military Affairs.*
AWW	*As We Were—the Story of Old Elizabethtown*, Thayer.
BHC	Burton Historical Collection, Detroit Public Library.
CHS	Cincinnati Historical Society
GWP	George Washington Papers [microform], Series 4, Film 1883.
HPCL	*The Harmar Papers from the Clements Library.*
IC	*Indian Captivity*, O.M. Spencer. Lane & Sandford.
JME	*Journals of the Military Expedition of Major General John Sullivan Against Six Nations of Indians in 1779.*
LFP	Ledyard Family Papers, Cornell University.
LRSW	Letters received by the Secretary of War, Registered Series.
NJJ	*New Jersey Journal.*
TWS	*The Western Spy.*
NWTT	Northwest Territory Transcripts.
OHS	Ohio Historical Society.
PCC	Papers of the Continental Congress.
PWHH	The Papers of William Henry Harrison, [microform].
RABSP	Records of Ante-Bellum Southern Plantations, Series I, Part 2, Nathaniel Evans.
RMSIA	Records of the Michigan Superintendency of Indian Affairs.
USBIA	United States Bureau of Indian Affairs, Piqua Agency.
WGW	*The Writings of George Washington.*
WSP	*Winthrop Sargent Papers.*

xi *Then to have sat down:* Baily, 103.

Chapter One, Colonel Spencer's Journey West

1 *a wild lush land:* IC, 32-33.
2 *the family tannery:* Gales, 14; *AWW,* 166.
2 *two ships:* Inspection roll of Negroes, 23 April, 1783, M332, Miscellaneous PCC, 1774-1789; Robert Spencer is listed as Master of the Dove, 22 January, 1785, Pennsylvania Court of Admiralty, Historical Society of Pennsylvania; British Headquarters Papers, Box-20, #4241, Box-36, #9183, New York Public Library. The sloop Spencer, Foster, master, Burlington, is arrived at Baltimore, *New York Gazetteer,* 5 Sept 1786, in Wilson; Schermerhorn, 303.
2 *"a most violent hurricane":* NJJ, January 23, 1788.
3 *"[He] sailed from hence":* Oliver Spencer to the Honorable Samuel Spencer, Esq., 12 Aug, 1788, *LFP.*
3 *Their ancestor Gerard:* Bremer, 1; Spencer, *Spencers of the Great Migration*; Jacobus, 81
3 *"left England on account of the persecutions":* IC, 5-6.
4 *"Come over and help us":* Emerson, 31.
4 *Lecar:* "Oliver Lecar Spencer" signer of a petition relating to roads, 14 Feb, 1764, *Calendar of the NJ State Library Ms. Collections.*
4 *descendant of Puritans:* Earle, 224.
4 *Elizabethtown, New Jersey:* Westergaard, 89.
5 *Uncle Elihu Spencer:* Hatfield, 395; Drake, *Dictionary of American Biography,* 447; Pilling, 158.
5 *"bleed, plead, or preach":* Symmes to Robert Morris, 2 March, 1796, in *Intimate Letters of John Cleves Symmes,* 82.
5 *"good wives Deserve good Husbands":* Oliver Spencer to Calvin Spencer, 19 Aug, 1789. Princeton Archives.
5 *Samuel...died of smallpox:* Cone, 69; Gales, 9.
5 *Machimoodus:* Stofko, 1.
6 *"enlarged and liberal ideas":* Gales, 10.
6 *"[s]laves, Servants, apprentices,":* AWW, 112.
6 *tannery:* TWS, 2 Feb, 1811.

Chapter Two, Earning a Reputation

7   *a Major in the NJ militia:* New Jersey Adjutant-General's Office, 355.

7   *battle of Springfield, 1776: TWS,* 2 Feb 1811; Meisner, Chapter VIII.

8   *"Waldeckers":* Meisner, Chapter VIII.

8   *"Blue Mountain Valley":* Hatfield, 410; M247, r 82, i68, p89, PCC; Gales, 12; Coriell, 2: 207.

9   *"at the Minisink":* To Lord Stirling, 16 Nov, 1778, *WGW;* To Brigadier General Edward Hand, 20 Nov, 1778, *WGW;* To Count Pulaski, 26 Nov, 1778, *WGW;* Manning, 277, 279.

10   *a base for launching raids:* Forry, 158; Graymont, 172.

10   *"making or repairing roads":* To Colonel William Malcom, 17-18 April, 1779, *WGW.*

10   *"such character and rank":* To The President of Congress, 3 March,1779, *WGW.*

11   *"Altho I wish to serve my country":* Colonel Oliver Spencer to George Washington, 14 April, 1779, GWP.

11   *"injury to the service":* To Colonel William Malcolm, 17, 18 April, 1779, *WGW.*

11   *Malcom decided:* To Colonel Oliver Spencer, 29 April,1779, *WGW.*

12   *"Robert, who was paymaster":* Robert Spencer was paymaster from 1 April, 1777 to 12 May, 1779, Genealogy Society Revolutionary War slips (pension), Rejt. #8097 (Wm. Penney), General Abstracts of Revolutionary War Pension Files, New Jersey State Archives, Trenton, New Jersey.

12   *the trouble continued:* To James Duane, 26 May, 1779, *WGW.*

12   *"rash measures":* Spencer to Washington, 30 April, 1779, GWP.

12   *Malcom's New York Companies of men:* To Colonel William Malcom, 29 April,1779, *WGW.*

12   *"confusion" and "dissatisfaction":* To Colonel Oliver Spencer, 29 April,1779, *WGW.*

12   *"a spirit, of which"*: To Colonel Oliver Spencer, 3 May, 1779, *WGW.*

13   *"The first object"*: To Colonel Oliver Spencer, 3 May, 1779, *WGW.*

13   *work on the roads:* To Colonel Oliver Spencer, 7 May, 1779, *WGW*; Hardenbergh, 14-16 May, 1779, and notes, 118; Detachment Orders, undated, EAOB, Spencer's Additional Regiment, No. 86, June 1779-24 July, 1779, Reel 7, 3.

13   *"just got acquainted"*: Spencer to Hand, 4 June, 1779, Emmet # 6722 (Oliver Spencer), New York Public Library.

14   *"his most sincere thanks"*: Detachment Orders, June 14, 1779, EAOB, No. 86, June 1779-24 July, 1779, Reel 7, 7-8.

14   *"The expedition...is to be directed"*: Stryker, *General Maxwell's Brigade*, 59-66.

14   *"The number of towns"*: Sullivan, *JME,* 303-304.

14   *the Iroquois fled:* G. Johnson to Col. Claus, Niagara, 31 Nov, 1779; D. Claus to John Johnson, Montreal, 26 June, 1780; D. Claus to Captain Matthews, Montreal, 30 Nov, 1780; Claus, Daniel and Family Fonds, C-1483, Reel 8; Howard, *Thundergate: The Forts of Niagara,* 140-141; Draper Mss., 4S40.

16   Coohcoocheeh is very similar to Nooch,coom,tha, the word for Grandmother. Telephone conversation with Don Greenfeather on 18 Feb, 1997; Thom, 273.

16   *last battle of the Revolution:* Gales, 20.

16   *"superintend the hospitals"*: Pracaness, 14 July, 1780, EAOB, No. 113, Reel 11.

16   *"commendation in lieu of half pay for life"*: PCC, M247, r163, i149, v3, p349.

CHAPTER THREE, STRUGGLE FOR OHIO

17   *Stites' settlement:* Ferris, 252-253.

17   *about the Shawnee:* Howard, *Shawnee!,* 1; Sugden, *Blue Jacket,* 10, 19, 25, 37-38; Hurt, *The Ohio Frontier,* 12; Calloway, *Shawnees and the War for America,* 44-

48, 59-64; Thwaites, 157-162. John Stuart's account originally from the Draper Manuscripts, 6NN105-12.

20   *land fever:* Hildreth, *Pioneer History,* 142.

20   *Joseph Brant, land confederation:* Graymont, 53; John Sugden, e-mail letter, 26 Aug, 2008.

21   *Moluntha:* Sugden, *Blue Jacket,* 68-69, 74-79; Downes, 298; Hurt, 98-99; Denny, 93-94.

23   *Benjamin Stites:* Ferris, no. 9: 252-253.

23   *Symmes and the land:* Symmes, *Correspondence,* 15, 46; Symmes, "Introduction," *Intimate Letters,* xv-xvii; "Judge John Cleves Symmes," *Ohio Historical and Arch. Quarterly* 30 (1921): 75-76; McBride, "John Cleves Symmes," *Pioneer Biography,* 2: 226-228; Ferris 1, no. 9, 254-258, 272, 274.

CHAPTER FOUR, SETTLING COLUMBIA

27   *George Ash, white captive:* Symmes, *Correspondence,* 58-59; Sugden, *Blue Jacket,* 121; Draper Mss. 13CC58.

27   *Lt. Jacob Kingsbury:* Heitman, *Historical Register and Dictionary of the United States Army,* Vol. 1.

28   *"Do not shoot":* Symmes, *Correspondence,* 59.

28   *Symmes gesture of peace:* Symmes, *Correspondence,* 47.

28   *"many curiosities they saw":* Ferris, *Pub.* 1, no. 9: 259-262.

29   *resourceful Kingsbury:* Symmes, *Correspondence,* 61.

29   *Picket fort:* Ferris, 1, no. 9: 262.

29   *Seven men:* McBride, "Thomas Irwin," *Pioneer Biography* 1: 110. Symmes, *Correspondence,* 60.

29   *difficult winter:* Ford, 47; Greve, 1: 178

30   *Northbend:* Symmes, *Correspondence,* 61-63, 75, 76; Ferris, 262.

30   *settlers crops:* Ferris, 264; McBride, "John Reily," *Pioneer Biography* 1: 12.

31   *Elder Stephen Gano: IC,* 30; McBride, "John Reily," *Pioneer Biography* 1: 28.

31   *Elder John Smith:* Dunlevy, 16-23.

31   *Jonathan Dayton:* "Jonathan Dayton,"; Symmes, *Correspondence,* 54.

31   *the attack anticipated:* Symmes, *Correspondence,* 96-97.

32   *Spencer's Bounty Land Warrant:* Craig, 5; Mss. No. 9901, pg. 130, Land Warrant No. 1994, New Jersey State Archives.

32   *Spencer "sets out tomorrow":* Dayton to Symmes, 16 May, 1789, in Symmes, *Correspondence.*

32   *"such a continued throng":* Symmes, *Correspondence,* 141

32   *a farm on the Ohio:* Symmes, *Correspondence,* 101.

32   *"There are very few hills":* Symmes, *Correspondence,* 79-80.

33   *Arthur St. Clair:* Heitman, Vol. 1; Simcoe, *Correspondence,* 1: 21, note.

34   *Joseph Brant believed:* Stone, 2: 284, 328-9.

34   *"From the misconduct":* Sword, 53-65.

34   *"A jealousy subsisted":* Stone, 2: 280.

34   *a copy of a letter:* Collins, 2: 433.

34   *"promise and flatter":* Symmes, *Correspondence,* 104

34   *Symmes chose Freeman:* Symmes, *Correspondence,* 92-93.

35   *"to rout these settlers":* Symmes to Dayton, 17 July, 1789. Symmes, *Correspondence.*

35   *never a legitimate purchase:* John Sugden, e-mail letter, 26 Aug, 2008

35   *peace and health:* Ferris, 264.

35   *he was very pleased:* Symmes, *Correspondence,* 264.

35   *well-built blockhouse:* Symmes, *Correspondence,* 103.

35   *Spencer bought land:* IC, 14

35   *428 acres:* Craig, *Columbia Township Hamilton County, OH Tax list—1796,* 5.

35   *Bounty Land Warrant:* BLW #1994-500-11, June 1789, Colonel in the New Jersey Line, no papers, in General Abstracts of Rev. War Pension Files, New Jersey State Archives; Mss. No. 9901, pg 130, Land Warrant No. 1994, 11 June, 1789, New Jersey State Archives.

35   *contracted to have a cabin:* IC, 7.

35 *"Col Spencer is accommodated":* Symmes to Dayton, 17 July, 1789, in Symmes, *Correspondence.*

36 *his horse became lame:* Symmes, *Correspondence,* 226.

36 *"Time is on the wing":* Oliver Spencer to Captain Calvin Spencer, Aug 19, 1789, in Princeton University Archives.

36 *Fort Washington:* Symmes, *Correspondence,* 235, 123, 129.

36 *John and Obadiah:* Ferris, 264-265; Jones, *History of Cincinnati and the territory of Ohio,* 59.

37 *when the Indians scalp:* Paraphrased from McBride, "Daniel Doty," *Pioneer Biography,* 2: 183.

37 *on a stake:* Jones, *History of Cincinnati and the territory of Ohio,* 59.

38 *"By information":* Report from H. Knox, Secretary of War, to the President of the United States, in *American State Papers, Class II, Indian Affairs,* 1:12-13.

39 *Antoine Gamelin:* "Mr. Gamelin's Journal," in *American State Papers, Class II, Indian Affairs,* 1: 93.

39 *Blue Jacket:* John Sugden, e-mail letter, 26 Aug, 2008; Sugden, *Blue Jacket,* 8, 24-27.

CHAPTER FIVE, THE FAMILY'S JOURNEY WEST

41 *Colonel Spencer's description:* IC, 7-8.

41 *"The affair is serious":* Thayer, 93-94.

42 *"a swashbuckling youth":* Thayer, 106.

42 *Francis Barber: Edwards, 19.*

42 *Aaron Ogden:* Thayer, 107-108; Ogden, "Autobiography," 13-31; Card catalog biography of Robert Ogden, NJ Hist. Soc., from *History and Directory of Warren County,* 78.

43 *The whole town:* Thayer, 120.

43 *The first few days...of their journey:* IC. 8-10.

44 *Before the application of steam:* IC, 10-11.

45 *Harmar's army:* ASPMA 1:20-21, 24-25; Denny, 146-149.

46 *The people at Columbia:* Ferris, 279.

46 *"I hope sir you":* Symmes, *Correspondence,* 133-135.

47   *"inviting to a charm":* Ibid, 133-135.

47   *a melancholy pleasure: IC,* 11-13.

CHAPTER SIX, BURNING ABNER HUNT

49   *The broad and extensive plain: IC,* 13-15.
49   *both church and school:* Ferris, 267.
49   *Turkey bottom: IC,* 34; Greve, 1:78.
50   *making do:* Ferris, 273-274.
50   *Wickerham's floating mill: IC,* 31.
51   *The boys began school:* Ferris, 321.

51   *John Reily: A Sketch of the Life and Character of John
      Reily, Dec'd.*

51   *girls learned at home:* Earle, *Child Life in Colonial Days,* 95.
51   *Benjamin Davis's cabin:* Greve, 1: 180.
51   judge of county court: "Proceedings of Oliver Spencer,
      Judge of Probate in & for the county of Hamilton,
      Territory of the U.S. Northwest of the River Ohio,"
      Abstract of Book 1 & Book A, Probate Record, 1791-1826.
51   *officers of the army:* Ferris, 322.
51   *planning a siege:* Jacob Kingsbury to Josiah Harmar,
      12 Jan, 1791, *HPCL,* 290-291.
51   *Big Bottom: ASPIA,* 1: 121.
51   *remaining two hundred warriors:* Sword, 126; Greve, 1:
      285.
52   *four surveyors:* Cone, "Indian Attack on Fort Dunlap,"
      Ohio Arch. and Hist. Quarterly, 17: 65; McBride, "John
      Reily," *Pioneer Biography,* 1: 13-22.
52   *Fort Dunlap:* Scamyhorn, 65.
52   *the surveyors:* Greve, 1: 285.
52   *Hunterdon Co.:* Indentures in 1790 show that Daniel Hunt
      of Lebanon Township and Ralph Hunt of Maidenhead
      Township were both of Hunterdon County, New Jersey.
      Daniel and Ralph Hunt were cousins, as stated in John
      Cleves Symmes to Daniel Hunt, 17 Nov, 1788. Then
      Symmes to Daniel Hunt, 6 June, 1789, shows that Ralph
      Hunt was Abner's brother. Also see footnote 34. William
      Hunt Family Papers, Ms. 1000, OHS.

52 *purchased land:* Symmes, *Symmes Purchase Records,* 96.

52 *Along with his father:* Burress, , 13; and Proceedings of Oliver Spencer, Judge of Probate, *Abstract of Book 1 & Book A, Probate Record,* 42.

52 *in exchange for land:* Symmes, *Correspondence,* 86.

52 *Abner associated with Symmes:* Symmes, "Gentlemen who managed the lottery," in *Symmes Purchase Records,* 16.

52 *surveyor: Sketch of the Life and Character of John Reily, Dec'd,* 4; and Symmes to Daniel Hunt, 6 June, 1789, "...Abner has been over [the Miami lands] several times...[and agrees] that it is a most excellent tract of land," William Hunt Family Papers, Ms. 1000, OHS.

52 *The Indians frequently:* Hildreth, 169-176.

53 *"I despise such low cunning:* John Cleves Symmes to Daniel Hunt, 6 June 1789, William Hunt Family Papers, Ms. 1000, OHS.

54 *the attack on Fort Dunlap: IC,* 15-17, Cone, "Indian Attack on Fort Dunlap," *Ohio Arch. & Hist. Society Quarterly* 17: 65-69; Greve, 1: 284-286; Scamyhorn, 67; McBride, "John Reily," *Pioneer Biography,* 1: 17-20; Jacob Kingsbury to Josiah Harmar, 12 Jan, 1791, in Harmar, *The Harmar Papers from the Clements Library, Ann Arbor, Michigan,* 290-291; 10 January, 1791 was a Monday; Ellicott, *Ellicott's Maryland and Virginia almanac, and ephemeris, for the year of our Lord 1791;* Symmes to Dayton, 1 Jan, 1790, 9 Jan, 1790, and 30 April, 1790, in Symmes, *Correspondence; IC,* 15-16; Ferris, 269-270; *A Sketch of the Life and Character of John Reily, Dec'd,* 4.

60 *Captain Trueman:* Heitman, 1: 972.

61 *splendid ball: IC, 28-29.*

61 *to encourage settlement:* Blum, 48: 10.

63 *attack on Spencer cabin:* Cist, 173; *IC,* 17-18; McBride, "John Reily," *Pioneer Biography,* 1: 25.

64 *pursued the trail:* Including Captains Flinn and Kilby, John Reily, and Thomas Irwin. McBride, "John Reily," *Pioneer Biography,* 1: 26; *IC,* 19.

65 *March 27:* Cist, 173.

65   *Plasket's boat:* OM Spencer mentions the attack on
      Plasket's boat in his response to an inquiry from Dr.
      Daniel Drake for an anniversary celebration in Cinci.,
      OM Spencer to Dr. Daniel Drake, 23 Dec, 1831.
      Draper Mss. 1O15 to 15-3.
65   *"Yonder comes a flatboat":* Ferris, 284-285.

CHAPTER SEVEN, THE LARGEST DEFEAT

67   *"The Indians kill":* Symmes, *Correspondence*, 143.
67   *Charles Scott:* Ward, 96, 105; *IC,* 17.
67   *James Wilkinson:* Jacobs, 123.
67   *attack on Wabash Indians:* Jacobs, 2-14, 68-69, 74, 76,
      79, 81, 84, 106-109, 128-129; Coombs, vii-viii; Ferris,
      262; *IC, 17.*
68   *battle of St. Clair: IC,* 20-22, 25; Sargent, *"Winthrop
      Sargent's Diary,"* 33: 342, 252.
69   *"Our fathers used to do":* Sugden, *Shawnee in
      Tecumseh's Time*, 57.
70   *General Butler bio:* Denny, 7-8 of the introduction.
70   *Now Butler responded:* Denny, 164-165; Sargent,
      "Winthrop Sargent's Diary," 33: 257-258; Michael
      McDonald to Patrick McDonald, 12: 66-68.
71   *lounge in their tents: IC,* 22.
71   *blue skies:* Sargent, *"Winthrop Sargent's Diary,"* 33: 253.
71   *"damnedest noise imaginable":* Michael McDonald to
      Patrick McDonald, 12: 66-68.
71   *the battle:* Sargent, *"Winthrop Sargent's Diary,"* 33: 253,
      259-261, 268-269; *IC, 22-25;* Denny, introduction 15-18,
      165-167; Michael McDonald to Patrick McDonald, 12: 66-
      68; Buchman, 40;
76   *men coming in from the woods:* Ferris, 290; Greve, 1: 339.
77   *dismay throughout the region:* John Cleves Symmes to
      Dr. Boudinot, 12 Jan, 1792, in Symmes, *Intimate
      Letters*, 123.
77   *"a good gun":* McBride, "Daniel Doty." *Pioneer
      Biography*, 2: 186-186.
78   *Winthrop Sargent:* Sargent to Spencer, 9 March, 1792,
      NWTT, OHS (*NWTT* microfilm edition, roll 1: 451);

Pershing,, "Winthrop Sargent: A Builder in the Old

Old Northwest," 6, in The WSP. [microform], Reel 1, Frame 004.

78 *"alleging that we ourselves are in danger"*: Spencer to Sargent, 10 March, 1792, WSP [microform], Reel 3, Frame 354-5.

78 *Columbia "will be greatly exposed"*: Sargent to Spencer, 11 March, 1792, *NWTT*, OHS (*NWTT* microfilm edition, roll 1: 452-453).

79 *frequent drafts of the militia*: Spencer to Sargent, 11 March, 1792, WSP [microform], Reel 3, Frame 356-7.

79 *Indians more active*: Spencer to Aaron Ogden, 31 Aug 1792, Gratz, Historical Society of Pennsylvania.

79 *Alcott, Newell, and Ball*: IC, 17; Ferris, 315-317

CHAPTER EIGHT, THE CAPTURE

81 *futility of resistance*: ASPIA, 1: 229-230

81 *An early and delightful spring*: IC, 32-35.

84 *made his own arrangements*: Spencer to Aaron Ogden, 31 Aug, 1792, Gratz, Historical Society of Pennsylvania.

85 *three peace messengers*: Heckewelder, 269.

85 *"Soon after my arrival"*: Putnam, 272-274.

87 *two days playing*: IC, 36-38; Ferris, 322.

87 *awash in goods*: Heckewelder.

87 *"the class that congregates"*: Finley, 105.

87 *Saturday*: Banneker, *1792*.

87 *his sisters had already gone*: Ferris, 322.

88 *"food for the Indians"*: Ferris, 322.

90 *the capture*: IC, 36-45.

94 *treatment from the Army surgeon*: Heckewelder, 271.

95 *"If they have determined"*: Ferris, 323; IC, 46.

95 *Mrs. Coleman*: Military History of Ohio, Logan Co., 118; McBride, *Pioneer Biography*, "John Reily," 1: 38.

95 *shocked and alarmed*: Ferris, 323.

96 *"I send to apprize you"*: Wilkinson to John Armstrong, 7 July, 1792, in Cist, *Cincinnati Miscellany*, 46.

96 *feelings of his parents*: IC, 47

CHAPTER NINE, ESCAPE!

98   *dawning of July 8: IC,* 48.

98   *"It would be some relief":* Ferris, 324.

99   *"so good natured":* Draper Mss., 14CC13-16, report of James Boushy (Beasley?), who arrived some months after the capture and lived 15 miles below Cincinnati. Boushy was confused as to the status of the other boy living with the Spencers. He thought that the boy was their nephew, not Ollie's.

99   *"Yesterday a canoe":* Rufus Putnam to Henry Knox, there is a note on the final page of the letter from the Historical Society of Pennsylvania saying that the following letter was enclosed in a letter to GW from Knox on 5 Aug, 1792, George Washington Papers, Series 4, 1792 May 8 - 1793 Jan 9.

99   *cream-colored horse: IC,* 48-50.

101   *"Truth-Bearer":* Howard, 180; *IC,* 50.

101   *blue silk vest: IC,* 86.

101   *tornado: IC,* 51-52.

102   *"On the 7th":* Wilkinson to Knox, 9 July, 1792, in Knopf, *Wayne Papers,* Historical Society of Pennsylvania, Vol. 20.

104   *old black horse: IC,* 53.

105   *escape: IC, 53-57.*

CHAPTER TEN, PUNISHMENT

108   *The sun set: IC, 57-61.*

109   *"I have been out picking raspberries": IC,* 61.

109   *punishment: IC, 61-65.*

110   *continued travels: IC, 65-73.*

115   *"greasy leather leggings": IC,* 86.

116   *Jonathan Alder:* Alder, 3-4, 8, 11-20.

CHAPTER ELEVEN, A NEW MOTHER

120   *Meecheway:* Telephone conversation with Don Greenfeather on 18 Feb, 1997; *IC,* 116.

120 *Simo-ne and So-tone-goo: IC,* 78.

121 *the Iroquois: IC,* 74-76; Richter, 9-10, 14-15, 17-19, 23-24, 32-39, 52-53, 55-56, 59, 62, 115-116, 125, 136-137; Snow, 1, 5, 15, 21, 29, 54, 58-62, 80, 82-83, 96-98, 109-110, 114-116, 121, 125.

125 *Cokundiawthah: IC,* 76-78.

126 *Coohcoocheeh's bark cabin: IC,* 78-81.

129 *all produce was theirs:* Hurt, 22.

129 *given up hope of escaping: IC,* 82-83.

129 *Black Swamp:* Gordon, 24.

130 *native dress: IC,* 84-86.

132 *visit to the Shawnee village: IC,* 86-89.

133 *description of Girty:* Butterfield, 323, 6-9.

135 *Katepakomen:* Johansen, "Girty, Simon (Katepakomen) (Seneca-Wyandot), 1741-1818," in *Encyclopedia of the Haudenosaunee.*

135 *General Hand and Squaw campaign:* Thwaites, 2, note 3; Hand to Crawford, 5 Feb, 1778, 202; Hand to Ewing, 7 March, 1778, 215; 217-220; Forry, 141-144; Butterfield, 50-54, 61-62, 79.

137 *"He was good to me":* Butterfield, 80.

137 *As a league warrior:* Johansen.

138 *"able to trepan him":* Butterfield, 89.

138 *Simo-ne: IC,* 78.

138 *Girty's wives:* Johansen, 115-116; Butterfield, 55.

CHAPTER TWELVE, WILLIAM MOORE AND
THE GREEN CORN FESTIVAL

140 *George Ironside:* Ironside Family File; Hay, 228, note 40; e-mail, Myrtle Anderson-Smith, 16 Feb. 1996; *IC,* 90-91.

141 *burned their homes themselves:* "David Morris's Account," Draper Mss., 4JJ4.

141 *Miamitown:* 221-225, 233.

142 *people at The Point: IC,* 90-91.

142 *British storehouse:* Buchman, 34.

143 *"no fear of GOD":* Jones, *A Journal of two visits,* 9.

143   *"Would it not stamp disgrace":* Wayne to Knox, 3 Aug, 1792, in Knopf, *Wayne Papers*, Vol. 20.

144   *"I have received your favor":* Knox to Sargent, 8 Aug, 1792, Winthrop Sargent Papers, Reel 3, Frame 523-4.

144   *Colonel John Francis Hamtramck:* Heitman, Vol. 1.

144   *"I condole with Colonel Spencer":* Hamtramck to Sargent, 9 Aug, 1792, Winthrop Sargent Papers, Reel 3, Frame 525.

144   *his townsman William Moore: IC,* 91-93.

144   *William Moore a Baptist:* Burress, 51.

144   *William Moore a Pennsylvanian:* Drake, 115; Draper Mss. 1O22-1.

146   *William Moore's gauntlet: IC,* 94.

147   *Green Corn Festival: IC,* 95-106.

148   *"Me kill um": IC,* 26.

153   *Roasting Ear Dance:* Sugden, *Shawnee in Tecumseh's Time,* 76.

154   *Drunken song: IC,* 102-103.

Chapter Thirteen, Becoming Indian

155   *The family was not too worried:* Spencer to Aaron Ogden, 31 Aug, 1792, Gratz, Historical Society of PA.

155   *Samuel H. Parsons drowned: NJJ,* 31 Dec, 1789.

156   *"step by step":* Spencer to Sargent, 15 Sept, 1792, Winthrop Sargent Papers, Reel 3, Frame 543.

156   *September 14 birthday: IC,* 106; Jacobus, 181-183.

156   *Minister Plenipotentiary:* Bindoff, 184.

156   *"Agreeably to your request":* Knox to Washington, 16 Sept, 1792, Henry Knox Papers.

156   *private request:* Spencer Family File, CHS, 9.

156   *shooting fish: IC,* 103, 82-83.

158   *William Wells:* Hamtramck to Sargent, 6 Feb, 1793, WSP; Draper Mss. 21S57; Draper Mss. 23S62, Darius Heald interview; John Johnston to Sec. Of War Eustis, 6 Nov, 1810, Letters Received by the Secretary of War, Registered Series, Roll 38, Jan. 1810-Oct. 1811; Young, 179; Draper Mss.

13CC146, W. Curry, Jr. interview; Hamtramck to Eustis, Enclosure in William Wells to Eustis, 25 Jun, 1809, LRSWRS; Heckewelder, 271.

158   *conversation with William Wells: IC,* 107-108; Simcoe, *Correspondence of Lt. Gov. John Graves Simcoe,* 5: 18-19.

159   *nexus of peoples:* Sugden, *Blue Jacket,* 135; Buchman, 28, 30, 32.

160   *"there were so many nations":* Butterfield, 274.

160   *Cornplanter:* Johansen, *Encyclopedia of Native American Biography,* 83-85.

160   *native positions:* Buchman, *The Confluence,* 46-48; John Sugden, e-mail letter, 26 Aug, 2008.

161   *"We do not want compensation":* Sugden, *Blue Jacket,* 138.

161   *the Seneca and 1793 conference:* Buchman, 67-68.

161   *"raise hell to prevent a peace":* ASPIA, 1: 244; Butterfield, 272.

162   *Coohcoocheeh's divination: IC,* 108-109.

163   *attack on Fort St. Clair:* McBride, *Pioneer Biography,* 1: 219-224; Butterfield, 274; Ehler, Ralph B. "The Story of Fort St. Clair." *Ohio Archaeological and Historical Quarterly* 32 (1923): 518.

164   *Catawa-waqua's attack:* Spencer Family File, 8.

164   *"I have forwarded":* Simcoe to Hammond, *Correspondence of Lieut. Governor John Graves Simcoe,* 1: 262.

165   *killing a wildcat: IC,* 110-113.

166   *lynx:* Canadensis, Raf., was numerous in the county up to 1845. The animal is forty inches in length, of a grayish color, having ears with a narrow black margin on the convexity, and tipped with a black pencil, and the end of the tail terminating in black brush. "The limbs of the lynx are very powerful, and the thick, heavily made feet are furnished with strong, white claws that are not seen unless the fur be put aside. It is not a dangerous animal except when attacked, when it is a match for more than half a dozen dogs." Williamson, 373-374.

168   *beaver's song: IC,* 114.

169   *troublesome Indians:* Spencer to Aaron Ogden, 31 Aug. 1792, Gratz, Historical Society of PA.

169 *"you also well know"*: Aaron Ogden to Jonathan Dayton, 10 Dec, 1792, New Jersey Parks Department.

169 *"Immediately after"*: R.G. England to J.G. Simcoe, 29 Dec, 1792, in *Correspondence of Lieut. Governor John Graves Simcoe*, 1: 271.

170 *On a very cold morning: IC, 115-117.*

171 *immerse himself:* Wells, "Indian manners and customs," *The Western Review*, 2 (Feb 1820): 45-46; Sugden, *Shawnee in Tecumseh's Time*, 43.

171 *narrowly escaped death: IC, 103-104.*

CHAPTER FOURTEEN, RANSOMED

173 *"I enclose for Your perusal"*: Simcoe, *Correspondence of Lt. Gov. John Graves Simcoe*, 5: 18-19.

173 *"Will you be so good"*: Hamtramck to Sargent, 6 Feb, 1793, WSP.

173 *near the close of February: IC, 117-122.*

177 *Joseph Blanche: IC, 122.*

178 *George Sharp:* George Sharp biography, BHC.

178 *Matthew Elliott:* Nelson, 46-49, 52; Horsman, 1-21, 32.

180 *his hapless situation: IC, 122.*

183 *they reached the rapids: IC, 127.*

183 *storehouse at the Rapids:* Horsman, 60-70.

183 *Alexander McKee:* Nelson, 24-32, 49, 62, 88-101, 110, 114, 127-129, 160.

184 *John Brickell:* Brickell, 1: 46-50.

185 *at the Wyandot camp: IC, 127-129.*

CHAPTER FIFTEEN, A JONAH

187 *bread and butter, a bath, Mrs. Andre, Detroit: IC, 129-134.*

191 *sloop Felicity: IC, 135;* Local History Index, BHC.

192 *"It gives me much pleasure"*: R.G. England to J.G. Simcoe, 17 March, 1792, in *CJGS*, 1: 302.

193 *Wapawaqua's attack:* Draper Mss., 6S186-192.

196 *attempts to cross Lake Erie: IC, 136-143.*

202   *Niagara Falls: IC,* 143, 146-148.

203   *Seneca at Niagara:* Kalm, 1: 703-707.

204   *"You may privately mention":* J.G. George Hammond to
      E.B. Littlehales, 16 April, 1793, in *Correspondence of
      Lieut. Governor John Graves Simcoe,* 1: 314.

205   *"infected by Republicanism":* Van Steen, 72.

Chapter sixteen, home again

206   *Lt. and Mrs. Hill: IC,* 143-146.

208   *Fort Niagara: IC,* 146-148.

209   *"miserably little wooden house":* Van Steen, 129.

209   *Simcoe a young British officer:* Riddell, 40-43; 69, note
      6; 76, 80.

209   *account of the battle: The Battle of Brandywine,* Smith,
      Samuel Stelle.

209   *Colonel Spencer at Battle of Brandywine:* Spencer was in
      Conway's Brigade under General Stirling at Brandywine.
      General Orders. May 26, 1777. The Papers of George
      Washington, Revolutionary War Series, 9, Dorothy
      Twohig, editor. Pg. 531.

209   *Simcoe's captivity and escape plans:* Simcoe, *Military
      Journal,* 109-117, 264-288.

211   *Simcoe after the war:* Riddell, 81.

211   *"species of banishment":* Fryer, 120.

211   *Mr. Morris made some inquiries: IC,* 149.

212   *conduct of Elliott: IC,* 149-150.

212   *questionable practices:* Horsman, 117.

212   *Mrs. Simcoe: IC,* 150; Van Steen, 14-17.

213   *"to participate in the honor":* Oberholtzer, 265, 303-307.

213   *journey to Canandaigua: IC,* 150-151.

214   *native Canandaigua:* Early American Orderly Books, No.
      93, Reel 9; Cook, *Expedition:* Burrowes, 7 Sept, 1779,
      47; Nukerck, 10 Sept, 1779, 217; Jenkins, 10 Sept,
      1779, 174.

214   *time in Canandaigua and journey to New York City: IC,* 151-
      154.

218   *newspaper announcement of Ollie's return: IC,* 155; *NJJ,*

Wednesday, 17 July, 1793.

218   *an exhibition of wild beasts: IC,* 155.

219   *becoming Indian:* Ackerknecht, 29, 34.

CHAPTER SEVENTEEN, DEFEAT OF THE SHAWNEE

220   *watchman on the walls of Zion, IC,* 30.

220   *freshly taken Indian scalp:* Greve, 1:180.

220   *pan-Indian conference:* Sugden, *Blue Jacket,* 142-160.

221   *Wayne's camps:* Simmons, 19.

221   *Fort Recovery:* Sugden, *Blue Jacket,* 162-171.

222   *"Fasting, Humiliation, and Prayer":* Spencer to Sargent, 31 July, 1794, Winthrop Sargent Papers, Reel 3, Frame 862-863.

222   *Colonel Spencer's cannon:* Wayne to Spencer, 15 March, 1794, Wayne Papers, 699, Historical Society of Pennsylvania.

222   *Battle of Fallen Timbers:* quoted and paraphrased from Anthony Wayne's report, *ASPIA,* 1: 491.

224   *William Moore's escape:* Ford, 399.

224   *Shawnee after the war:* Sugden, *Blue Jacket,* 182-213

225   *Ollie's return to Ohio: IC,* 156-157.

CHAPTER EIGHTEEN, STRUGGLING TO THRIVE

226   *"characterized by a peculiar urbanity":* Cincinnati Daily Gazette, 6 June, 1838.

226   *O.M. elected county recorder and leaving for Natchez:* Hall, 8: 236-237.

226   *militia Quartermaster:* 12 July, 1803, RABSP.

226   *Oliver H an army surgeon:* Hall, 8: 236; Oliver H. Spencer to Winthrop Sargent, 6 Feb, 1803, The Winthrop Sargent Papers, Reel 6, Frame 319-320; Claiborne to Henry Dearborn, Sec. of War, 20 May, 1804, in Claiborne, *Official Letter Books of WCC Claiborne,* MS Territorial Archive, 2: 153.

226   *"The troops take possession":* O.H. to Evans, 20 Dec,

1803, RABSP.

227 *flag ceremony:* Marbois, 333.

227 *"I mounted the first guard":* O.M. to Evans, 3 Jan, 1804, RABSP.

227 *"I have not yet seen the ladies":* O.M. to Evans, 3 Jan, 1804, RABSP.

228 *Colonel Alexander Oliver:* Burress, 201.

228 *clerk at MEC:* Hall, 8: 239.

228 *Miami Exporting Company:* Katzenberger, 44: 206-207; 5 Dec, 1836, *Journal of the House,* 35th; Hall, 8: 243; Huntington, 24: 258-260.

229 *O.M. County Recorder:* Hall, 8: 239.

229 *"Colonel Spencer engaged to pay":* Joseph Bloomfield to Jonathan Dayton, Esq., 17 Nov, 1799. From the Collections of the Society of the Cincinnati.

229 *"In the county of Hamilton":* St. Clair to Timothy Pickering, Cincinnati, 30 Mar, 1800, in *St. Clair Papers,* 2: 495.

229 *Colonel Spencer's obituary:* Western Spy, 26 Jan, 1811; Symmes, "Sketch of the Life of Col. Oliver Spencer," *Western Spy,* 2 Feb, 1811.

230 *O.M.'s "solemn vow" to become minister:* Spencer Family File, CHS, 9; Hall, 8: 244;

230 *four year trial:* Conversation with Susan Cohen, Oct 1, 1996, Librarian, Ohio Wesleyan Methodist Archives.

230 *"Entre nous":* O.H. to Evans, Oct, 1813, RABSP.

230 *history of banking and land fever:* Huntington, 24: 267, 271; 5 Dec, 1836, *Journal of House 35th,* State Library of Ohio, 188.

230 *O.M. coped:* O.M. to Evans, 22 March, 1815, RABSP.

231 *native aims:* McAfee, 17-18.

231 *chiefs visited President Jefferson:* Sugden, *Blue Jacket,* 229.

231 *Captain Lewis:* Ohio Native Genealogy Cards, Center for Archival Collections, Bowling Green State U.; McKenny, 2: 55-57; Sugden, *Blue Jacket,* 229.

232 *Tecumseh, the Prophet, attempt at native revival:* Sugden, *Blue Jacket,* 231-252; Sugden, *Tecumseh, A Life,* 121, 136-137; McAfee, 17-18.

234   *"object of this Shawnese Prophets":* Wells to Dearborn, 25
        April, 1807, Letters Received by the Secretary of War,
        Registered Series, v.14 (May 1806-Jun 1807 [W76-W300]).

234   *Prophet removed to Wabash:* McAfee, 19-20.

234   *Blue Jacket died in 1808:* Sugden, *Blue Jacket,* 254.

234   *Tecumseh recruiting for the Prophet:* Sugden, *Tecumseh,
        A Life,* 181; McAfee, 19-20, 25-26.

235   *"to ratify all the treaties":* Liberty Hall, 4 Sept, 1811.

236   *Battle of Tippecanoe:* McAfee, 26-44.

236   *"Agrarian cupidity":* Roseboom and Weisenburger, 79-80.

CHAPTER NINETEEN, WAPAWAQUA AND THE AMERICAN CAUSE

237   *"There is not any danger":* 26 May, 1812, John
        Johnston letters, VFM 4875, OHS.

237   *protecting the Indians:* Perrin, 364.

237   *General William Hull:* Heitman, 553.

237   *Tecumseh at Fort Malden:* Sugden, *Tecumseh, A Life,* 285.

237   *Hull's invasion of Canada:* Horsman, 35-41.

238   *Harrison's army:* Roseboom, 81.

238   *"furnishing the Shawanoese":* Johnston to Harrison, 23
        Oct, 1812, *Messages and Letters of William Henry
        Harrison,* 2: 186.

238   *Catawa-waqua an American spy: IC,* 104

238   *"The [hostile] Indians":* Johnston to Harrison, 23 Oct, 1812,
        Messages and Letters of William Henry Harrison, 2: 186.

238   *"Malden to defend":* Harrison to Brig. Gen. Howard, 24
        May, 1813, in Letters received by the Secretary of War,
        Registered Series, 1801, 1860, Roll 53, Dec 1812-May
        1814 (G-H).

239   *O.M.'s "best gifts":* Spencer, "A Masonic Sermon
        delivered by brother O.M. Spencer, on the anniversary
        of St. John the Baptist, June 24th, A.L. 5813 A.D.
        1813," 3-10.

239   *"I rejoice to hear":* O.M. Spencer to Sarah B. Evans, 24
        Aug, 1813, RABSP.

239   *O.M.s Christian service:* 16 Sept, 1814, Methodist
        Episcopal Ohio Annual Journal, Mss. 1800-1826, 114;
        Hall, 8: 244.

239 *join war or move:* Klopfenstein, 26-27.

240 *Harrison and Proctor:* Slocum, 278-279; McAfee, 328.

240 *"Wyandots within our lines":* Johnston to Sec. of War, 3 Aug, 1813, *Messages and Letters of William Henry Harrison,* 2: 509.

240 *chiefs pledged warriors:* Knopf, *Document Transcriptions of The War of 1812 in the Northwest,* 5: 163.

240 *"conduct of the Shawanese":* 4 Sept, 1813, The Papers of William Henry Harrison, [microform] 19 Aug, 1813-19 March, 1814, Reel 9: 60.

241 *Battle of Lake Erie:* Roseboom, 81-82.

242 *progress of Army:* Slocum, 278-285.

242 *"take hold of the same tomahawk":* Harrison to Armstrong, 10 Oct, 1813, in LRSWRS, Roll 53, December 1812-May 1814 (G-H); Harrison Papers, [microform] 19 Aug, 1813-19 March, 1814, Reel 9: 402.

242 *Americans killed Tecumseh:* Slocum, 286-289; Knopf, *Document Transcriptions of The War of 1812 in the Northwest,* 5: 242; Roseboom, 81-82.

243 *discharged friendly Indians:* PWHH, 19 Aug, 1813-19 March, 1814, Reel 9: 560.

243 *"pay of the Indians":* Hill, 76.

243 *Brigadier General Lewis Cass:* www.aoc.gov/capitol-hill/national-statuary-hall-collection/lewis-cass

243 *Cass and band of select warriors:* Cass to Armstrong, 25, July, 1814, LRSWRS, Roll 60.

243 *natives did not want to fight other tribes:* McArthur to Armstrong, 31 Aug, 1814, LRSWRS, Roll 64.

243 *so alarm the country:* Cass to Monroe, 13 Aug, 1814, LRSWRS, Roll 60.

243 *plundering, but killing no one:* McArthur to Armstrong, 21 Aug, 1814, LRSWRS, Roll 64.

243 *requested more select Indians:* McArthur to Armstrong, 21 Aug, 1814, LRSWRS, Roll 64; McArthur to Monroe, 10 Sept, 1814, LRSWRS, Roll 64.

243 *seventy-four Shawnee:* McAfee, 481.

243 *Brigadier General Duncan McArthur:* Bio of Duncan McArthur at Ohio History Central,

www.ohiohistorycentral.org/entry.php?rec=256

244 *American attack on Canadian mills:* Slocum, 300-302; McAfee, 482-487.

245 *Indians cared for sick and wounded:* McArthur to Sec of War, 15 May, 1815, RMSIA, Letters Received and Sent, 1814-1818, Vol. 1.

245 *"I visited these Indians":* James Hughs to Gov. Worthington, Urbana, 20 May, 1815, John Johnston Papers, (microfilm edition, Roll 2, Frame 980), Box 2/ Folder 13, OHS.

246 *"collect the Indians":* Hill, 95.

246 *Wapawaqua commenced an annual visit: IC,* 157.

246 *O.M.'s thousands of acres:* Receiver Ledger W, Cincinnati Land Office, 1815-1829, OHS.

246 *Rum Creek:* Perrin, 562-563.

246 *O.M. and banking history:* Hall, 8: 244-245; Huntington, 24: 282, 298-299.

247 *O.M.'s service:* "Valuable Purchase," 4: 24; Hall, 8: 245.

247 *"That being out of business":* O. M. Spencer to General James Findlay, 7 April, 1826, in Torrence Papers. Historical and Philosophical Society of Ohio, CHS.

247 *O.M. on boards:* Wright, 55: 11; Perko, 38: 98.

247 *no scarcity of money:* Huntington, 24: 344.

248 *"Brother and the family":* Dorothy Meeks to Sarah Evans, 29 March, 1832, RABSP.

CHAPTER TWENTY, THE SHAWNEE JOURNEY WEST

249 *small Ohio reservations:* Klopfenstein, 32-33.

249 *"Quitawepea":* Ohio Native Genealogy Cards, Center for Archival Collections, Bowling Green State U.

249 *Lewistown reservation:* Kappler, 2: 145-155, 162-63.

249 *"emphasis on elevating":* Schoolcraft, 6: 737, Table IV.

249 *As O.M. wrote: IC,* 73.

249 *paid the warriors:* Wayne Agency, 1 Jan,1817, 24 April, 1817, RMSIA, Letters Received and Sent, 1814-1818, Vol. 2, April 24, 1817-June 3, 1818; Detroit, 18 April, 1819, RMSIA, Letters Sent, 1818-1823, Vol. 3, June 6, 1818-April 25, 1822.

250 *compensated for land improvements:* Cass to John Johnston, Detroit, 6 Aug, 1819, RMSIA, Letters Sent, 1818-1823, Vol. 3, June 6, 1818-April 25, 1822.

250 *"Under any circumstances":* Governor of Michigan territory to Sec of War, WH Crawford, Detroit, 11 May, 1816, RMSIA, Letters Received and Sent, 1814-1818, Vol. 1, May 31, 1814-April 17, 1817.

250 *"I do hope":* Cass to John Johnston, Detroit, 17 April, 1820, RMSIA, Letters Sent, 1818-1823, Vol. 3, June 6, 1818-April 25, 1822.

250 *"We are surrounded":* Jahoda, Chapter 1.

250 *Captain Lewis's confederacy:* Foreman, 184-198.

251 *"Wa pa Moek or White Loon":* Shawanoes and Senecas of Lewistown To his Excellency James Monroe President of the United States and the Honorable J.C. Calhoun, Secretary of War, Lewis Town, 10 Feb, 1824, USBIA, Roll 21, frame 270.

251 *"now that there is no publick":* Johnston to J.C. Calhoun Sec of War, 19 Jan, 1824, USBIA, Roll 21, frames 293-296.

251 *council with eastern Indians:* Foreman, 184-198.

251 *"The Indian Lewis":* Johnston to Thos. L. M. Kenny Esqr., Indian Office, Piqua, April 11, 1825, Records. USBIA, Roll 21, frame 428.

251 *"Since the year 1818":* Johnston to J.C. Calhoun Sec of War, Piqua, 11 Feb, 1824, USBIA, Roll 21, frame 301.

252 *"The earlier a permanent provision":* Johnston to J.C. Calhoun Sec of War, 28 April, 1824. Records. USBIA, Roll 21, frame 325.

252 *their Reservations:* 18 Nov, 1828, John Johnston Papers, (microfilm edition, Roll 2, Frame 157), Box 2, Folder 3, OHS.

252 *"their thirst for strong drink":* John McElvain, Indian Agent to Col. TL McKenney, November, 1829, 829, Washington. Records. USBIA, Roll 21, frame 648.

252 *dividing their annuity:* Johnston to McKenney, 14 May, 1829, Records. USBIA, Roll 21, frame 600.

252 *"Our Great Father":* Shawnee Chiefs to the President, Wapa-koneta, 30 Jan, 1830. Records. USBIA, Roll 21, frame 862.

253   *"The lands owned":* Johnston to Thos. L. M. Kenny Esq., Indian Office, 14 May, 1829. Records. USBIA, Roll 21, frame 601.

253   *"told the Indians":* Hughes, "The Removal of the Shawnee Indians from Ohio," Master's Thesis at Indiana University.

253   *two of his adult sons:* "Treaty with the Seneca, etc., 1831," in Kappler, *Indian Affairs. Laws and Treaties,* 2: 327.

253   *"their uniform attachment":* Johnston to J.C. Calhoun Sec of War, 11 Feb, 1824. Records. USBIA, Roll 21, frame 301.

253   *funds for their removal:* Harvey, 210-214.

254   *"Shawanoese, Senecas, and Ottawas":* Diary, 12 Sept, 1828, John Johnston Papers, (microfilm edition, Roll 2, Frame 037), OHS.

254   *account of Shawnee removal:* Gibson, *The Indian Removals. Document 512,* 1: 686-693.

257   *James McPherson:* Downes, 270; McPherson File, Logan County Historical Society.

270   *"Last of Shawanese":* Diary, 12 Sept, 1828, John Johnston Papers, (microfilm edition, Roll 2, Frame 042), OHS.

270   *"a number of half-breed Indians"* Perrin, 562-563.

CHAPTER TWENTY ONE, OMEGA

271   *O.M. had published: IC,* title page and introduction.

271   *Spencer, Strong and Blachly:* Hall, 8: 248.

271   *"Brother has been quite sick":* DE Meek to SB Evans, 18 June, 1835, RABSP.

271   *another financial crash:* Huntington, 24: 384-387.

272   *four of his adult sons:* Woodruff, 163.

272   *Colonel Spencer's war pension:* Meeks to Evans, 14 Aug, 1837, RABSP.

272   *"My Dear Uncle":* SB Evans to Aaron Ogden, kept with copy of Meeks to Evans, 14 Aug, 1837, RABSP.

275   *"a large and commodious house": Cincinnati Daily Gazette,* 5 May, 1838.

275 *O.M. kept his faith:* Paraphrased from OM Spencer to Sarah B. Evans, 24 Aug, 1813, RABSP.

276 *O.M. died of a stroke:* Records of Spring Grove Cemetery.

276 *O.M.s obituary: Cincinnati Daily Gazette,* 6 June, 1838.

276 *O.M.s and Electra's children:* Family Data Collection-births-AncestryLibrary.com, OHS.

276 *"I do not wish to leave":* 22 March, 1815, RABSP.

277 *Samuel was a farmer:* Ford, 1: 654.

277 *John and Francis "at sea":* Spencer, *Raphael Semmes: The Philosophical Mariner,* 76; Supreme Court Journal of Logan Co., 1845-50, Vol. B: 25.

277 *Alexander Oliver Spencer:* Spencer File at the Logan County Historical Society, info taken from the Weekly Examiner, 1 July, 1904 and 9 Sept, 1904.

277 *O.M.'s daughter Anne Elizabeth:* Raphael Semmes to his daughter Electra, 26 March, 1861; Semmes to wife, 28 May, 1861, 7 July, 1862; Post War letters, No Date, Anne to a daughter; and Historical Note. Alabama Department of Archives and History, Semmes Family Papers, 1859-1913, [Microform]; Spencer, *Raphael Semmes: The Philosophical Mariner,* 168.

278 *"left England on account":* IC, 5-6.

278 *Eastern Shawnee:* Howard, *Shawnee!,* 19-20.

Illustration Sources

Cincinnati Daily Gazette: 276.

New Jersey Journal: 21, 23, 47, 218.

Janet E. Nelson Rupert: cover, xi, 89, 131, 199, 215.

Spencer, O.M., Carleton & Lanahan: 93, 157.

MANUSCRIPT COLLECTIONS

Askin, John. Papers. Burton Historical Collection, Detroit Public Library.

British Headquarters Papers, New York Public Library.

Spencer to Hand, 4 June, 1779, Emmet # 6722 (Oliver Spencer), New York Public Library.

Calendar of the New Jersey State Library Manuscript Collections in the Cataloguing Room, State Library, Trenton, New Jersey.

Claus, Daniel, and Family Fonds, Correspondence of Gen Haldimand and his Sec Captain Mathew, with Colonel Claus of the Indian Department, also letters from Langan, Guy, Johnson, etc. 1777-1784. C-1485, Reel 8. Library and Archives Canada.

Collections of the Society of the Cincinnati, Society of the Cincinnati Library, Washington, DC.

"Jonathan Dayton," Boxwood Hall State Historic Site, Department of Environmental Protection & Energy, Division of Parks and Forestry, New Jersey.

Draper MSS, [Microform], State Historical Society of Wisconsin.

General Abstracts of Revolutionary War Pension Files, New Jersey State Archives, Trenton, New Jersey.

Gratz Collection, Historical Society of Pennsylvania.

Harrison, William Henry, Douglas E. Clanin, and Ruth Dorrel. The Papers of William Henry Harrison, 1800-1815. [Microform]. Indiana Historical Society, Indianapolis, Indiana.

Hunt, William, Family Papers. Ohio Historical Society, Columbus, Ohio.

Inscriptions. First Presbyterian Church Cemetery, Elizabeth, N.J.

Ironside Family File. Farrow Early Immigrant Research Society.

Johnston, John. Letters. VFM 4875. Ohio Historical Society, Columbus, Ohio.

Johnston, John. Papers. [Microform]. Ohio Historical Society, Columbus, Ohio.

Knox, Henry. Papers. [Microform]. Owned by the New England Historic Genealogical Society and deposited in the Massachusetts Historical Society.

Ledyard Family Papers, Cornell University, Ithaca, New York.

Land Warrant No. 1994, MSS. No. 9901: 130, New Jersey State Archives, Trenton, New Jersey.

Letters Received by the Secretary of War, Registered Series, 1801-1860.

McPherson File. Logan County (Ohio) Historical Society, Bellefontaine, Ohio.

Methodist Episcopal Ohio Annual Journal. MSS 1800-1826. Ohio Wesleyan Methodist Library, Delaware, Ohio.

New Jersey Genealogical Society Revolutionary War slips (pension). New Jersey State Archives, Trenton, New Jersey.

Northwest Territory Transcripts, (microfilm, roll 1), Ohio Historical Society, Columbus, Ohio.

Ogden, Aaron to Jonathan Dayton, 10 Dec, 1792, New Jersey Parks Department.

Ogden, Robert. Card catalog biography. New Jersey Historical Society, Newark, New Jersey.

Oliver Spencer to Calvin Spencer, Aug 19, 1789. Princeton Archives.

Ohio Native Genealogy Cards. Center for Archival Collections. Bowling Green (Ohio) State University.

Pennsylvania Court of Admiralty, Historical Society of Pennsylvania, Philadelphia.

Receiver Ledger W. Cincinnati Land Office, 1815-1829. Ohio Historical Society.

Records. Spring Grove Cemetery. Cincinnati, Ohio.

Records of Ante-Bellum Southern Plantations from the Revolution through the Civil War, Series I, Selections from the Louisiana and Lower Mississippi Valley Collection Louisiana State University Libraries, Part 2, Louisiana and Miscellaneous Southern Cotton Plantations, Nathaniel Evans, 1791-1865+, Wilkinson County, Mississipp and West Feliciana and St. Mary's Parishes, Louisiana. [Microform].

Sargent, Winthrop. Papers. Microfilm Publication: Number 1. Ed. by Frederick S. Allis, Jr. Boston: Massachusetts Historical Society, 1965.

Semmes Family Papers, 1859-1913. [Microform]. Alabama Department of Archives and History. Montgomery, Alabama.

Spencer Family File. Cincinnati Historical Society.

Spencer File. Logan County (Ohio) Historical Society.

St. Clair, Arthur. Papers. 1746-1882. [Microform]. Ohio Historical Society.

Supreme Court Journal of Logan County, Ohio.

The Papers of George Washington, Revolutionary War Series, 9, Dorothy Twohig, editor. University Press of Virginia: Charlottesville and London.

Torrence Papers. Historical and Philosophical Society of Ohio. Cincinnati Historical Society.

United States, Bureau of Indian Affairs. Records of the Indian Agency, Piqua, Ohio, 1824-1830. (Selections from Record Group 75). Microfilm, Roll 21. Washington, DC: National Archives.

United States, Continental Army. 1779-1780. Early American Orderly Books, 1748-1817. [Microform]. New York Historical Society.

United States, Continental Congress. Inspection roll of Negroes, April 23, 1783. Miscellaneous Papers of the Continental Congress, 1774-1789. M332. Washington, DC: National Archives Trust Fund Board, National Archives and Records Administration, 1988.

United States, Continental Congress. Papers of the Continental Congress, 1774-1789. M247. Washington, DC: National Archives.

United States of America. Letters Received by the Secretary of War, Registered Series, 1801-1860, (Record Group 107), Microcopy M221. Washington, DC: National Archives.

United States of America. Letters Received by the Secretary of War, Unregistered Series, 1789-1860, (Record Group 107), Microcopy M222. Washington, DC: National Archives.

United States of America. Records of the Michigan Superintendency of Indian Affairs, 1814-1851. Records of the Bureau of Indian Affairs. (Record Group 75.) Microcopy M1. Washington, DC: National Archives, 1942.

Washington, George. Papers. [Microform] Series 4, Film 1883. Washington: Library of Congress, Manuscript Division, 1964.

BOOKS, ARTICLES, DISSERTATIONS

A Sketch of the Life and Character of John Reily, Dec'd. Hamilton, O., 1850.

Abstract of Book 1 & Book A, Probate Record: Probate Record, 1791-1826. Cincinnati, Ohio: Hamilton County Chapter, Ohio Genealogical Society, 1977.

Ackerknecht, Erwin Heinz. "'White Indians,' psychological and physiological peculiarities of white children abducted and reared by North American Indians." *Bulletin of the History of Medicine* 15 (January 1944): 14-36.

Alder, Jonathan, and Johnda T. Davis. *The Journal of Jonathan Alder.* Johnda T. Davis, 1988.

American State Papers: Indian Affairs. 2 Vol. Washington, DC: Gales and Seaton, 1832-1834.

American State Papers: Military Affairs. 7 Vol. Washington, DC: Gales and Seaton, 1832-1861.

Baily, Francis. *Journal of a Tour in Unsettled Parts of North America in 1796 & 1797*. Southern Illinois University: Carbondale.

Banneker, Benjamin. *Benjamin Banneker's Pennsylvania, Delaware, Maryland and Virginia almanack and ephemeris, for the year of our Lord, 1792*. Baltimore: William Goddard and James Angell, 1791. Electronic resource, Web-E book through Ohio State University library catalog.

Bindoff, S. T., E. F. Malcolm-Smith, and Sir Charles K. Webster. *British Diplomatic Representatives, 1759-1852*. London: Offices of the society, 1934.

Blum, Carol Jean. "'A Devotion to the West': The Settlement of Cincinnati, 1788-1810." Queen City Heritage 48 (Spring 1990): 2-19.

Bremer, Francis J. *The Puritan Experiment, New England Society from Bradford to Edwards*. Hanover and London: University Press of New England, 1995.

Brickell, John. "Narrative of John Brickell's Captivity Among the Delaware Indians," *The American Pioneer* 1 (February 1842): 43-56.

Buchman, Randall, L. *The Confluence: "the site of Fort Defiance."* Columbus: Publication for the Ohio American Revolution Bicentennial Advisory Commission by the Ohio Historical Society, 1976.

Burr, Aaron, and J. J. Coombs. *The Trial of Aaron Burr for High Treason*. Notable Trials Library. New York, New York: Leslie B. Adams, Jr., 1992.

Burress, Marjorie Byrnside. *Early rosters of Cincinnati and Hamilton County: a collection of pioneer rolls*. North Bend, OH, (3289 Triplecrown, North Bend 45052): M.B. Burress, 1984.

Butterfield, Consul Willshire. *History of the Girtys: being a concise account of the Girty brothers*. Columbus, OH: Long's College Book Co., 1950.

Calloway, Colin G. *The Shawnees and the War for America*. The Penguin Library of American Indian History. New York: Viking, 2007.

Cist, Charles. *The Cincinnati Miscellany, or Antiquities of the West; and Pioneer History and General and Local Statistics*. Comp. from the Western General Advertiser, from October 1, 1844 to April 1, 1845. Vol. 1. Cincinnati: Caleb Clark, Printer, 1845.

Collins, Lewis. *Collins Historical Sketches of Kentucky: history of Kentucky by the late Lewis Collins*. Vol. II. Covington, KY: Collins & Co., 1874.

Cone, Stephen Decatur. "Indian Attack on Fort Dunlap." *Ohio Archaeological and Historical Quarterly* 17 (1908): 64-72.

Cone, William Whitney. *Some account of the Cone family in America principally of the descendants of Daniel Cone, who settled in Haddam, Connecticut, in 1662. Comp. by William Whitney Cone.* Topeka: Printed by Crane & Co., 1903.

Cook, Frederick, George S. Conover, and New York State. *Journals of the Military Expedition of Major General John Sullivan Against Six Nations of Indians in 1779.* Auburn, NY: Knack, Peck & Thomson, Printers, 1887.

Coriell, Mrs. Abner S. "Major-General Elias Dayton." *Proceedings of the Union County Historical Society* 2 (1923- 1924): 203-211.

Craig, Robert D. *Columbia Township Hamilton County, OH Tax list—1796.* Cincinnati: Robert D. Craig, 1963.

Crumrine, Boyd. *Virginia Court Records in Southwestern Pennsylvania; records of the District of West Augusta and Ohio and Yohogania counties, Virginia, 1775-1780.* Baltimore: Genealogical Pub. Co., 1974.

Denny, Ebenezer. *The Military Journal of Major Ebenezer Denny, An Officer in the Revolutionary and Indian Wars.* Philadelphia: J.B. Lippincott & Co., for the Historical Society of Pennsylvania, 1859.

Downes, Randolph C. *Council Fires on the Upper Ohio, A Narrative of Indian Affairs in the Upper Ohio Valley until 1795.* University of Pittsburgh Press, 1989.

Drake, Daniel. *Notices Concerning Cincinnati.* Cincinnati: Printed for the author at the press of John W. Browne & Co., 1810.

Drake, Francis Samuel. *Dictionary of American Biography.* Boston: Osgood and Co., 1872.

Dunlevy, A.H. *History of the Miami Baptist Association.* Cincinnati: Geo. S. Blanchard & Co., 1869.

Earle, Alice Morse. *Child Life in Colonial Days.* New York: Macmillan and Co., 1899.

Edwards, William H., comp. *Timothy and Rhoda Ogden Edwards of Stockbridge, Mass., and their descendants.* Cincinnati: Robert Clarke Co., 1903.

Ehler, Ralph B. "The Story of Fort St. Clair." *Ohio Archaeological and Historical Quarterly* 32 (1923): 518.

Ellicott, Andrew. *Ellicott's Maryland and Virginia almanac, and ephemeris, for the year of our Lord 1791.* Baltimore: Printed and sold, wholesale and retail, by John Hayes, Market-

Street, 1790. Electronic resource, Web-E book through Ohio State University library catalog.

Emerson. *Letters from New England.*

Ferris, Ezra. "The Early Settlement of the Miami Country." *Indiana Historical Society Publications* (Indianapolis: Bowen-Merrill) 1, no. 9 (1897).

Finley, James B. *Autobiography of Rev. James B. Finley, or, Pioneer Life in the West*, ed. by W.P. Strickland. Cincinnati: Methodist Book Concern, 1853.

Finley, Rev. James B., and W.P. Strickland, D.D. *Sketches of Western Methodism, Biographical, Historical, and Miscellaneous, Illustrative of Pioneer Life.* Cincinnati: The Methodist Book Concern, 1854.

Ford, Henry A., and Kate B. Ford, compilers. *History of Hamilton County, Ohio, with illustrations and biographical sketches.* Cleveland, O.: L.A. Williams & Co., 1881. Reprint, Evansville, IN: Unigraphic, Inc., 1974.

Forry, Richard Reuben. "Edward Hand: His Role in the American Revolution." Ph. D. diss., Duke University, 1976.

Fryer, Mary Beacock, and Christopher Dracott. *John Graves Simcoe, 1752-1806: A Biography.* Dundurn, 1998.

Gibson, George. *The Indian Removals.* Vol. 1. *Document 512, Correspondence on the subject of the Emigration of Indians between the 30th November, 1831, and 27th December, 1833.* Reprint, New York: AMS Press, 1974.

Graymont, Barbara. *The Iroquois in the American Revolution.* Syracuse, NY: Syracuse University Press, 1972.

Greve, Charles Theodore. *Centennial history of Cincinnati and representative citizens.* Vol. 1. Chicago: Biographical Company, 1904.

Hall Virginius C. "Oliver M. Spencer, Man and Boy." *Bulletin of the Historical and Philosophical Society of Ohio* 8 (October 1950): 233-257.

Harmar, Josiah. *The Harmar Papers from the Clements Library, Ann Arbor, Michigan*, transcribed by Richard C. Knopf. Anthony Wayne Parkway Board, 1954.

Harvey, Henry. *History of the Shawnee Indians, from the year 1681 to 1854, inclusive.* Cincinnati: Ephraim Morgan & Sons, 1855.

Heckewelder, John Gottlieb Ernestus. *Thirty Thousand Miles with John Heckewelder*, ed. by Paul A. Wallace. Pittsburgh: University of Pittsburgh Press, 1958.

Heitman, Francis B. *Historical register and dictionary of the United States Army, from its organization, September 29, 1789 to March 2, 1903.* Vol. 1. Washington: Government Printing office, 1903.

Hildreth, Samuel P. *Pioneer History.* 2 Vols. Cincinnati: H.W. Derby;   New York: A.S. Barnes & Co., 1848.

Hill, Leonard U. *John Johnston and the Indians in the land   of the three Miamis, with recollections by John Johnston.* Piqua, Ohio, 1957.

Huntington, C. C. "A History of Banking and Currency in   Ohio before   the   Civil   War." *Ohio Archaeological and Historical   Quarterly* 24 (1915): 235-239.

Jacobs, James Ripley. *Tarnished Warrior, Major-General James Wilkinson.* New York: The Macmillan Co., 1938.

Jacobus, Donald Lines. "The Four Spencer Brothers: Their Ancestors and Descendants." *American Genealogist* 27   (April 1951): 81; 29 (July 1953): 181-183.

Jahoda, Gloria. "Tahlonteskee Goes West and Quitewepea Brings an Invitation." Chap. 1 in *The Trail of Tears.* New York: Wings Books, 1975.

Johansen, Bruce E., and Barbara Alice Mann. *Encyclopedia of the Haudenosaunee (Iroquois Confederacy).* Westport, Conn: Greenwood Press, 2000.

Jones, A. E. *Extracts from the History of Cincinnati and the territory of Ohio.* Cincinnati: Cohen & Co., 1888.

Jones, Rev. David. *A Journal of two visits made to some nations of Indians on the west side of the River Ohio in the years   1772 and 1773.* Chillicothe, OH: Ross County Historical   Society, 1946.

Kappler, Charles Joseph. *Indian Affairs, Laws and Treaties.* Vol. II. Washington: Government printing office, 1904.

Katzenberger, George A. "Martin Baum." *Ohio Archaeological and Historical Quarterly*   44 (April 1935):   204-219.

Klopfenstein, Carl Grover. "The Removal of the Indians from Ohio, 1820-1843." Ph.D. diss., Western Reserve University, 1955.

Knopf, Richard, C. *Document Transcriptions of The War of 1812 in the Northwest.* Vol. V, *The National Intelligencer Reports The War of 1812 in the Northwest.* Columbus, OH: The Ohio Historical Society, 1958.

Manning, Clarence Augustus. *Soldier of Liberty, Casimer Pulaski.* New York: Philosophical Library, 1945.

McAfee, Robert. B. *History of the Late War in the Western Country, by Robert McAfee, 1816.* Bowling Green, OH: Historical Publications Co., 1919.

McBride, James. *Pioneer Biography, sketches of the lives of some of the early settlers of Butler County, Ohio.* 2 Vol. Cincinnati: Robert Clarke & Co., 1869-1871.

McKenney, Thomas L. "Quatawapea, or Colonel Lewis," *History of the Indian Tribes of North America, with biographical sketches and anecdotes of the Principal Chiefs*, in three volumes. Vol. II. Philadelphia: Rice, Rutter & Co., 1865.

Military History of Ohio, Its border annals, its part in the Indian wars, in the War of 1812, in the Mexican war, and in the War of the rebellion. Logan County. New York: H. H. Hardesty, 1886.

Nelson, Larry L. *A Man of Distinction Among Them: Alexander McKee and the Ohio Country Frontier, 1754- 1799.* Kent, Ohio, and London: Kent State University Press, 1999.

New Jersey, Adjutant-General's Office, William S. Stryker, and James Wall Schureman Campbell. *Official register of the officers and men of New Jersey in the Revolutionary War.* Baltimore: Genealogical Pub. Co., 1967.

Oberholtzer, Ellis Paxson. *Robert Morris, Patriot and Financier.* New York: Macmillan, 1903.

Ogden, Colonel Aaron. "Autobiography." *Proceedings of the New Jersey Historical Society,* 2nd ser., 12 (January 1892): 13-31.

Perko, Michael. "The Building Up of Zion: Religion and Education in Nineteenth Century Cincinnati." *Cincinnati Historical Society Bulletin* 38 (Summer 1980): 96-114.

Perrin, William Henry, and J. H. Battle. *History of Logan County and Ohio.* Chicago: O. L. Baskin, 1880. Reprint, Evansville, Ind.: Unigraphic, 1980.

Pilling, James Constantine. *Bibliography of the Iroquoian Languages.* Washington: Govt. Printing Off., 1888.

Putnam, Rufus. *The Memoirs of Rufus Putnam and certain official papers and* correspondence, comp. by Rowena Buell. Boston and New York: Houghton, Mifflin and Co., 1903.

"Random History Notes." *Bulletin of the Historical and Philosophical Society of Cincinnati* 12 (January 1954): 65-70.

Richter, Daniel K. *Ordeal of the Longhouse: The Peoples of the Iroquois League in the Era of European colonization.* Chapel Hill & London: Published for the Institute of Early American History and Culture, Williamsburg, Virginia, by the University of North Carolina Press, 1992.

Riddell, William Renwick. *The Life of John Graves Simcoe, the first lieutenant-governor of the province of Upper Canada, 1792-1796.* Toronto: McClelland & Stewart, Ltd., 1926.

Roseboom, Eugene H., and Francis P. Weisenburger. *A History of Ohio.* Columbus: The Ohio Historical Society, 1996.

Sargent, Winthrop. "Winthrop Sargent's Diary while with General Arthur St. Clair's Expedition Against the Indians." *Ohio Archaeological and Historical Quarterly* 33 (1924): 237-273.

Scamyhorn, Richard, and John Steinle. *Stockades in the Wilderness: the frontier defenses and settlements of southwestern Ohio, 1788-1795.* Dayton, OH: Landfall Press, 1986.

Schermerhorn, William E. *The History of Burlington, New Jersey.* Burlington, NJ: Enterprise Pub. Co., 1927.

Schoolcraft, Henry Rowe. *History of the Indian Tribes of the United States.* Vol. 6. Philadelphia: J. B. Lippincott & Co., 1857.

Simcoe, John Graves. *Simcoe's Military Journal: A History of the Operations of a Partisan Corps, called the Queen's Rangers, commanded by J.G. Simcoe.* New York: Bartlett & Welford, 1844.

Simcoe, John Graves, E.A. Cruickshank, and Ontario., Lieutenant Governor, 1791-1796 (John G. Simcoe). *The Correspondence of Lieut. Governor John Graves Simcoe, With Allied Documents relating to his administration of the government of Upper Canada. Vol. I. 1789-1793.* Toronto: Ontario Historical Society, 1923.

Simmons, David A. *The Forts of Anthony Wayne.* Fort Wayne, IN: Historic Fort Wayne, Inc., 1977.

Slocum, Charles Elihu. *The Ohio Country, Between the Years 1783 and 1815.* New York: G.P. Putnam's Sons, 1910.

Snow, Dean R. *The Iroquois.* Cambridge, MA: Blackwell, 1994.

Smith, Samuel Stelle. *The Battle of Brandywine.* Monmouth Beach, NJ, 1976.

Society of the Cincinnati in the State of New Jersey and Weston Spies Gales. "Colonel Oliver Spencer." In *Historical papers read before the Society of the Cincinnati in the state of New Jersey, July fourth, 1900.* Brooklyn, NY: Printed for the society by Collins & Day, 1900.

Spencer, Jack Taif, and Edith Woolley Spencer. *Spencers of the great migration.* Vol. I. Baltimore, MD: Gateway Press; Dekalb, IL: J.T. Spencer [distributor], 1997.

Spencer, Oliver M. (O.M.). *Indian Captivity: a True Narrative of the Capture of the Reverend O.M. Spencer by the Indians, in the neighbourhood of Cincinnati.* New York: G. Lane & P.P. Sandford, 1842.

————*Indian Captivity: a True Narrative of the Capture of the Reverend O.M. Spencer by the Indians, in the neighbourhood of Cincinnati.* New York: Carlton & Lanahan, [n.d.].

————*A Masonic Sermon delivered by brother O.M. Spencer, on the anniversary of St. John the Baptist, June 24th, A.L. 5813 A.D. 1813.* Cincinnati: J. Carpenter & Co., 1813.

Spencer, Warren F. *Raphael Semmes: The Philosophical Mariner.* Tuscaloosa: University of Alabama Press, 1997.

St. Clair, Arthur. *The St. Clair Papers. The Life and Public Services of Arthur St. Clair,* arranged and annotated by William Henry Smith. Vol. II. Cincinnati: Robert Clarke & Co., 1882.

Stofko, Karl P., and Rachel I. Gibbs. *A Brief History of East Haddam Connecticut.* East Haddam Historic District Commission, 1977.

Stone, William L. *Life and Times of Red Jacket, or Sa-go-ye-wat-ha; being the sequel to the history of Six Nations.* New York, London: Wiley and Putnam, 1841.

Stone, William L. *Life of Joseph Brant, (Thayendanegea).* 2 Vol. Albany, NY: J. Munsell, 1865.

Stryker, William S. *General Maxwell's Brigade of the New Jersey Continental Line in the expedition against the Indians in the year 1779.* Trenton, NJ: W.S. Sharp, printer, 1885.

Sugden, John. *Blue Jacket: Warrior of the Shawnees.* Lincoln & London: University of Nebraska Press, 2000.

————*The Shawnee in Tecumseh's Time.* Nortorf, Germany: Abhandlungen der Völkerkundlichen Arbeitsgemeinshcaft, eft 66, 1990.

————*Tecumseh, a Life.* New York: Henry Holt, 1998.

Sullivan, John. *Letters and Papers of Major-General John Sullivan, Continental Army, edited by Otis G. Hammond.* 3 Vol. Concord, N.H.: New Hampshire Historical Society, 1930-39.

Sword, Wiley. *President Washington's Indian War: The Struggle for the Old Northwest, 1790-1795.* Norman and London: University of Oklahoma Press, 1993.

Symmes, John Cleves. *Symmes Purchase Records, a verbatim copy of the entry book, pamphlet, and forfeiture records of John Cleves Symmes,* transcribed by Chris McHenry. Lawrenceburg, Ind.: C. McHenry, 1979.

Symmes, John Cleves, Beverley W. Bond, and Anna Symmes Harrison. *The intimate letters of John Cleves Symmes.* Cincinnati: Historical and Philosophical Society of Ohio, 1956.

Symmes, John Cleves, Jonathan Dayton, and others. *The Correspondence of John Cleves Symmes,* ed. by Beverley

Bond. New York: Pub. for the Historical and   Philosophical Society of Ohio by Macmillan Company, 1926.

Thayer,   Theodore.   *As   We   Were: The   Story   of   Old Elizabethtown.* Elizabeth, NJ: Pub. for The New Jersey Historical Society by Grassmann Pub. Co., 1964.

Thom,   Dark   Rain.   *Kohkumthena's   Grandchildren: The Shawnee.* Indianapolis, IN: Guild Press of Indiana, 1994.

Thwaites, Reuben Gold, and Louise Phelps Kellogg. *Frontier Defense on the Upper Ohio, 1777-1778.* Madison: Wisconsin Historical Society, 1912.

"Valuable Purchase," *Bull. Hist. and Phil. Soc. of Ohio,* 4   (Sept 1946).

Van Steen, Marcus. *Governor Simcoe and His Lady.* Toronto and London: Hodder & Stoughton, 1968.

Ward, Harry M. *Charles Scott and the "Spirit of '76".* Charlottesville: University Press of Virginia, 1988.

Wayne Papers, transcribed by Richard C Knopf. Vol. 20-24, 26-52. Historical Society of Pennsylvania, 1995.

Wells, William. "Indian manners and customs." *The   Western Review and miscellaneous magazine* 2 (Feb 1820): 45-46.

Westergaard, Barbara. *New Jersey: A Guide to the State.* New Brunswick, NJ: Rutgers University Press, 1998.

Williamson, C. W. *History of Western Ohio and Auglaize County.* Columbus, Ohio: W. M. Linn & Sons, 1904. Reprint, Evansville, Ind.: Unigraphic, Inc., 1974.

Wilson, Thomas B. *Notices from New Jersey Newspapers, 1781-1790.* Lambertville, NJ: Hunterdon House, 1988.

Woodruff,   J.H.   *Cincinnati   Directory   Advertiser,   1836-7.* Cincinnati: J.H. Woodruff, 1836.

Wright, Steven L. "The 1826 Company with 21st Century Ideas." *Queen City Heritage* 55 (Fall 1997): 9-40.

Young, Calvin, M. *Little Turtle (Me-she-kin-no-quah): the great chief of the Miami Indian nation.* Greenville, Ohio: Young, 1917.

NEWSPAPERS

Cincinnati Daily Gazette
Liberty Hall
New Jersey Journal
Western Christian Advocate
Western Spy

WEBPAGES AND COMPUTER FILES

Cass, Lewis, biography, http://www.aoc.gov/capitol-hill/national-statuary-hall-collection/lewis-cass

Harrison, William Henry, White House biography, http://www.whitehouse.gov/history/presidents/wh9.html7u/

McArthur, Duncan, biography, Ohio History Central, http://www.ohiohistorycentral.org/entry.php?rec=256

Meisner, Marian. "The War Comes to Millburn." Chap. VIII in *A History of Millburn Township*. eBook jointly published by the Millburn/Short Hills Historical Society and the Millburn Free Public Library, 2002.
http://www.millburnlib.net/ebook/eBook.pdf.

Ohio History Society, Family Data Collection-births-AncestryLibrary.com

www.ingramcontent.com/pod-product-compliance
Lightning Source LLC
Chambersburg PA
CBHW020453100426
42813CB00031B/3355/J